COAT OF ARMS OF
THE MERCHANT ADVENTURERS OF ENGLAND
1296

THE EARLY
CHARTERED COMPANIES

(A.D. 1296—1858)

BY

GEORGE CAWSTON
BARRISTER-AT-LAW

AND

A. H. KEANE, F.R.G.S.
HON. MEMBER OF THE VIRGINIA HISTORICAL SOCIETY

THE LAWBOOK EXCHANGE, LTD.
Clark, New Jersey

ISBN 978-1-58477-196-8

Lawbook Exchange edition 2002, 2017

The quality of this reprint is equivalent to the quality of the original work.

THE LAWBOOK EXCHANGE, LTD.
33 Terminal Avenue
Clark, New Jersey 07066-1321

*Please see our website for a selection of our other publications
and fine facsimile reprints of classic works of legal history:*
www.lawbookexchange.com

Library of Congress Cataloging-in-Publication Data

Cawston, George.
  The early chartered companies (A.D. 1296-1858) / by George Cawston
and A.H. Keane.
    p. cm.
  Originally published: London ; New York: E. Arnold, 1896.
  Includes bibliographical references and index.
  ISBN 1-58477-196-8 (cloth: alk. paper)
    1. Great Britain—Commerce—History. 2. Colonial companies. I. Keane, A. H.
(Augustus Henry), 1833-19 12. II. Title.

HF485 .C4 2001
382'.0942—dc2l   2001041393

Printed in the United States of America on acid-free paper

THE EARLY

CHARTERED COMPANIES

(A.D. 1296—1858)

BY

GEORGE CAWSTON
BARRISTER-AT-LAW

AND

A. H. KEANE, F.R.G.S.
HON. MEMBER OF THE VIRGINIA HISTORICAL SOCIETY

EDWARD ARNOLD
𝔓𝔲𝔟𝔩𝔦𝔰𝔥𝔢𝔯 𝔱𝔬 𝔱𝔥𝔢 𝔍𝔫𝔡𝔦𝔞 𝔒𝔣𝔣𝔦𝔠𝔢

LONDON   NEW YORK
37 BEDFORD STREET   70 FIFTH AVENUE
1896

PREFACE

In November, 1893, on the invitation of the late Sir Charles Mills, I delivered a lecture on South Africa at the Imperial Institute, and I included in that lecture a brief account of some of the early Chartered Companies.

My friend Mr. J. H. Reddan, of the Foreign Office, kindly assisted me in preparing the lecture, and we decided that the result of our researches should also be used as materials for a systematic treatise on the subject. We found, however, that the manuscripts in the British Museum alone, without referring to the foreign libraries and private collections, were far too extensive to be dealt with by either of us, even had Mr. Reddan's services not been required in connection with the urgent question of the boundary between British Guiana and Venezuela. I was therefore glad to accept Professor Keane's offer to utilize as much of the available printed and manuscript material as might suffice to present an intelligible summary of the more important companies. How he has acquitted himself of the somewhat thankless task must be left to the judgment of the reader.

The object was to give a clear picture of the inner workings of these associations, especially in their direct relations to the rise and spread of British Commercial and Political Power from the time that these islands began to take a share in the general progress of the civilized world. For this purpose the abundant, and for the most part trustworthy, information scattered in a somewhat fragmentary way over the six volumes of Anderson and Coombe's ' Origin of Commerce ' has been freely used. Other recognised authorities have also been consulted, amongst them Wheeler's ' History of the Merchant Adventurers,' 1601, and Mr. H. H. Bancroft's great work on the ' Pacific States of North America,' the latter of which has supplied copious data for the important chapter on the Hudson Bay Company. In the Appendices will be found several original documents of considerable interest, such as the full texts of charters of various periods, selected as specimens of such documents from Mr. Reddan's collections.

There is reason to believe that a large number of

manuscripts bearing on the origin and history of the Chartered Corporations are dispersed amongst the private collections of England. It would be deemed a great favour if the owners would give facilities for consulting or copying these treasures, with a view to an enlarged edition of the present work.

The labour expended in the preparation of this work will not be regretted, should it have the effect of awakening public interest in our great historical Chartered Companies, and of inducing others to enter on this almost unexplored field of research. I believe the results will prove that what I stated in my lecture is true, viz., that 'most of the colonial possessions of this Empire were in the first place settled through the agency of Chartered Companies, and that our foreign trade and commerce principally originated in the same manner.'

The anonymous author of a pamphlet written about the year 1820 has truly remarked that 'individuals cannot extend society to distant places without forming a compact amongst themselves, and obtaining some guarantee for its being observed.' All the old and most successful British colonies in America, Virginia, Massachusetts, Connecticut, Rhode Island, Pennsylvania, Maryland, and Georgia, which formed the basis of that most wonderful country, the United States of America, were founded by individuals whose public spirit, prudence, and resolution were not otherwise assisted by the Government of their country. The charter from the Crown simply erected each of those bodies of individuals into a corporation, with authority required for accomplishing, to use the words of several of these charters, ' their generous and noble purpose.'

The present work was projected long before the unfortunate position created by recent events in South Africa.

GEORGE CAWSTON.

June, 1896.

CONTENTS

CHAPTER I.

CHAPTER II.

CHAPTER III.

CHAPTER IV.

CHAPTER V.

CHAPTER VI.

APPENDIX I.

APPENDIX II.

APPENDIX III.

THE

CHARTERED COMPANIES

CHAPTER I.

CHARTERS AND CHARTERED CORPORATIONS—THE HAN-
SEATIC LEAGUE — REGULATED AND JOINT - STOCK
COMPANIES.

A CHARTER, so named from the material on which it is
drafted (Lat. *charta*, paper), may be defined as a
written instrument by which the State confers certain
privileges on corporate bodies, either to protect them
in the exercise of their lawful avocations at home, or
else to encourage and sustain them in their more
hazardous ventures abroad.

Charters were first granted to municipalities and
guilds of all sorts, whose operations were necessarily
limited to particular localities within the State. Such
documents were needed to protect the trades and
industries of the country in times of almost chronic
civil commotion, feudal oppression, and general law-

I

lessness. Under such conditions these concessions were soon found—especially in England—to be as mutually advantageous to the Crown as to the privileged corporations. Thus it came about that during the periods of border warfare with Scotland and Wales, and later during the disastrous Wars of the Roses, numerous privileges were granted to the great trade guilds, which had hitherto been merely private bodies, acting in concert only in self-defence or in the common interests of their crafts, but which now received many immunities, privileges, and monopolies in return for corresponding services and money grants often made to the Crown in times of great emergency. As early as the year 1327 the Goldsmiths obtained a well-earned charter, followed successively by others in favour of the Mercers in 1393, the Haberdashers in 1407, the Fishmongers in 1433, the Vintners in 1437, and the Merchant Taylors in 1466.

Such charters, with which we are not here further concerned, may be said to stand in the same relation to the *trades* as those charters did to *trade* which were issued in favour of the merchant classes. In the natural order of events, these came later, for there could be no regular interchange of commodities abroad until the home industries had been sufficiently developed to support a general export and import movement. The revival of local industries after everything had been swept away by the irruption of the Northern barbarians, and the chaos following on the fall of the Western

Empire, took place in Italy, Germany and the Low Countries at a much earlier date than in Britain. Hence it is that for several centuries England had little to offer in exchange for foreign wares, except such raw materials as hides, fish, tin, lead, and the fine wools for which the island had always been famous.

But communities exclusively engaged in the production of raw materials—that is, in purely agricultural and pastoral pursuits—are seldom traders in the strict sense of the term. They hold a somewhat passive position in all that concerns international traffic, for their profits in such transactions are greatly inferior to those acquired by buyers of *produce* and sellers of *products*. These sellers of the products of skilled labour accumulate wealth far more rapidly than the sellers of the produce of unskilled labour, and are consequently also in a better position to secure the further advantages derived from the carrying trade over land and water. But when they thus extend their operations beyond the seas, when they develop commercial relations between their own and foreign countries, these operations in semi-barbarous times become risky, and need the protection both of their own rulers and of the foreign States where they have established themselves somewhat in the envious character of intruders, monopolists, and interested opponents of all incipient industrial enterprise.

It is not, therefore, surprising to find that the first great trading corporations grew up on the mainland,

and that some of the first trading charters issued by the Crown of England were granted, not to private companies which were still non-existent, but to branches already established in Britain of the renowned Hanseatic League, in every way the most powerful and widely ramifying commercial association of mediæval times. It may not be amiss here to give a brief account of this league so far as regards its relations with this country.

The Hanseatic League derived its name from the old German *hansa*, meaning either a guild or corporate body, or a union of such bodies. The name, therefore, indicates that the association was a union, not of individual burghers engaged in trade, as is commonly supposed, but of the burghs themselves, towns, and municipalities banded together against the rapacity of kings, princes, and other local potentates—both civil and ecclesiastical—as well as against the land and sea robbers, by whom the highways, estuaries, and coasts of Northern Europe were infested far into the fourteenth century. The oldest extant written records of the League appear to date from about 1239, when Hamburg formed an alliance for mutual self-defence with Ditmarsch and the Hadeln district. The union was extended in 1241 to Lübeck, in 1247 to Brunswick, and thereafter to many other places in rapid succession. Before the close of the thirteenth century its ramifications extended eastwards to Novgorod in Russia, northwards to Bergen in Norway, and westwards to

London. At that time the confederated towns num-
bered over seventy, and the League had already become
a sort of *imperium in imperio*, strong enough to raise
troops, wage war in distant parts, strike alliances with
many potent rulers, and secure its position in foreign
States by concessions as beneficial to the Hanseatics as
they were often burdensome to the natives. An immense impulse was thus given to commerce, and when
the League had in the seventeenth century to yield to
the disintegrating forces of the times, it still continued
to be represented by several ' Free Hanse Towns,' three
of which—Hamburg, Bremen, and Lübeck—still survive as autonomous members of the German Empire.

In England, ' the Emperor's men '—that is, traders
out of Germany—appear to have already held a recognised position in Anglo-Saxon times, and at a very
early date had their station at the so-called Steelyard
on the banks of the Thames, where now is Thames
Street. Here was their only trading post in the
Thames basin, from 900 to 1597, when it passed into
the hands of the League and became their factory.
They, with pardonable pride, retrospectively identified
themselves with the earlier ' Germans of the Steelyard,'
who, ' coming with their ships, were accounted worthy
of good laws and might buy in their ships ; but it is not
lawful for them to forestall the markets from the
burghers of London.'*

* Dr. Howell, quoted by Anderson (i. 125) on some laws made
by King Ethelred in 979 relating to customs on ships and mer-

In 1232 Henry III. had granted a charter to certain merchants of Flanders and of the Hanse towns (Lübeck, Hamburg, Bremen, Cologne), giving them exclusive possession of the old German Steelyard station, and, moreover, enlarging their privileges, as usual for services rendered, and again in 1236 additional privileges for further services. Then follows what must be regarded more as a treaty between two States than as a mere charter, granted about 1266 to the Easterlings, as these German traders were commonly called. Having lost in a storm the whole of their fleet, which had been engaged on the side of the English against the French, and being unable to obtain full compensation, they made an agreement with Henry III. 'that they would entirely remit all this debt to the King on condition that he and his successors would grant free liberty to the Easterlings to import and export all merchandise whatever at no higher a duty or custom than one per cent., which was the then rate paid.' Thanks to this important charter, the Hanseatics continued to flourish in England for fully three hundred years, although their privileges were at times curtailed by onerous conditions, such as the obligation imposed upon them by Edward I. of keeping in repair the gate known as 'the Bishop's Gate,' and contributing one-third part to its defence, in case London should at any time be besieged

chandise which paid toll at Blyngesgate (Billingsgate), then the only quay in the port of London, near the old wooden bridge (London Bridge) already existing there.

by an enemy. Having apparently been somewhat remiss in this duty, we find it stated in Stowe's ' Survey of London' that in 1282 the Steelyard Company was called upon to pay 210 marks for the repair of Bishopsgate, and to be more diligent in future.

Over a century later (1399) they were threatened with a total withdrawal of all their privileges, the complaint being that under pretence of their English charters they had afforded shelter to other outlandish merchants, whereby the King had suffered loss in his customs. It was also reported at this time that the English merchants trading with Lübeck and other Hanse towns had sustained great loss and injury from their German rivals. Thereupon a proclamation was issued by Henry IV., importing that ' whereas the privileges and freedom of commerce granted to the German merchants of the Steelyard were on condition that the English should enjoy the like in Germany, wherefore the said Hanse towns were summoned to answer before the King and his council for the said injuries, and to make due satisfaction for the same.' Thus was for the first time clearly announced the principle of reciprocity, by which the trading relations of all civilized peoples were afterwards regulated.

But the Hanseatics may truly be said to have rushed upon their own fate. Impelled by jealousy of all foreign rivals, they committed many unheard-of outrages, especially against the English, one hundred of whom were shortly before this time seized by their

armed bands at Windford in Norway, bound hand
and foot, and thrown into the sea, so that all
perished.

'At certain other times,' complains King Henry IV.,
'both in our own reign, and in that of King Richard II.,
those Hanseatics violently seized the effects of English
merchants at Bergen, and assaulted them in their
houses, being in such violences connived at by the
Danish Court (Norway being at that time subject to
Denmark), because of their great commerce thither.'
Thus, as Anderson remarks, their overbearing and
insolent carriage towards other nations trading to any
of their factories, or to other ports whose trade they
had engrossed, 'contributed not a little to their own
downfall' ('History of Commerce,' i. 553).

Then followed a series of vicissitudes which need not
detain us here: the inevitable friction with the Merchant
Adventurers and other rising English companies, wars
of tariffs between England and the Empire, a series of
hostilities carried on not unsuccessfully by the Hanseatics for three years against Edward IV., revocations
and restitutions of their chartered rights, and so on.
At last came the crash in 1578, when all their ancient
immunities were finally abrogated by Elizabeth, and
their Steelyard itself closed for ever in 1597. The
reason given is characteristic and instructive. Finding
that the privileges of these aliens were in many respects
pernicious and hurtful to the growing commercial interests of her kingdom, the Queen did in the year 1597

direct 'a Commission to the Mayor and Sheriffs of London to shut up the house inhabited by the merchants of the Hanse towns at the Steelyard in London; and, moreover, ordered all the Germans there and everywhere else throughout England to quit her dominions on the very day on which the English were obliged to leave Staden' by order of the Emperor Rudolf. Henceforth the Steelyard, which had been the trading-station of the Teutons for about seven hundred years, ceased to be used by them, and became lost in the vast system of wharfs and quays developed in later times along Bankside.

Thus was the commercial soil of England disincumbered of its foreign obstructions at the very time when the country was rapidly awakening to its destinies as immeasurably the greatest trading and colonizing nation that the world has ever seen.

The trading associations that were now springing up and clamouring for the ægis of 'the most high, mightie and magnificent Empresse Elizabeth' were constituted on two distinct principles. First in the natural and actual order came the so-called *Regulated Companies*, which were suitable to the first efforts of the nation to acquire a share of the world's trade, but destined eventually to be superseded by the far more powerful and efficient *Joint-Stock Companies*. For a long time all belonged to the first category, and even so late as the end of the seventeenth century there existed in England only three founded on the joint-stock principle, although these three—the *East India*, the *Royal African*, and the *Hudson Bay*—were perhaps more important than all the rest put together.

In the 'regulated' companies, at that time chiefly represented by the *Russia*, the *Turkey*, and the *Eastland*, every member or 'freeman' traded solely on his own account, subject only to the 'regulations' of the association. In fact, they may be regarded as growing out of the trade guilds, modified to meet the requirements of their more enlarged sphere of action. In the guilds each member purchased a license to ply his trade in his own district at his personal risk, the guild itself being irresponsible for his liabilities in case of failure. On the other hand, he enjoyed all the advantages of membership in an incorporated trade, which could not be exercised by outsiders, even though residents in the district. In the same way no subject of the Crown could trade in any foreign 'district' where a regulated company was established without first acquiring membership by the payment of a fee.

Even in the earliest of these chartered bodies the principle of apprenticeship was enforced, so that, as in the guilds, he who served his time to a member acquired *ipso facto* the privilege of membership; or if a fine was exacted, it was either nominal or of much less amount than that imposed on outsiders. The fines exacted helped towards the general working expenses of the company, including the support of consuls in the foreign ports where they enjoyed exclusive rights.

It is thus seen that in the very elements of their constitution the regulated companies were merely a development of the local guilds adapted for trading purposes beyond the seas. And as in those days the local industries needed the protection of royal charters, so the commercial bodies trading outside the kingdom needed at first the shelter of the Crown against home rivalries and foreign aggression. Without such guarantees it is hard to see how any foreign trade could have been at all developed. Although some of these regulated associations, such especially as the Merchant Adventurers, rose to great power and influence, nearly all had ceased to exist by the close of the eighteenth century, not, however, without leaving a deep mark on the commercial and national records of England. When their work was done, they disappeared, yet the forces by which they were brought into being were not dissipated, but only diverted into fresh channels.

Then came the time when, with the growth of wealth and experience, these pioneer traders in foreign lands acquired a deeper consciousness of their latent powers, a greater sense of their higher destinies, and especially that mutual confidence in each other which was needed for the adoption of the joint-stock principle. As in the regulated associations each member retained his personal independence, and mainly acted on his own account—'traded on his own bottom,' as was the phrase —so in the 'joint' concerns the individual was largely

merged in the corporate body, all working together
primarily for the common good rather than for their
direct personal advantage.

There were other differences, all tending to strengthen
the organization as a whole and make it a more efficient
instrument in the hands of able and far-seeing directors.
Thus, in the regulated bodies no member could transfer
his interests or introduce a new member who had not
'served his time,' without the consent of the whole
association; nor could he, without due notice, withdraw
from the society and claim his share in the common
funds. Moreover, in the later regulated companies, when
they began to lose the character of mere guilds, each
member was liable to the whole extent of his means for
the debts contracted by the company.

All this was different in the joint-stock concerns,
where no shareholder could at any time demand back
the amount of his share, but was under no circumstances
liable for more than that amount. He could, however,
at any time, and without the consent of the body
corporate, transfer his share to another person, who
thus became a member without serving his time.
Hence the complaint of the regulated Turkey Company in 1681, that its rival, the joint-stock East India
could not 'breed up any person under the notion of an
East India merchant, because anyone who is master
of money may purchase a share of their trade and
joint stock.'

But it was this very freedom from the old restraints

of the guilds, combined with the other above-enumerated advantages, that caused the regulated system to fall more and more into abeyance, while the joint-stock rose steadily in the public favour.   On this very occasion the East Indians were able to retort that ' it cannot be denied by a reasonable man that a joint stock is capable of a far greater extension as to the number of traders and largeness of stock, than any regulated company can be.   Because, in a joint stock, noblemen, gentlemen, shopkeepers, widows, orphans, and all other subjects, may be traders, and employ their stock therein ; whereas in a regulated company, such as the Turkey Company is, none can be traders, but such as they call legitimate or bred merchants.'   Hence it is not surprising that after all questions of shareholders' personal liability were clearly defined by the Legislature, and especially by the Companies Acts, the regulated system was universally supplanted by the joint-stock principle, which appears to be now permanently established as a main promoter and safeguard of public credit.

It was by the general adoption of this principle that the great chartered companies acquired their enormous expansion, and in some memorable instances were by the force of circumstances gradually transformed from mere commercial associations of Adventurers into powerful political organizations.

No class of the community were held in greater honour than these Merchant Adventurers, whose enterprising spirit was always at the disposal of their country.

Through the agency of the companies they founded (whose history this book attempts to write), they secured the fairest lands of the earth for our race, laying the foundations of our great Colonial Empire, and thus have secured an undeniable claim to the gratitude of all succeeding generations of Englishmen.

CHAPTER II.

THE MERCHANTS OF THE STAPLE.

THIS association is usually regarded as the first English
corporate body which received a charter from the Crown
for purely trading purposes. Their early records, however, are not always to be clearly distinguished from
those of the *Brotherhood of St. Thomas à Becket*, with
whom they appear to have been later amalgamated.
Besides the first English royal charters, which cannot
now be recovered, they are stated to have received
privileges in the year 1248 from John, Duke of Brabant,
to trade in the Netherlands, whither they had begun to
import English wools, lead, and tin, taking in exchange
the fine woollen cloths for which Flanders was already
famous.

The Notable Merchants, of whom mention frequently occurs in the statutes and ordinances of these
times, seem to have been almost exclusively members
of the Staple. But it is specially noteworthy that these
staplers were at first all foreigners, as appears from
Magna Charta, as well as from the statute issued in

1253 in favour of the Staple, prohibiting English merchants from carrying staple commodities out of the
realm.   This intolerable enactment, however, was
revoked in 1362, when the English traders were placed
on the same footing as the aliens.   Hence it is difficult
to understand how the association can be regarded as
an English corporate body before this time.   Before
the middle of the fourteenth century they could have
been little more than a foreign society, licensed to
carry on as much of the export and import trade of
England as was not already monopolized by the Hanseatics.   Nevertheless, it is stated by Gerard Malynes*
that the merchants of the Staple, whose official title
was 'The Mayor, Constable and Fellowship of the
Staple of England,' ' were the first and ancientest commercial society in England, so named from their exporting the staple wares† of the Kingdom long before
the Company of Merchant Adventurers existed.   Those

* 'The Centre of the Circle of Commerce,' 1623.

† In mediæval Latin documents the common expression for
staple is *stabile emporium*, a staple (fixed mart), where such
wares had to be brought ; hence the assumed derivation of *staple*
from *stabile.*   But the word is current in various allied meanings
in the Germanic languages, as in O. Eng. *stapol, stapul*, a prop or
post, from *stapa*, a step ; Dutch *stapel*, a pile ; Low Ger. *stapel*, a
heap, a warehouse ; whence also O. Fr. *estaple, estape* (N. Fr. *étape*),
a station, a stage, generally a town or mart where certain wares
were brought on sale, and hence called 'staple wares,' or simply
'staples.'   The original idea, therefore, appears to be, not so much
a *staple* or fixed place, as a post or raised platform approached by
steps, and arranged for a convenient sale of goods.

staples were then only the rough material for manufacture, viz., wool and skins, lead and tin. The society
was put under sundry regulations for the benefit of the
public, and was the means of bringing in considerable
wealth, as well before as after the making of woollen
cloth here, and was privileged by many succeeding
kings, viz., Henry III. (1267), Edward II. (1319),
Richard II. (1391), Henry IV. (1410), and Henry V.
(1422).

But no privileges could save from natural extinction
a corporation which depended mainly on its exclusive
right to export local produce, which produce, especially
wool, was in course of time required by the rising manu-
facturing industries at home. Hence the Staplers
received a fatal blow when the exportation of wool
began to be prohibited by the State. 'The Merchant
Adventurers gradually gained the ascendant over the
Staplers' Company, although in the charters both of
Queen Elizabeth and King James I. to the Merchant
Adventurers there is a reservation to the merchants of
the Staple of full liberty to trade into the limits of those
charters. And when at length it was judged expedient
to enact a total prohibition of the exportation of our
wool, it is no wonder that the Staplers' Company
dwindled to nothing. At this day, 1762, they are only
a mere name, without any virtual existence; nevertheless, they keep up the form and show of a corporation,
by continuing annually to elect the officers of their
company, as directed by their ancient charters. Those

2

who deal in wool, still called wool-staplers, keeping up
this nominal corporation, and holding at this time, in
their corporate capacity, a small sum of money in the
public funds, the interest whereof serves to defray the
expense of their meetings and elections.   But they
never had a hall or particular house or office of their
own within the City of London like other trading companies, although the Inn of Chancery, near Holborn
Bars, is so denominated from their warehouses being
anciently situated there, as was also an office and warehouse of theirs which, since the erection of the new
bridge at Westminster, has lost its very place, as well
as an ancient name of Wool-staple, at the upper end of
Canon, commonly called Channel Row.'—Anderson,
i. 303.

It is interesting to note that the staple for the Port
of London stood originally on the site of the present
Houses of Parliament, whence it was removed in 1375
to the Inn of Chancery in Holborn, which afterwards
became known as Staple Inn.   Abroad, the Staplers
appear to have been for a long time confined to one
mart in the Netherlands or neighbouring districts, this
restriction being imposed on them in order to facilitate
the collection of the customs raised by the Crown on
their trade.

The first of these marts seems to have been Antwerp,
which is already mentioned as their staple for the Low
Countries so early as the year 1312.   At that time the
ports of export for English wool were, by an injunc-

tion of Edward II., in 1320, confined to Weymouth, Southampton, Boston, Yarmouth, Hull, Lynn, Ipswich, and Newcastle, so that in those days England stood in her trading relations with the Continent somewhat in the same position as China does with England at the present time. Later, the Staplers, under the pressure of the times, shifted their headquarters backwards and forwards between the towns of Antwerp, St. Omer, Brussels, Louvain, Mechlin, and Calais, and when this last place was lost to England in 1558, they ominously migrated to Bruges, without, however, succeeding in saving either themselves or that once renowned emporium from decay and extinction.

CHAPTER III.

THE FRATERNITY (BROTHERHOOD) OF ST. THOMAS À
BECKET, LATER CALLED THE COMPANY OF THE
MERCHANT ADVENTURERS OF ENGLAND.

IT was above stated that the early records of the companies of the Staplers and the Merchant Adventurers
are somewhat entangled. This point is well brought
out by the statement regarding their origin made by
the Adventurers in 1638 before the House of Commons,
when defending themselves against the charges brought
against them by private traders, at that time branded as
'Interlopers.' On that occasion they claimed to have
sprung from the London Guild of Mercers, a company
of English merchants who started the first woollen
manufacture in England in 1296, and obtained
privileges from John, Duke of Brabant, enabling them
to settle in Antwerp in association with all other
English merchants resorting thither. But we have
seen that it was the Staplers who obtained privileges
from John of Brabant, while it is certain that there
were no chartered Adventurers before the year 1505,

when this body became officially recognised as the Company of Merchant Adventurers of England.

Before that time they, or their immediate fore-runners, bore the name of the Fraternity or Brother-hood of St. Thomas à Becket, a society which was flourishing about the year 1358, when they are stated to have received ample privileges from Louis, Count of Flanders, for fixing their staple for the sale of English woollen cloth at Bruges. No doubt Edward III. had already selected this place in 1341 as his staple for wool, leather, and tin; but the two statements may perhaps be reconciled by the consideration that such wares had ceased to be largely exported after this time, so that the Staplers, as exporters especially of wool, might have now been replaced at Bruges by dealers in general commodities. Such were emphati-cally the merchants of St. Thomas à Becket, who, by adapting themselves to the changing conditions of international intercourse, gradually engrossed the trade in cloth, which was now being manufactured in in-creasing quantities in England. Thus, as cloth was taking the place of wool as the principal export busi-ness, so the new company began to supersede the old Wool-staplers.

No special privileges, however, were granted to them by the Crown till the year 1406, when they re-ceived their first charter from Henry IV. Even this document conferred no exclusive rights on the corpora-tion beyond that of choosing their own governor and rectifying their own abuses. By paying a 'freedom fine' of an old noble (about 18s. 6d. of modern money) any person might consort with them; hence Malynes (p. 86) asserts that 'of their privileges all the merchants and marines of England and Ireland were to be equally partakers without exception.' They would thus appear to have been at first an open trading association, and did not become a strictly regulated company till they began later to lay taxes on woollen goods and mulcts on their own members, as well as to exclude (wrongly, as was charged against them) all outsiders from their fellowship except on payment of large fines for admission.

But this abuse of power was probably connived at 'for a consideration' by the charter of 1430, by which all their former immunities [and usurped rights?] are stated to have been confirmed.

Like the Staplers, the 'Brotherhood' frequently changed their central stations abroad, and we are told by their secretary, John Wheeler ('Treatise of Commerce,' 1601) that when they removed in 1444 from Middelburg to Antwerp 'they were met by the magistrates and citizens without the town, and conducted with solemnity to an entertainment.' The writer, perhaps with a pardonable exaggeration, goes on to say that the 'English Nation,' as they were called, were the founders of the greatness of that city, which soon after their arrival became a most flourishing seaport, so that 'houses therein, which used to be let for

40 or 60 dollars, were now let for 300 or 400 and some for 800 dollars yearly rent.'

The chief exporters at this time were the English, who had already begun to deal less in produce and more in products, such as woollen cloths of diverse kinds, pewter ware, brasswork, crockery, gloves, stockings, various articles of dress, saddlery, hangings, and cutlery. Towards the close of the fifteenth century the competition with foreign wares had become so keen that protective duties began to be imposed on some of these English goods imported by the Brotherhood. This led to much recrimination, and occasionally to international commercial treaties drawn up quite in the modern spirit. Thus, in a treaty (1494) between Henry VII. and Archduke Philip, Sovereign of the Netherlands, it is stipulated that 'the new duty of one florin on every English woollen cloth, and also whatever other new imposition had been laid thereon, was now absolutely annulled, and English cloth was hereby freely permitted to be imported and sold in all the Archduke's counties (Flanders only excepted) free of the said duty of one florin, and of all other new impositions.'

A dispute, which continued for nearly two hundred years from this time, now broke out between the chartered bodies and private traders—that is, the above-mentioned 'Interlopers.' A clear idea of the main points at issue is afforded by an Act of Parliament passed in 1497, providing, among other things, that 'every Englishman shall have free recourse to certain foreign marts without exaction to be taken by any English fraternity or fellowship, excepting only the sum of ten marks' (£6 13s. 4d.).

There appears to have been some ground for the complaints against the fellowship, as the free course of commerce may have been somewhat obstructed by their privileges. However, after an examination of the complaint had been made, the result was very favourable to the company, and the Legislature appears to have decided that the time had not yet come when our infant foreign trade could be left to its own devices.

Full effect was given to the decision in the year 1505, when a fresh charter was granted to the Fraternity, now recognised by the proud title of the Merchant Adventurers of England. Under this charter the export trade in woollen goods was retained in their hands, and they were also authorized 'to hold courts and marts at Calais, provided, however, that they exacted no more than the 10 marks of any merchant whatever for his freedom in this fellowship for trading to Flanders, Brabant, Holland, Zealand, and the countries adjacent under the Archduke's Government, hereby enjoining all merchant adventurers to come into the freedom of this fellowship.'

This last clause needs a word of explanation. At that time not only the Fellowship, but also all private traders abroad, called themselves Merchant Adventurers, because they ventured their merchandise into foreign parts, and all such transactions were still and for long after in the nature of risks. It is here, therefore, provided that the private adventurers shall cease altogether to trade on their own account, and join the Company of Adventurers. At the same time, the justice of the case is met by keeping the entrance-fee at a low rate, whereby the subscribers had ample return for their money in the greatly-increased security of membership with a powerful corporate body.

How great was this corporate advantage, as opposed to their previous independence, and how strong the company itself had become for the general weal about the middle of the sixteenth century, was made evident in connection with the history of the Netherlands in those dark days of religious fanaticism. While all the surrounding lands were made desolate by the fiery persecutions of the Spaniards, aided by the recently-introduced sanguinary tribunal of the Inquisition, peace and security for life and property still reigned in Antwerp, which the Merchant Adventurers had chosen as the centre of their operations in the Low Countries. And when the Emperor Charles V. wished to establish the Inquisition in that city also, these English Adventurers stood forward as the champions of liberty of conscience.

Such was their influence at the time that they were able to save this great emporium, 'a general storehouse for the whole world,' from such a dire catastrophe, simply by threatening to close their factories and quit the place, should the Emperor carry out his intention. Charles, who with all his bigotry had still an eye to the main chance, found by inquiry that the departure of the company would be the ruin of the provinces, where Wheeler assures us that the Adventurers maintained or employed some twenty thousand persons in Antwerp alone, besides thirty thousand in other parts of the Netherlands. And thus did the company vindicate their right to their own chartered liberties by manfully preserving those of the people with whom they maintained commercial intercourse.

A few years later (1564) Camden states in his 'History of Queen Elizabeth' that our general trade with the Netherlands amounted to 12,000,000 ducats, of which 5,000,000 was for English cloth alone. This was perhaps the best reply to those who still continued their angry polemics against these privileged Adventurers, whose immunities were confirmed by several charters issued in their behalf during the reign of Elizabeth.

Then came a crisis in the affairs of the company, which, after the seizure (1568) of its effects by Alva to the value of £100,000 in Antwerp, had perforce to quit the Netherlands and establish itself first in Hamburg and then in Staden. Here they resided intermittently till 1597, greatly to the benefit of this trading place, which up to that time was quite unknown.

In consequence of this movement, their charter of

privileges was extended (1586) to Germany, where they were authorized to hold their courts and exercise their trade, to the exclusion of all interlopers, as before. But here they had much to contend with owing to the machinations of the Spanish envoys, and still more to the open opposition of the Hanseatics, jealous of their growing influence in the North. This is very clearly shown in a letter (1591) of the Elector Palatine to Queen Elizabeth, explaining, in reply to her remonstrances, that the action taken against the Adventurers in Staden 'was violently obtained by means of the Spanish ambassadors and of certain factious Hanseatics, who are only grieved that they do not enjoy the advantages which the said contract procured for Staden,' the reference being to an agreement permitting the company to settle in that place. But their enemies prevailed at last, and, by combining their interests at the Imperial Court, were successful in procuring (1597) the expulsion of the company, not only from Staden, but from the whole of Germany. Indeed, the Adventurers must have now either closed their accounts or else directed their energies to more distant lands, but for the friendly intervention of the now independent United Provinces, whence they received urgent invitations from Groningen, and from as many as a dozen other places, to settle amongst them.

Wheeler gives an interesting account of the general condition about this time of the company, which 'consists of a great number of wealthy merchants of divers great cities and maritime towns, etc., in England, including London, York, Norwich, Exeter, Ipswich, Newcastle, Hull. These of old time linked themselves together for the exercise of merchandise, whereby they brought much wealth home to their respective places of residence. Their limits are the towns and ports lying between the river of Somme in France, and along all the coasts of the Netherlands and Germany within the German Sea.'

They exported annually at least sixty thousand white cloths, worth at least £600,000, forty thousand coloured cloths, worth £400,000 — in all, £1,000,000 sterling, besides what went to the Netherlands from England of lead, tin, hides, tallow, corn, beef, etc. The company imported from Holland and Germany wines, copper, steel, iron and copper wire, gunpowder, and all things made at Nuremburg (toys, small ironware, etc.); from Italy silks, velvets, and 'cloth of gold.'

But now trouble arose out of 'Cockayne's patent,' and the dyeing industry, which caused no little noise in the early years of the reign of James I. It is curious to read that the English, who were already the best cloth-weavers in the world, had not yet learned the much simpler craft of colouring the products of their busy looms. The consequence was that their white cloths had to be shipped to Holland, whence they came back dyed and finished. Reflecting on this anomalous state of things, Alderman Sir William Cockayne suggested to the King that this needless waste might be stopped by having the business done at home. For this purpose he easily obtained an exclusive patent, his Majesty reserving to himself the monopoly of the sale of such home-dyed goods.

But this ingenious plan had the disadvantage of throwing everything connected with the textile industries out of gear. In the first place, the Merchant Adventurers complained of the loss of their carrying trade in white cloths, which, despite their chartered right, they were now forbidden to export out of the kingdom. Then the Hollanders and Germans retaliated by prohibiting the importation of all English dyed fabrics, so that most of the foreign trade in these goods suddenly collapsed, to the dismay and ruin of the manufacturers. These were to some extent appeased by the permission to export a limited quantity of the white cloths. But it was then discovered that the home-dyed goods were worse done and yet dearer than those finished in Holland. Under these accumulating evils James had to give way, annulling Cockayne's patent and restoring their privileges to the Adventurers (1617).

The company were accused of constantly making handsome ' New Year's gifts ' to the Ministers of State for the continuance of their interest. Thus, in 1623 the Lord Treasurer received two hundred gold pieces of twenty-two shillings each, and a piece of plate, and other presents were at the same time made to the Duke of Buckingham, the Archbishop of Canterbury, the Lord Keeper, the Lord President, the Secretaries of State, etc. It would thus appear that, while persons of influence mulcted the company, the company indemnified itself by raising the fees of admission into the corporation.

During the disorderly time of the Civil War, this process went on apace, until it threatened to assume colossal proportions. By an ordinance of the Lords and Commons, made in the year 1643, the Adventurers were authorized to double their freedom fines—that is to say, £100 for a Londoner and £50 for those of the outports, with further power to imprison those refusing to pay said fines. But it is stated that this ordinance, one of the first issued without the royal assent, was made in consideration of the enormous sum of £30,000 advanced to Parliament by the company.

About this time (1647) they transferred their chief factory from Delft to Dort, the centre of their operations abroad having been located in Holland ever since their expulsion from Germany. But after courteously declining two pressing invitations to settle in Bruges, especially on the ground that freedom of religious worship was not guaranteed them, the Adventurers now again betook themselves to Germany. This was no doubt partly owing to the political troubles between the English and Dutch Republics, which broke into open warfare in 1652, and partly because there was henceforth little more to fear from the rivalry of the now moribund Hanseatic League. But whatever the cause, Hamburg presently became their chief, and soon after their sole, staple town for the English woollen trade, and so continued till the extinction of the company. It was on this account that they became henceforth generally known as the Hamburg Company, although the old official title of Merchant Adventurers was retained to the last in all their records.

Henceforth also their history appears to have been absolutely uneventful. They continued to enjoy considerable privileges, and to carry on a great trade in English woollens and other manufactures. Hamburg thus served as the chief distributing place for our commodities over a great part of Europe throughout the latter half of the seventeenth and the whole of the eighteenth century, and, indeed, to some extent down to the present time. Only the trade is now free to all comers, no longer needing the adventitious aid of charters and immunities.

CHAPTER IV.

THE RUSSIA COMPANY.

IT was towards the close of the reign of Edward VI.
that efforts were for the first time made to open direct
trading relations with Russia (or Muscovy, as it was
then more commonly called) by the route leading round
North Cape to the White Sea. This route was already
known in Anglo-Saxon times, at least by report from
the famous Norse trader and seafarer Ohthere, who was
the first to round North Cape and penetrate into the
Polar waters as far as the Cwen (White) Sea. On his
return Ohthere visited England and related his adven-
tures to King Alfred, who embodied them in his transla-
tion of Orosius. Here we read how the daring Norse
explorer said that he wished to find ' how far the land lay
right north, or whether any man dwelt north of the waste.
Then he went right north near the land, having all the
way the waste land on the right, and the wide sea on
the left for three days. The land was uninhabited all
the way on his right, save by fishers, fowlers and
hunters, who were all Finns (Lapps, still so called by

the Norwegians); and there was a wide sea always on his left; but farther on the land was well peopled by the Beormas (Biarmians, Permians). He went thither to see the land, and also for the horse-whales (walruses), which have very good bone in their teeth, and of these teeth they brought some to the King, their hides also being very good for ship-ropes.'

But all this was forgotten in the 'dark ages,' and the way round Norway had to be rediscovered by the expedition of Sir Hugh Willoughby in 1553, which was equipped by a number of gentlemen and merchants to cut out the Portuguese spice trade with the Moluccas by opening direct communication with Cathay (China) by the north-east passage. This north-east passage remained unvisited till the Nordenskjold expedition of our own times; but meanwhile the 'gentlemen and merchants' had learnt enough from the few survivors of Willoughby's disastrous venture to form themselves into an association for the purpose of further research and profitable trade, if not with China, then with the intervening lands of Tsar John Vasilivich (Ivan the Terrible). In this they were the more encouraged that Richard Chancellor, Captain of one of Willoughby's ships, had reached Archangel on the White Sea, and had been well received by the Tsar, who not only showed himself inclined to grant the English consider-able privileges at Archangel, but also furnished Chancellor with letters to King Edward giving effect to that intention.

When Chancellor reached London by the overland return route, Edward had already passed from the scene, and it was consequently from Queen Mary that the company received in 1554 their first charter of incorporation. In this document they are characteristically styled the ' Merchant Adventurers for the Discovery of Lands, Countries, Isles, etc., not before known or frequented by any English '; and the here indicated twofold purpose of trade and discovery gives the keynote to the whole history of these daring pioneers in the Far East. This somewhat cumbersome official title was replaced by the more convenient name of the *Russia Company*, by which they are usually known.

In the preamble, itself an interesting historic sketch, it is stated ' that the Marquis of Winchester, the Earl of Arundel, the Earl of Bedford, the Earl of Pembroke, the Lord Howard of Effingham, etc., had already fitted out ships for discoveries northward, not as yet frequented by any other Christian monarchs in friendship with us. And whereas one of the said ships (Chancellor's) set forth last year (1553), arrived safe and wintered in the dominions of our cousin and brother Lord John Basilowitz, Emperor of all Russia, who entertained them honourably and granted them letters to us, with license freely to traffic in his country, with other privileges under his signet ; wherefore we grant the corporation liberty to resort not only to all parts of that Emperor's dominions, but to all other parts not known to our subjects, none of whom but such as shall be free of, or licensed by this company, shall frequent the parts aforesaid under forfeiture of ships and merchandise, one half to the crown, and one half to the company.'

A first start under their charter was made the very next year, when Chancellor sailed with two ships to the river Dwina, making his way from Vologda in sledges to Moscow, where the party was entertained by the Tsar, and from him received for themselves and their successors many important privileges. Such were freedom to trade in any part of his dominions without safe conduct or license; immunity from arrest except for debt; power to choose and control or punish their own brokers, skippers and other servants; jurisdiction over all the English settled in Russia. Due punishment was to be inflicted for assault or murder; the company's goods were to be exempt from forfeiture in case an Englishman should wound or kill a Russian subject; and Englishmen arrested for debt were to have the right of bail.

About this time Captain Stephen Burrough, in the company's service, made a first attempt to reach Novaya Zemlia, but was unable to pass Waigats Strait owing to the pack-ice. The two ice-bound ships of the Willoughby expedition were, however, soon afterwards brought away. The crews had all been frozen to death, and Sir Hugh himself was found seated in his cabin, with his diary and other papers lying on the table.

In 1558 the company's agent, Anthony Jenkinson, attempted to open a new channel for trade through Russia into Persia. Sailing down the Volga to Astrakhan, he made his way thence by the Caspian Sea to the Persian town of Boghar, where he found traders from Russia, India, and even distant Cathay, which was stated to be at that time a nine months' journey from Boghar. On his return to England he published the first known map of Russia, and afterwards again traversed the same route no less than six times. Yet after his time the road was again closed till 1741, when it was reopened by Act of Parliament in favour of the Russia Company.

Other routes, however, were attempted with varying success, and in 1566 they obtained from the Sophy (Shah) exemption from all customs on their goods, as well as full protection for their persons and property. In the same year the company received the sanction of a formal Act of Parliament, always regarded as more effective than a royal charter. One object of the Act was to protect from interlopers the precincts of the company, which was now officially renamed 'The Fellowship of English Merchants for Discovery of New Trades.' Within these precincts were also now included 'the countries of Armenia, Media, Hyrcania, Persia, and the Caspian Sea.' It was at the same time provided in the general interest of British trade and industries that the company should employ English ships alone, with a majority of English crews, and that they should export to Russia, etc., 'no woollen goods or kersies unless they be well dressed, and for the most part dyed within this realm,' both provisions under heavy penalties.

Another provision was also introduced in favour of the northern seaports of Newcastle, Hull, and Boston, as well as the city of York, by which they could acquire the freedom of the company on exceptionally easy terms. The concession was made in this statute, which was the first to establish an exclusive mercantile corporation, on the ground that the navigators of those northern towns had been amongst the earliest to take part in the efforts now being made to force the north-east passage.

The company was also made an effective instrument for the encouragement and reward of those early sea voyages by which British enterprise was fostered and a good beginning made in the discovery of those Arctic regions whose secrets have not yet been wholly re-vealed.

How great were the risks above referred to may be seen from the catastrophe which occurred during the company's renewed efforts to keep open the Persian trade in the years 1568-73. As recorded by Hakluyt, these efforts would have proved exceedingly profitable had their ships not been plundered by Cossack pirates on the return voyage across the Caspian Sea. The fleet was laden with a rich cargo of Persian raw silk, wrought silks of divers kinds, gall-nuts, carpets, East

Indian spices, turquoise gems, and other commodities to the value of about £40,000, very little of which was ever recovered.

All this time English interests were in the safe keeping of Sir Thomas Randolph, Queen Elizabeth's Ambassador at the Court of Russia. In 1569—that is, one year after his arrival in Moscow—he obtained, after much waiting and ceremony, all his demands in favour of the company. The concessions were embodied in a regular commercial treaty between the two countries, in which they were granted an exemption from all customs, with renewed leave to transport their wares through Russia to Persia, whereas others were not allowed to trade beyond the city of Moscow. In those times the English conveyed their goods in dug-outs up the Dwina to Vologda, thence overland to the Volga, down that river to Astrakhan, across the Caspian and through the Turkestan desert to Kasbin and other Persian towns, whence they still hoped ultimately to reach China. But, says Camden, by reason of the war between the Turks and Persians, and the robberies of the barbarians (the Turkoman nomads and Turki Cossacks), the Londoners—that is, the company— 'were discouraged from pursuing this glorious enterprise.'

In fact, the fortunes of the company were about this time at a very low ebb, and instead of spreading farther afield, they needed all their energies to maintain their footing in Muscovy amid the disorders caused by the oppression and butcheries of Ivan the Terrible. During a revolt of the nobles (1571) against this savage ruler's cruelties, Moscow was captured and burned by the Tartars, the company losing in the conflagration no less than 400,000 roubles, or, say, about £60,000. No doubt Ivan promised to indemnify them, but deprived them of their privileges instead.

Such was the state of affairs when Jenkinson arrived for the fourth time in Russia, now in the capacity of Queen Elizabeth's Ambassador. This was sufficient to secure the respect even of Ivan, who was, moreover, induced by the representations of that most able diplomatist to restore the company's privileges, and make satisfaction for at least a part of their recent losses. But they had also suffered by shipwrecks, by Polish pirates in the Baltic, by bad debts, and other mishaps, so that it was some time before they recovered from this run of ill-luck.

Nevertheless, and despite the action of the separate traders already encroaching on their sphere, both in the Baltic and round North Cape to Kola in Russian Lapland, they remained true to the spirit of their constitution by again attempting the North-east Passage in the year 1576. But, as is recorded in Hakluyt, they were again baffled by the great accumulation of ice in the Waigats, or Kara Strait, flowing to the Kara Sea between Novaya Zemlia and Waigats Island.

The company went to great expense in fitting out this expedition, which, even had it surmounted the

initial difficulties, could never have established direct
trading relations with China. They were, however,
somewhat recouped for the outlay by turning their
attention to the deep-sea and fresh-water fisheries in
these high latitudes, which must have been very profitable, as, in addition to fish-oil, the company's ships
in successful seasons brought home as many as ten
thousand salmon. Hence they strove hard to maintain this exclusive trade, not only against English
interlopers, but also against the Dutch, who had
begun about the year 1578 to encroach upon the
company's preserves along the coast of Russian Lapland.

But it is difficult to see how foreigners could be
affected by an English charter of privileges. Hence,
although in 1582 as many as 'eleven ships well armed'
were despatched thither 'for fear of enemies and
pirates'—by 'enemies' are no doubt to be understood
English interlopers, bound by royal charters, and still
more by Acts of Parliament (see above), and not the
Dutch or other foreigners lawfully trading in those
waters. Friction might no doubt arise between the
crews of diverse nationalities, as is even now of not
rare occurrence on the Dogger Bank. But such cases,
attended at times by bloodshed and other outrages,
would have to be settled on equal terms in the courts
of the respective combatants.

Such, however, was the policy of those times that,
as Camden tells us, Queen Elizabeth was obliged in

1583 to make a treaty with the King of Denmark, in which permission was given to the Russia Company to freely navigate the North Sea round by the coasts of Scandinavia to the White Sea, and in case of foul weather to take refuge either in Iceland or in the Norwegian seaports. Even the havens hitherto closed to them were now thrown open, though not for trading purposes, with the King's special license, procurable on the annual payment of 100 rose nobles.

On the other hand, Sir Jerome Bowes, despatched in 1583 to the Court of Ivan's successor, Tsar Feodor Yanowich, failed to obtain a renewal of the company's exclusive privileges in Muscovy. Nor was Dr. Fletcher much more successful, when he went thither on a like errand in 1588, although a promise was made to remit in favour of the company half of the Customs imposed on other foreign traders, in consideration of their having been the first discoverers of the sea-route round by North Cape.

At that time the company traded chiefly in woollens, silks, velvets, coarse linen cloth, mercery, cutlery, and miscellaneous wares in considerable variety. But 'what with expense of the first discovery and the large presents since bestowed on the Tsar and his Ministers, and the false dealings of others there, it had cost the company about £80,000 before it could be brought to any profitable account; and even at this time, from the fickle temper of the Tsar and his people, the encroachments of the Hollanders and the expense of ambassadors, etc., all borne by the company, this trade now stood on a very precarious bottom.'* This last statement is a striking proof of the immense benefits directly and indirectly conferred on the English nation by the enterprising spirit of these early chartered corporations. But for them, our people would not have been so much as heard of in those remote Eastern regions, whither the Crown could not have afforded to send envoys had not all the expenses been defrayed by the companies. It is a matter of history how the dignity and prestige of the State was upheld by these envoys (Jenkinson, for instance, at the Court of Ivan the Terrible) amongst those way-ward and dangerous autocrats, Sophy, Tsar, and Sultan.

But the benefits were mutual, as seen by the action of Elizabeth's Ambassador, Jerome Horsey, who in 1584 was successful in his intercession on behalf of the company. The Tsar not only restored but increased their immunities, and also sent Horsey back by the overland route laden with costly presents for the Queen. On Horsey's return by the sea-route, he was received with all honours at Archangel, and, moreover, 'saluted with the cannon of the Dutch and French ships,' so respected had the name of England already become in those parts.

Two years later he obtained a renewal and further extension of the company's privileges, though it would

* Anderson, ii., p. 107.

seem these were no longer of an exclusive character, but rather, as we should now say, on the footing of 'the most favoured nations.' Such were the Dutch and the French, who had also by this time begun to take a share in the Russian trade, after the road had been opened by the English over thirty years before. It is curious to find Sir Walter Raleigh complaining at the beginning of the reign of James I. that the Dutch were everywhere outstripping the English, and especially monopolizing the carrying trade 'by the structure or roominess of their shipping, holding much merchandise, though sailing with fewer hands than our ships could, thereby carrying their goods much cheaper to and from foreign parts than England can; whereby the Dutch gain all the foreign freight, whilst our own ships lie still and decay, or else go to Newcastle for coals.'*

Raleigh takes a somewhat pessimistic view of the company's business in Muscovy, remarking that 'for seventy years together we had a great trade to Russia, and even about fourteen years ago we sent store of goodly ships thither; but three years past we sent out four thither, and last year but two or three ships; whereas the Hollanders are now increased to about thirty or forty ships, each as large as two of ours, chiefly laden with English cloth, herrings taken in our seas, English lead, and pewter made of our tin,

* 'Observations Concerning the Trade and Commerce of England with the Dutch and other Foreign Nations,' 1603.

besides other commodities, all which we may do better than they. And although it [Russia] be a cheap country, and the trade very gainful, yet we have almost brought it to nought by disorderly trading.'*

The picture was probably not quite so black as it is here painted, although the affairs of the company were beyond question in a somewhat precarious state for some time after the accession of James I. But then came a revival, and hopes were for a time greatly raised by the ambitious project of Sir Henry Neville, who in 1613 proposed to extend the company's operations, not merely to Persia, as had already been done by Jenkinson, but even to India itself, and this at a time when the very geographical conditions were but imperfectly known. In this daring scheme, as communicated through John Chamberlain to Sir Ralph Winwood, it was proposed to divert the whole trade of Persia and of the Indian peninsula up the river Hydaspes overland (that is, over the Hindu-Kush) to the river Oxus, which was described as flowing at that time, not to the Aral Sea, but to the Caspian. The Oxus certainly has during the historic period twice shifted its course between the Aral and the Caspian, and we know that ' in the time of Strabo it was a sort of eastern continuation of the Kura water-highway, affording a continuous trade route from Georgia across the Caspian and the Khwarezm desert under

* 'Observations Concerning the Trade and Commerce of England with the Dutch and other Foreign Nations,' 1603.

the 39th parallel, to Charjui, and so on to Baktra (Balkh) under the Hindu-Kush.'*

This was obviously the route that Neville had in view. But although the Oxus appears to have again been diverted from the Aral to the Caspian in the fourteenth century, its course beyond all question has since that period been, as at present, directly to the Aral Sea. Hence it is not surprising that nothing further was heard of the project, except so far as regards the Persian section across the Caspian. This route continued to be used at intervals by the company, especially for the importation of raw silk, till it was closed by the political convulsions of the eighteenth century, when Persia was first wasted by the Afghans, and when the tide of conquest was afterwards rolled back under Nadir Shah right away to India and Delhi, then the capital of the Mogul Empire.

Meanwhile, a fresh source of revenue was found in the development of the whale fishery in the Greenland waters. Although this region was included in the original charter obtained from Queen Mary (see above), the company, in order to make assurance doubly assured, induced James to grant them another in the year 1613 of a more stringent and exclusive character, whereby not only the English but also foreign skippers were excluded. In order to give practical effect to this provision, as many as seven armed vessels were at once equipped and despatched to Spitzbergen, where the

* A. H. Keane, 'Asia,' 1896, vol. i., p. 117.

company set up a cross with the King's arms on it, thus annexing the Archipelago to the British Empire under the name of ' King James's Newland.'

This appears to be one of the first recorded instances of a purely commercial chartered corporation taking possession of new territory, nor was it effected without a struggle, for we read that with their seven armed ships the company ' drove from those seas not only fifteen sail of Dutch, French, and Biscayners [Basques from the Bay of Biscay], but even four English separate fishers, to whom they gave the Dutch appellation of interlopers.* And they obliged certain French ships, which they had permitted to fish there, to pay a tribute of eight whales.'† ' Every one,' adds this authority, ' will at once see the absurdity of King James's pretensions to a monopoly of the fishery for whales in that extensive ocean, as well as calling a land his Newland where no human creature ever did nor even can subsist for the space of one winter, although twice fatally attempted.'‡

The point was already raised, without being settled, in the year 1614, when King James addressed a protest through his Ambassador Extraordinary, Sir Henry Wootton, to the United Provinces, concerning the

---

* This word is a curious outcome of Dutch hybridism, being compounded of the Lat. *inter*=between, and the Dutch *looper*= runner, hence one who illegally intercepts, forestalls, or cuts out another, especially in trade ; *loopen*=to run, is cognate with the Eng. *leap*, and corresponds exactly with the Germ. *laufen*=to run.

† Anderson, ii., p. 343.   ‡ *Ibid.*

differences that had arisen between the subjects of the two nations, ' on account of the fishery in the North Sea, near the shores of Greenland, of right solely belonging to us and our people, but interrupted by the said Hollanders.' The question would doubtless turn on the meaning to be given to the little word ' near,' which was obviously susceptible of diverse interpretations — rigid or elastic, according to the different interests involved. Pending a diplomatic solution, ' the said Hollanders' settled the matter in their practical way by sending that very year eighteen ships to those seas, ' four of which were ships of war of the States, where, in spite of our company's exclusive claim [and also in spite of the company's thirteen ships, presumably not armed], they fished there by main force.'*

These quarrels lasted many years, the Dutch, on the whole, having the best of it. In 1617 they seized a quantity of the English oil, and also of the ' fins ' or whalebone, of which mention is now for the first time made.

About this time the newly - founded East India Company formed a kind of alliance with the Russia, so as to constitute one joint association for the whale fishery. But although thirteen ships were despatched to the Spitzbergen waters in 1618, the Hollanders again proved superior, overpowering, plundering, and dispersing the English vessels, ' most of which returned home empty.'

* Anderson, ii., p. 346.

It may be interesting to describe how this dangerous industry was carried on in those days. The whales, having hitherto been little disturbed, still continued for some years freely to resort to the bays and inlets round the coasts, so that they were often captured in great numbers without having to be pursued and harpooned from open boats on the high seas. The blubber was thus also easily landed on the shore, and boiled down in the so-called 'cookeries,' that is, coppers, which are erected on the spot and left standing from year to year. Thus only the purified oil was brought home, together with the whalebone. The English having been the first to arrive on the scene, had possessed themselves of all the best havens, so that the Dutch, coming next, were obliged to seek for suitable bays still farther north. Then followed the Danes, who got in between their two predecessors, and were successively followed by the French and the Basques, all adopting the same process of 'cooking' as had first been introduced by the English.

But then the schools gradually became thinner and thinner, so that the inshore grounds were at last deserted, and the huge monsters had to be sought at great distances from the land. Hence the cooking business also came to an end, for it was found more convenient to cut up the blubber at the ship's side, and transfer it directly to casks, in which it was brought home to be boiled down and purified. But this deep-sea fishing proving too dangerous in those high latitudes, it was abandoned by the Russia Company; nor do the English appear to have returned to these grounds till the next reign.

They, however, continued to fish in the more southern waters about the small island of ' Trinity,' which would appear to be the Cherie (Cherry) Island, now more commonly known as Bear Island, midway between Spitzbergen and Norway. But even here they met with opposition on the part of their own countrymen, the fishers from Hull, by whom the island had just been discovered. In fact, it is stated by Camden ('Annals') that this island was in 1618 granted by King James to the Corporation of Hull for their whale-fishing; hence the people of Hull now refused to recognise the exclusive right of the chartered company to pursue the whale in these waters. Thus, whichever way they turned they seemed to meet with nothing but misfortunes, and the tenacity with which they continued for so many years manfully to struggle against all these obstacles may well excite our admiration and sympathy for an association, which had already carried the name and fame of England into remote dominions of the Tsar and the Sophy, and which long continued to be a safety-valve for the overflowing energies of our nation.

In 1620, with a view to revive or further develop the Persian trade, Mr. Hobbs, one of the company's agents, made a journey from Moscow by the old Caspian route to Ispahan, at that time capital of the Sophy's dominions.

In his letter to his employers, this shrewd 'traveller and trader' has left on record an interesting account of his experiences, always with a view to the main object of the expedition. We are told of the great trade in raw silk at that time carried on at various ports on the Caspian Sea, and it is pointed out how easily the company might monopolize that profitable trade by attracting the wholesale dealers to Russia. We are further informed that the Persian vessels, which have so long disappeared from the Caspian waters, still brought to Astrakhan their dyed silks, calicoes, and Persian textiles, taking in exchange sables, martens (that is, the costly furs of these animals), red leather, for which Russia was already famous, and old Russia specie. Mr. Hobbs also draws attention to the difficulty that would have to be contended with, thanks to the rivalry of Turks, Arabs, Armenians, and Portuguese, who were severally plotting against the company's trade with Persia.

The Portuguese more especially are stated to have been our greatest competitors on all occasions. Their rivalry, however, soon ceased, because before the close of the seventeenth century they had been swept from the western parts of the Indian Ocean by the Arabs of Oman, whose empire now comprised the southern shores of Arabia, parts of the Persian coastlands and the East African seabord from Cape Guardafui nearly to the Zambesi estuary. It was this empire that was later (1856) split into two, the northern section remaining under the so-called ' Imams ' of Mascat, while the African section was constituted the Sultanate of Zanzibar under a branch of the Imam's dynasty.

Mr. Hobbs' journey soon bore fruits in the treaty of amity and commerce concluded in 1623 between King James and Tsar Michael Feodorovich, in which the company's privileges were renewed, though not in an exclusive sense. The Persian branch of their trade was specially recognised and safeguarded by the article in which it is provided that ' if either Prince shall have occasion to send such [envoys, messengers, etc.] into other countries through the countries of the other con- tracting parties . . . or unto and from Persia, Turkey, and other parts of the East, not in open hostility with either party, they shall pass freely with all their goods and people, and have due convoy by land and water.'

In general, this treaty establishes complete freedom of trade between England and Russia, but 'for all such merchants only, and none other, as are allowed on the part of Great Britain to trade into the dominions of Russia by the license of their Sovereign, and according to the gracious letters and privileges granted and to be granted hereafter to the English merchants by his renowned Majesty of all Russia and the Right Reverend great Lord and Holy Patriarch of all Russia.' The effect of this clause, of course, was that the im- munities of the Russia Company were doubly secured —on the part of England by their charters, on the part of Russia by the official recognition of those charters.

As above stated, the whale fisheries were resumed in the reign of Charles I., who in 1636 renewed the exclusive rights granted them by James I., further directing, 'for the encouragement of that company and the increase of navigation, that none, whether natives or foreigners, shall import any whole fins or whale-oil but the said company only, and this in their joint stock capacity alone in respect to the whale fishery, "all under heavy penalties."' As we hear little more of troubles and disputes connected with the fisheries, it may be presumed that this industry was henceforth continued in a peaceful way, until it was at last brought to a close, when the whales became so reduced in numbers as to make their pursuit no longer profitable.

Meanwhile, fresh troubles arose in Russia, where the execution of Charles I. had caused great indignation, and was made at least a colourable pretext for depriving the company of its immunities. Before that event the English had become complete masters of the trade to Archangel, and their rights had been fully confirmed by Alexis Michaelovich on his accession to the throne in 1645. But now everything was changed, and the Dutch, taking advantage of the general feeling of resentment against 'the English regicides,' acquired such influence at the Russian Court as to completely supplant their rivals. They were stated some years later to have employed as many as two hundred agents in Archangel alone.

Even after the Restoration the same attitude of hostility was maintained against the English, or, perhaps it would be more correct to say, was kept alive by the intrigues of the Hollanders at the Imperial Court. Hence the failure of the Earl of Carlisle's Embassy, sent in 1663 by Charles II. to obtain a renewal of the company's privileges. Amongst the specious pretexts put forward for refusing this favour was the statement that ' all the English merchants to whom the privileges were first granted were dead, and that their privileges expired with them.' It was useless for Lord Carlisle to protest that the privileges 'were granted to the English nation, and not to any particular set of individuals, and were therefore perpetual.' After long and tedious negotiations, in which it was urged that the English had been the first to open a profitable trade for the two countries, that they had fought the enemies of Russia in the East (Baltic) Sea when the neighbouring princes had leagued together to close the port of Narva, that they furnished both commanders, men, and money for the Russian wars, and so forth, the Envoy had to return in 1669, having barely succeeded in obtaining leave for the company to trade with Russia on the same footing as the Dutch.

The real interest in these diplomatic missions, whether successful or not, lies in the consideration that but for the chartered trading associations there would have been no such missions at all. In those barbaric Eastern lands England must have long continued the mere echo of a name, had not its growing power and influence in the Western world been made manifest by the enterprising spirit of these corporate bodies. Thus were at an early date created those 'British interests' which, being exposed to the jealousy of foreign competitors, needed the watchful care of the mother-country, and the despatch of embassies from time to time to those Oriental potentates. And as the consuls and other political agents in the Netherlands, France, and Germany were at first supported by the companies, so these first embassies to the Far East were similarly equipped at the expense of the great corporations needing their intervention.

See in Thurloe's 'State Papers' (ii. 558) the language which William Prideaux, 'Messenger of his Highness the Lord Protector to his Imperial Majesty the Tsar,' addresses in 1654 to the then Governor of Archangel. It had been reported from the Hague that the English had been banished from Archangel at the request of the Lord Culpepper, agent for Charles II., then abroad; thereupon a fleet of merchant vessels was sent thither, accompanied by Cromwell's messenger, Prideaux, who addressed a letter to the Governor, stating, amongst other things, that 'whereas there hath been a distance from commerce for some time by the English merchants to the said port of Archangel, they are now come hither with their ships laden with goods. So it is required of the Governor, in the name of the Lord Protector of the Commonwealth of England, Scotland, and Ireland, to know if trade shall be permitted with freedom, and if granted, on what terms.' Thereupon the White Sea port was again thrown open to the English nation, the Governor declaring that 'the English Company is licensed by his Imperial Majesty of all Russia to trade in Archangel in all unprohibited goods, they paying the same custom as other strangers do.'

This was a great concession, considering the prevailing hostility to the Western Republicans, fomented by the machinations of the Dutch. It is not, therefore, surprising that a rider was added, ' that as soon as the English have done trading at that port, they must go beyond sea [return home], and not be permitted, as anciently, to go up to Moscow, nor to any other part of Russia ; but what goods shall be left unsold may either remain at Archangel or be carried back to England. Mr. Prideaux, however, is permitted to go to Moscow, to acquaint his Imperial Majesty with his said commission from the Protector.' That the Tsar should, under the circumstances, consent to receive a messenger at all from the ' regicide ' is not a little remarkable. The incident shows the respect, if not the love, in which a ruler was held, even by Eastern autocrats, who was possessed both of the power and will to uphold the rights of the English nation the world over.

In the last year of the seventeenth century a change

was introduced into the constitution of the Russia Company, which had the object of rendering it more elastic, and thus of bringing it more into harmony with the liberal tendency of the times. It was accordingly enacted that 'every subject desiring admission into that fellowship shall pay no more than five pounds for the same.' The practical result of such a provision was to throw the corporation open to all British subjects wishing to trade with Russia under such advantageous conditions as the company still enjoyed. A large and profitable business was evidently at that time carried on in naval stores of all kinds, for in the same year—1699—it was enacted that the 'Commissioners of the Customs shall in every session of Parliament lay before both Houses an account of all naval stores which shall have been imported by any person from Russia into England.' It is not quite clear why this statute was framed, unless it was because, as suggested by Anderson, 'the then legislature had in their thoughts the promoting of the importation of naval stores from our American plantations' (iii. 198). If so, an illustration may be thus afforded of the way in which the development of our colonies in the New World was already beginning to react on the commercial relations in the Eastern Hemisphere.

Meanwhile, however, the imports from Russia continued to increase to such an extent that the balance of the exchanges was said to be largely in favour of that country towards the middle of the eighteenth century.

In his ' New Geography of Russia,' Dr. Burching shows that in 1749 the foreign exports of Petersburg (Peter the Great had not yet been canonized) were valued at 3,184,320 roubles, and the imports at 2,942,200 roubles, showing a slight difference to the credit of Russia. But with respect to Great Britain the exchanges stood thus :

	Roubles.
Exports from Petersburg to Great Britain - -	2,245,573
Imports to Petersburg from Great Britain - -	1,012,209
Balance against Great Britain - -	1,233,364

But these returns, of which so much has been made, are not conclusive, because no account is taken of the trade of the Russia Company with Archangel. Nor is there any clear reference to the indirect trade through Russia with Persia.

In this connection it should be mentioned that a few years previously (1741) the long-standing but often interrupted Persian trade was revived by an Act of Parliament obtained by the company ' for opening a trade to and from Persia through Russia.' For this purpose a clause was introduced granting exemption from the Act of 12 George II., forbidding the importation of merchandise except from the place of its growth, production, or manufacture, or from those parts where it was usually wont to be shipped. But as raw silk and other Persian commodities had not for some time been brought to England through Russia, it was now enacted that they might be so imported in British ships, being purchased by barter with woollen or other British wares, upon paying the same Customs as were paid by the Levant (Turkey) Company on such goods brought from the Levant.

For some years this revived trade continued to flourish, as appears from the statute of 1750, confirming the Act of 1741, and reserving to all freemen of the Russia Company, and to them only, the right to import 'raw silk of the growth of Persia' through Russia on the conditions aforesaid. The overland intercourse with Persia through the Tsar's dominions appears to have been finally extinguished, and never since revived, by the civil strife and disorders that broke out in Persia soon after the death of Nadir Shah in 1746.

Thus one great source of profitable business was lost for ever to the Russia Company; and, as the whale fishery was now also being carried on mostly at a loss, little remained except the trade around North Cape with Archangel. But this precarious route, although never abandoned, could not pretend to compete with that of the Baltic, as soon as this shorter and more convenient highway became available for the pursuit of international commerce—that is, as soon as the encircling nations—Swedes, Danes, Poles, and Russians —had fought out their quarrels and settled down to peaceful ways. Strange as it may seem, this *pax maris clausi* may be said to have given its death-blow to the Russia Company, which, like all the other regulated corporations, died of inanition towards the close of the eighteenth century. It bequeathed no territory to the nation, not even ice-bound Spitzbergen or nebulous ' Trinity.' But it left an instructive record of a manful struggle long sustained against adversity and a rich inheritance of noble deeds and memories that will not be readily forgotten.

CHAPTER V.

THE EASTLAND COMPANY.

LIKE that of North Cape, the Baltic highway was already known to King Alfred from Ohthere's second voyage as far as Sleswig, and from Wulfstan's voyage into the 'East Sea' as far as Truso, near Danzig. The accounts the King received from both navigators were inserted in his Orosius, and afterwards translated (in part) by Lambarde for Hakluyt's Collection (second edition, 1598).

It would be pleasant to linger over these early and exceedingly interesting expeditions, that especially of Wulfstan, who, as a native of Anglen, might almost be claimed as an Englishman. But space forbids, and it must suffice here to state that, unlike the route round North Cape, that through the Sound to the Baltic, or the 'East Sea,' as it was always called by our fore-fathers, and is still by the Germans, was never forgotten by our seafarers. These inland waters continued to be frequented from time to time by English skippers trading on their own account under charters from the

Crown down to the time of Elizabeth, when the Baltic was constituted a closed sea in favour of an amalgamated English trading association, appropriately called the Eastland Company.*

This corporation received its first charter in 1579, being described as 'the Fellowship of Eastland Merchants.' By this document they are privileged 'to enjoy the sole trade through the Sound into Norway, Sweden, Poland, Lithuania (excepting Narva, which was reserved to the Russia Company), Prussia, and also Pomerania, from the river Oder eastward to Dantzick, Elbing, and Königsberg; also to Copenhagen, and Elsinore, and to Finland (here called an island), Gothland, Barnholm, and Oeland. They shall have a Governor, deputy, or deputies, and twenty-four assistants, who may make bye-laws, and impose fines, imprisonment, etc., on all non-freemen trading to those parts.'

It is stated that these exclusive privileges had for their chief object the encouragement of English enterprise in those waters in opposition to the still powerful

---

* This term 'Eastland' occurs in Alfred's text as the region beyond the Vistula, inhabited by the Estas; that is, the present Esthonians, a Finnish people still surviving on the south side of the Gulf of Finland. Alfred tells us that in his time it was a very extensive region, with a 'great many towns,' and 'over every town a king.' Now the Finnish domain is greatly reduced, most of the Baltic provinces being inhabited by Letts, Lithuanians, Germans and Russians. The terms 'Eastland,' 'East Country,' of the early records, have always reference to this land beyond the Vistula.

Hanseatic League. But, being a regulated company of a somewhat rigid type, the association appears to have from the very first caused much complaint on the part of private adventurers, who naturally felt aggrieved at being now excluded except on burdensome conditions from a region whither they had always been accustomed to resort.

It may, indeed, be questioned whether the policy of converting the Baltic into a closed sea could at that time be justified even on the ground of expedience. The Baltic had already become a sort of 'Northern Mediterranean,' round which were settled numerous nations in the enjoyment of a tolerably advanced degree of culture, and it had the further advantage of immunity from the attacks of corsairs to which the southern Mediterranean began to be again exposed after the occupation of Algiers by Barbarossa. No doubt the Baltic nations were frequently at war one with another, but all were at least Christians, and for the most part of kindred stock. Hence their wars were carried on in a civilized manner, and in any case all, excepting the Hanseatics, were generally well disposed towards the English merchants, from whom they were glad to take manufactured wares of all kinds in exchange for their raw produce.

It would really seem as if no charters were needed in the second half of the sixteenth century to protect English commerce in the East Sea, and still less in later times; hence the Eastlanders carried from the first the germs of disease in their system. They were not needed, and throughout their existence they were constantly engaged in bickerings with the private adventurers, who could not here fairly be stigmatized as 'interlopers.'

Nevertheless, they were at times prosperous, and, during the reign of the second Stuart, powerful enough to obtain full recognition of all their claims. In the year 1629 Charles issued on their behalf a famous proclamation, which is still interesting enough to be quoted at length :

'Whereas the Eastland Company have, by the space of fifty years at least, had a settled and constant possession of trade in the said Eastland parts in the Baltic Seas, and have had both the sole carrying thither of our English commodities, and also the sole bringing in of all the commodities of those countries, as, namely, hemp-yarn, cable-yarn, flax, pot-ashes, rope-ashes, Polonia wool, cordage, Eastland linen, cloth, pitch, tar, and wood, whereby our kingdom hath been much enriched, our ships and mariners set on work, and the honour and fame of our nation spread and enlarged in those parts.

'And whereas, for their further encouragement, the said company have had and enjoyed, by letters patent from Queen Elizabeth, the exclusive privileges above named, with general prohibitions and restraints of all others not licensed by the letters patents, we, minding the upholding of the said trade, and not to suffer the said society to sustain any violation or diminution of their liberties and privileges, have thought good to ratify the same.

'And we do hereby strictly charge and command all our customers, comptrollers, etc., that they suffer not any broadcloths, dozens, kersies, bayas, skins, or such-like English commodities, to be shipped for exportation to those parts, nor any hemp, etc. (as before named), or any other commodities whatsoever of those foreign countries wherein the said company have used to trade, to be imported by any but such as are free of that company.

'Provided always that the importation of corn and grain be left free and without restraint. We also strictly command that the statutes of the fifth of King Richard II., the fourth of King Henry VII., and the thirty-second of King Henry VIII., made against the shipping of merchandise in strangers' bottoms, either inward or outward, be duly put in execution; and that neither the said company nor any other whatsoever be permitted to export or import any of the above-mentioned commodities in any but English bottoms under the penalties in the said statutes contained.'

From the reference here made to previous statutes it would seem that certain provisions of the Navigation Act, framed to protect or encourage English shipping, had already been anticipated, not only by the first Tudors, but even by the last of the Plantagenets. It is also not a little remarkable that the importation of 'corn and grain' from the Baltic should have already acquired such a national importance under Charles I. as to be excluded from the privileges of the chartered company, and 'left free and without restraint.'

But a still heavier blow was aimed at this luckless corporation in the year 1672, when an Act of Parliament was passed reducing its immunities to a minimum. 'For the encouragement of the Eastland trade,' runs one of the clauses, with a sort of grim irony, 'it is hereby enacted that all persons, natives or foreigners, might from the first of May, 1673, have free liberty to trade into Sweden, Denmark, and Norway, anything in the Eastland Company's charter to the contrary notwithstanding.'

Thus, by a stroke of the pen, the whole of Scandinavia was removed from their jurisdiction, which was henceforth restricted to the more easterly, and for the most part less developed, coastlands along the south side of the inland sea.

And by another clause it was enacted that 'whoever, if an Englishman, shall henceforth desire to be admitted into the fellowship of the said Eastland Company, shall pay forty shillings and no more.' In other words, the freedom of the company was thrown open to all comers, or, at least, to all British subjects, for the nominal fee of £2.

These severe measures, which gave effect to the prevailing opinion that this chartered body was an anachronism, were justified by Sir Josiah Child, who declared at the time that 'the Eastland Company, by excluding others from their trade, not free of their company, had enabled the Dutch to supply all parts within the Baltic with most of the merchandise usually sent thither, and that the Dutch, who have no East-land Company, had ten times the trade thither that we had.'

Such an argument must at that time have seemed conclusive. In any case it proved beyond all cavil that a lucrative business could be carried on with the Baltic lands by any enterprising nation without the protection of charters. But it may be accepted as an axiom in political economy that where charters, that is, monopolies, are not needed, they must be regarded as an obstruction, and should be abrogated forthwith.

Such, in fact, was the fate of the Eastlanders, who, after a languid existence of little over a century, received their *coup de grace* by those articles in the Declaration of Rights (1689) in virtue of which all monopolies not actually confirmed by Parliament were practically abolished. The Eastland Company undoubtedly came within the scope of those provisions, and therefore from this time ceased to exist as a privileged trading corporation.

CHAPTER VI.

THE TURKEY (LEVANT) COMPANY.

IF the records of the Eastland Company may be taken as an object-lesson on the unwisdom of creating chartered bodies where they are not wanted, the history of our first efforts to develop a trade in the Mediterranean will serve even still better to show the wisdom of establishing such bodies where they may be needed. Our first feeble attempts to trade in this direction date from about the year 1413, when it is recorded that 'a company of London merchants laded several ships with much wool and other merchandise to the value of £24,000 towards the western parts of Morocco. But some Genoese ships, emulous of this commerce, made prize of those London ships outward bound, and carried them into Genoa. Whereupon King Henry IV. grants the sufferers reprisals on the ships and merchandise of the Genoese wherever they can find them.'*

Thus the first essays of these private adventurers were nipped in the bud, for 'letters of marque and

* 'Fœdera,' viii., p. 773.

reprisals on the bodies and goods' of powerful rivals could little avail in the hands of skippers unsupported by the prestige and resources of a corporate body. There was consequently no renewal of such disastrous enterprises until the period between 1511 and 1534, when we again read of 'diverse tall ships of London, and of Southampton and Bristol,' trading to Sicily, Candia, Chios, Cyprus, and even to Tripoli and Baruth (Beiruth) in Syria—that is, to the easternmost shores of the Levant. But the voyage, which generally took about a twelvemonth, was beset by all kinds of perils, so that one of those 'tall ships' barely escaping, 'was put into Blackwall dock and never more went to sea.'

For our Genoese rivals were now replaced by the Barbary corsairs, who had their origin in the expulsion of the Moors from Spain, and who, beginning by preying on their Spanish foes, ended by scouring the Mediterranean, and at times even the Atlantic, for wellnigh three hundred years.

Thus another suspension of operations ensued for about half a century, when Queen Elizabeth, desirous of opening direct relations with Turkey, sent William Harburn (Harebone) in 1579 on a mission to the Court of the Sultan Murad III., from whom permission was obtained for English merchants to resort freely to the Levant on the same footing as other nations. This preparatory step having been taken, Elizabeth granted in 1581 a charter of incorporation to Sir Edward Osborn, Thomas Smith, Richard Staper, and William

Garret, of whom Osborn and Staper are here stated to have 'at their own great cost and charges found out and opened a trade to Turkey, not heretofore in the memory of any man now living known to be commonly used and frequented by way of merchandise, by any the merchants or any subjects of us or our progenitors; whereby many good offices may be done for the peace of Christendom, relief of Christian slaves, and good vent for the commodities of the realm, to the advancement of her honour and dignity, the increase of her revenue, and of the general wealth of the realm.

'Her Majesty therefore grants unto those four merchants and to such other Englishmen, not exceeding twelve in number, as the said Sir E. Osborn and Staper shall appoint to be joined to them and their factors, servants and deputies, for the space of seven years to trade to Turkey. . . . The trade to Turkey to be solely to them during the said term' under three provisions: (1) That the Queen may at any time revoke this exclusive grant upon one year's previous notice; (2) that the Queen may herself add two members to the said number of patentees; and (3) that at the end of the said seven years the Queen may, at their desire, grant a renewal for other seven years, 'provided the said exclusive trade shall not appear to be unprofitable to the kingdom.'

Thus the interests both of Crown and nation were in every way safeguarded by this remarkably cautious charter of privileges. Referring to its immediate results, Sir William Monson, in his 'Naval Tracts,' 1635, asks how the English appeared to be so tardy in discovering this rich sphere of enterprise. We could not venture thither sooner, he says in reply, 'because of the great danger of falling into the hands of the Turks, the Barbary corsairs, who in those days were so ignorant of our nation as to think England to be a town in the kingdom of London.'

Such ignorance would probably have long continued but for the formation of this powerful chartered body at the right moment. The very next year (1582) we read of 'the Queen's letters to the Grand Seignior' being received with much courtesy from the hands of her Ambassador, Harebone, who was for the time being almost more the representative of these princely merchants than of their Sovereign. Acting under her instructions and on their behalf, he forthwith set about appointing consuls in the various seaports now thrown open to the English, and framing regulations for their guidance in opening trading relations throughout the Levant.* Thus an enormous impulse was given to British enterprise in a region where the name of England had scarcely been heard of since the time of Richard the Crusader. And these Eastern peoples

---

* *Levant*, from the Ital. *levante*, rising, simply means the east where the sun rises ; but it is applied in a special sense to the eastern parts of the Mediterranean, where the Italians (Venetians, Genoese) were formerly the dominant European people. In its widest sense it comprises Egypt, Syria and Palestine, Asia Minor, the Archipelago, and the western shores of the Ægean.

now learned to distinguish between *Feringhi* and *Ingliz*, and already perhaps unconsciously felt that the Ingliz was the coming race.

One of the first improvements following directly from the formation of this company affected the shipping interests; for it was now found necessary to build larger and stouter vessels for such a long voyage across the stormy Bay of Biscay and up the great inland sea. This was effected with as much rapidity as was the analogous change necessitated in our own times by the opening of the Suez Canal. Hence in the early days of the enterprise we read how the members of the association attending on the Queen and Council received great thanks and high commendation 'for the ships they then built of so great burthen,' with many encouragements also to go forward 'for the kingdom's sake.' This scene is worthy of the grand times of the great Queen Elizabeth, worthy also of the pencil of our great historic painter.

Another great advantage, affecting the general welfare and health of the nation, was the very considerable fall in the price of Eastern commodities soon after the Levantine trade began to be developed. Amongst these commodities were various kinds of drugs and fruits, such as currants, figs, raisins, dates, beside the coffee-berry. All this tended to greater general refinement, and helped soon to place the English nation on the same, and even a higher level in this respect than the other Western peoples.

But from the first this growing trade was beset with difficulties and perils, against which private adventurers could never have successfully contended. Contemporary writers dwell much on the dangers to which the company's fleets were exposed from the Barbary corsairs, who had constantly to be bought off by presents, as much as £2,000 yearly. They also speak of the exactions and hostility of the Venetians, who in this respect played somewhat the same part in the Mediterranean that the Hanseatics did in the North. But being a sovereign State, they had even more effective means of injuring our trade by the imposition of heavy duties on our imports to, and exports from, all territories under their dominion.

During the Spanish wars all these perils were intensified to such an extent that the company's vessels had to fight regular naval battles in defence of their rich treasures. A memorable engagement of this description took place in the Strait of Gibraltar in the year 1590, when ten of these homeward-bound ships were attacked by twelve Spanish galleys, each of which was strongly armed, and manned by a crew of three hundred hands. Yet after a stiff fight of six hours they were all put to flight badly damaged, and with the loss of many men, the English coming off scathless, and, as was reported, without losing a single man.

The company was reconstituted in 1593 under a new charter on a somewhat broader base, and for a period of twelve years, with the title of the Governor and Company of Merchants of the Levant. Their range of activity was now also enlarged, so as to embrace not only the Sultan's dominions 'by land and sea,' as well as those of the Venetian Republic, but also India itself—that is to say, 'through his [the Grand Seignior's] countries over land to the East Indies, a way lately discovered by John Newberry, Fitch, etc.'

This last clause, which caused so much trouble later, needs a word of explanation. It is a singular fact that, while the Portuguese were the first to reach India by the ocean highway (Vasco da Gama, 1497), the English had the now forgotten honour of discovering, or, rather, rediscovering, the overland route familiar to the ancients. The first Englishman known to have penetrated thither was Thomas Stephens, of the Jesuit College, Salsette (1579). But the first Englishmen who opened the overland trade route were the above-mentioned members of the Turkey Company, Newberry, Fitch, and Leedes, who in 1583 made their way with their cloth, tin and other wares from Aleppo to Bagdad; thence down the Tigris and Persian Gulf to Ormuz, and so on to Goa, Agra (then the Great Moghul's capital), Lahore, Bengal, Peru (for which read Pegu in Lower Burma), Malacca, and other parts of the ' Golden Chersonesus.'

They were the bearers of the Queen's recommendatory letters to the King of ' Cambaya ' (Cambay

on the north-west coast of India), and to the Emperor
of China, the Middle Kingdom being the goal of this
remarkable expedition.   But they got no farther than
Malayland, returning by much the same route through
Ormuz, and Bagdad, to Aleppo and Tripoli in Syria,
whence they sailed in one of the company's ships to
England, arriving in London in 1591.   The rich store
of information brought back by these pioneers on the
commercial relations of India at that time was no
doubt the main inducement to the renewal of the
charter in 1593, and especially to the extension of the
Turkey Company's jurisdiction to India by an overland route, which still left Persia free to the Russia
Company.

In this renewed charter provision was made for the
adequate protection of the trade by the equipment of
' four good ships with ordnance and munition, and with
200 English mariners' as escorts to the company's
fleets, but with a reservation of their withdrawal at
three months' notice should they be required ' for the
defence of the realm.'   A license was further given for
the company's vessels to fly ' the arms of England,
with a red cross in white over the same,' thus identify-
ing these Elizabethan trading corporations with the
general interests of the realm.

A further proof is afforded by the action taken by the
Crown in favour of the company against the heavy
Customs imposed on their merchandise by the Venetian
Republic, for redress whereof the Queen forbids the

subjects of Venice ' to import into England any manner
of small fruits called currants, being the raisins of
Corinth, or the wines of Candia, unless by this company's license under their seal, upon pain of forfeiture
of ship and goods, half to the Queen, and half to the
company, provided always that if the Venetian State
shall take off the said new imposts, then this restraint
touching currants and wines of Candia shall be void.'
Thus were the questions of prohibitive tariffs, free
trade, and 'fair trade' understood and settled in those
days. And in the same manner the interests of the
trading associations were regarded as national interests, to be safeguarded by the State against foreign
aggression.

On the expiration of the twelve years' charter (1605)
it was renewed in perpetuity by James I., the company
being now designated as *the Merchants of England to
the Levant Seas*. The entrance fees for all English
subjects were now also fixed at £25 for persons under
twenty-six years, at £50 for those over that age, and at
£1 for all their apprentices. Thus a most profitable
commerce to England was established in perpetuity, by
which great quantities of our woollen manufactures
and other merchandise were annually exported. The
Venetians had for many ages supplied Constantinople
and other parts of the Levant with woollen cloth and
other merchandise until the English commenced their
Levant trade; and as they were able to sell their cloth
cheaper than the Venetians, because they grew their

own wool, they drove the latter totally out of the cloth
trade to Turkey.   At this time the profits of the
Levant trade are stated to have been ' three to one.'

A natural sequel to the perpetual charter was the
appointment (1606) of a permanent English Minister in
Turkey.   The first so nominated was Thomas Glover,
described as King James's ' envoy and agent in the
dominions of Sultan Achmet, the Grand Seignior, who
has freely given his consent that our merchants may
trade to his dominions.   Liberty is hereby given to the
said Thomas Glover to reside in what part of Turkey
he shall think best, and to appoint Consuls for the
good government of the English in the other proper
ports.'   We see thus that, as in the case of Muscovy,
regular diplomatic relations were first established
between England and Turkey wholly in the interest of
British trade, which was at that time exclusively carried
on by a chartered corporation.

With the growth of this trade grew also the power
and influence of the King's representative, as seen by
the appointment (1619) of Sir John Eyre, who is no
longer an ' agent,' but a ' Minister,' and who no longer
resides ' in what part of Turkey he shall think best,'
but is henceforth attached to ' the Court of the Grand
Seignior at Constantinople.'   And his mission is again
declared to be ' for the settling of friendship and commerce between England and Turkey '; and the King
gives his Minister power to appoint consuls as before.
Most interesting in this connection is the account

given by Munn of our Levant trade in 1621, when ' of all the nations of Europe [England] drove the most profitable trade to Turkey, by reason of the vast quantities of broadcloth, tin, etc., which we export thither —enough to purchase all the wares we wanted in Turkey, and in particular 300 great bales of Persian raw silk yearly; whereas there is a balance in money paid by the other nations trading thither. Marseilles sends yearly to Aleppo and Alexandria at least £500,000 sterling, and little or no wares. Venice sends about £400,000 yearly in money, and a great value in wares beside. The Low Countries—that is, Holland— send about £50,000, and but little wares; and Messina —*i.e.*, Sicily—£25,000 in ready money; besides great quantities of gold and of dollars [thalers] from Germany, Poland, Hungary, etc. And all these nations take of the Turks in return great quantities of camblets [camlets, camelots, originally *camel*-hair cloth], grograms [Fr. *grosgrain*, coarse silks], raw silk, cotton, wool and yarn, galls, flax, hemp, rice, hides, sheep's wool, wax, corn, etc.'*

In 1643 a confirmation of previous rights, with a further extension of privileges, was granted by Parliament, presumably in return for certain sums advanced by the association to the State. The company was now empowered 'to levy moneys on its members, and on strangers, upon all goods shipped in English bottoms

* 'Discourse of Trade from England to East India,' p. 17 ; quoted by Anderson, vol. ii., p. 382.

or on strangers' bottoms, going to or coming from the
Levant, for the supply of their own necessary expense,
as well as for such sums of money as shall be advanced
for the use and benefit of the State, by the approbation
of Parliament.'

Such extensive powers were certainly not granted
without a material consideration, and it must be
evident, from the reference to money advanced ' for the
use and benefit of the State,' that the chartered corporations were at this time found to be a convenient, if
somewhat unconstitutional, means of raising revenue.
In this very year 1643 the Merchant Adventurers paid
£30,000 in return for renewal of privileges. But the
chief reasons given for these renewals and extensions
of immunity are the benefits indirectly derived by the
nation at large from the commercial activity of these
associations and the development of navigation.

A less justifiable step was taken in 1661 by Charles II.,
who in a supplementary charter, ratifying previous
rights and immunities, added a clause to the effect
that 'no person residing within twenty miles of
London, excepting noblemen and gentlemen of quality,
shall be admitted into the freedom of said company
unless first made free of the City of London.' Thus,
all ordinary subjects of the realm were absolutely excluded from trading into the Levant, except on the
unreasonable condition of residence in the London
district. It is not surprising to hear that later this
provision was the cause of much complaint, and, in

fact, tended greatly to prejudice the public against the Turkey Company.

Meantime the corporation continued greatly to prosper, and in 1675 were powerful enough to secure from Sultan Mahomet IV. a wide extension of their trade to the Levant, and even by the Black Sea or by land to Muscovy and Persia. In the remarkable treaty of commerce conferring these favours, all English subjects are granted leave to reside and trade under the company's flag in Turkey on the same footing as the French, the Venetians, or 'any Christian nation.' But it is further provided that the Dutch, and the merchants of Spain, Portugal, Ancona (Papal States), Florence, etc., trading thither, 'shall always come thither under the colours of England, and shall pay the dues to the English ambassadors and consuls, in the same manner as the English merchants do.'

To understand this last provision, it should be stated that this question of the protection of the flag had already given rise to some angry discussions between the English and French ambassadors at the Porte; and that the privilege previously conferred on the French was now transferred to the English. It affected the Dutch and the other above-mentioned nations, because these had hitherto concluded no commercial treaties with the Sultan.

In the same treaty, which was ratified by the English Ambassador, Sir John Finch, at Adrianople, heavier dues were imposed on the woollen cloths of Holland than on those of English make. A curious clause was also introduced whereby 'two ship-loads of figs and currants are annually allowed to be exported from Smyrna, Saloniki, etc., for the use of the King of Great Britain's kitchen, provided there be no scarcity of those fruits, paying only 3 per cent. custom for the same.'

That friction should sooner or later arise between this regulated association and its great rival, the joint stock East India Company, was inevitable. In 1670 the Levantines had already begun to complain of the East Indians for injuring their raw silk import trade by the large quantities now introduced from India. Then the matter was brought before Parliament in 1680 by Mr. Polexfen, and this action was followed in 1681 by a budget of grievances presented to the King in Council. In this document the Levantines set forth that they exported English wares to Turkey to the yearly value of about £500,000, taking in exchange raw silks, galls, grogran yarns, drugs, cotton, etc., all of which, being worked up in England, ' afford bread to the poor of the kingdom; whereas the East India Company export immense quantities of gold and silver with but little cloth, bringing back calicoes, pepper, wrought silks, and a deceitful sort of raw silk,' the woven goods being ' an evident damage to the poor of England and the raw silks an infallible destruction to the Turkey trade.'

Then follow the customary contrasts, that need not here be repeated, between regulated and joint stock concerns, the former being depicted in roseate hues, the latter in the darkest tints. It is further urged against the Indians that they have 'sent over to India throwsters, weavers, and dyers, and have actually set up there a manufacture of silk,' with all the dire consequences to the home industries, just like the 'wicked capitalists' of our own days, who have begun to run cotton-mills in Bombay and elsewhere in the peninsula, to the inevitable destruction of the Lancashire weavers.

To all this and much more to the same effect the Indians replied that, if they sent out less cloth, it was 'fine and more valuable' than the stuffs exported by the Levantines, who are also guilty of exporting much bullion for the purchase of their raw silks, that the trade developed under the joint stock principle has more than doubled his Majesty's Customs, while 'many generous chargeable [costly] and successful attempts' have also been made to open commercial relations with Siam, Cochin-China, China, and Japan; but their stock is now at least £1,700,000 clear of all debt, while their credit is so good that they can borrow at 3 per cent.; that since their importation of raw silks our silk manufactures have increased fourfold, while the quality is 'the same as with all other commodities on earth—good, bad, and indifferent'; that the Indian plain wrought silks, the strongest, most

6

durable, and cheapest in the world, 'are generally re-exported from England to foreign parts,' a profitable carrying and transit business being thus developed; that Indian flowered and striped silks may a little impede the English industry, but not nearly to the same extent as the imported raw silk 'doth advance it'; that the charge of sending to India throwsters, etc., is baseless, 'excepting only as to one or two dyers usually sent to Bengal, and this for the nation's as well as the company's advantage, especially as to plain black silks, generally exported again.'

The Turkey Company having also petitioned for leave to enter their rivals' domains at least to the extent of trading round the Cape of Good Hope into the Red Sea and all parts of the Sultan's territory in Africa and Arabia, the Indians contented themselves with scornfully replying that they 'cannot help admiring at the confidence [vulg. 'cheek'] of the proposers.' They, however, condescended vehemently to protest against certain interloping ships (flying the Levantines' flag) that had, during the last three years, penetrated into the Indian seas, urging that, as their forts and forces cost about £100,000 annually, it would be impossible to carry on a profitable trade, if interlopers be tolerated.

This first passage of arms may be described as a drawn battle, no decided action having been taken either by Crown or Parliament. One venture of a certain Captain Thomas Sands, with a cargo of some

£50,000, was indeed stopped by the King, who, after a protracted trial, obtained from Chief Justice Jeffreys a decision in favour of the Indians, so that ship and cargo had to be sold at a great loss to the owner. But, on the other hand, the interlopers not only continued their voyages to India, but also had the 'confidence' to raise the constitutional question as to whether the Crown could at all legally obstruct them by any exclusive charter whatsoever, unless its provisions were sanctioned by an Act of Parliament. As a set-off against Jeffreys' decision, they obtained the opinion of several leading lawyers on their side, and we have already seen how these matters were summarily disposed of by the Declaration of Rights eight years after.

In 1701 the French Board of Trade, established the year before, presented a memorial to the King on the trade of the world, in which occurs the subjoined interesting reference to the affairs of the English Turkey Company at that time: 'The English carry on that trade with much more advantage than the French, their woollen cloths being better and cheaper. The English also carry to the Levant lead, pewter, copperas, and logwood, which are goods they are masters of, together with a great deal of pepper. And that they may not drain their country of its gold and silver, they also take in dry fish of their own catching, sugar of their own colonies, and other goods of their own product, which they sell on the coasts of Portugal, Spain, and Italy for pieces of eight, which they carry to the

Levant to make up a stock sufficient for purchasing their homeward cargoes.' In confirmation of this account it may be mentioned that, in the single month of August, 1730, as many as two hundred thousand pieces of broadcloth are stated to have been shipped in four vessels to the Levant by the Turkey Company.

But the period of inevitable decline was already approaching. For some time past the French had been making serious inroads on the company's trade, partly owing to the more convenient position of the rising seaport of Marseilles, but much more through their more carefully studying the market and its requirements. They thus discovered that a lighter and more showy woollen fabric was best suited for the climate, and this they were naturally able to produce at a lower rate than the more substantial and really finer English make.

After the Treaty of Paris (1763) the affairs of the company continued steadily to decline, mainly, as would appear, because the French were now able to turn their attention once more to the peaceful pursuits of commerce in the Levant. During the late war, which left the English masters of the ocean highways, the Mediterranean basin had perforce been somewhat neglected, and it was now, perhaps, too late to recover ground in those inland waters. Things came at last to such a pass that long before the close of the century the company had become virtually bankrupt, and must have closed all its factories but for the monetary assistance which it was fain to accept from Government from time to time. Thus, amongst the supplies granted by Parliament in the year 1780 was an item of £10,000 'to the Levant Company,' this time not in return for any special service rendered to the State, but merely to keep it afloat in the assumed interest of the public weal.

But no corporate body could hope to maintain itself long by such adventitious aid. The time had now also come for throwing open the trade of the Mediterranean, which had been cleared of the Barbary corsairs, at least for a considerable period, by the bombardment of Algiers by Lord Exmouth in 1816. Hence the Turkey Company, not perhaps unwillingly, surrendered all their rights and privileges in 1825, which year marks the close of their existence as a chartered association. The summarized history of most of these privileged commercial societies — charter, prosperous trade, keen competition, encroachments, decline, debt, difficulties, disappearance—applies in a special manner to the rise and fall of the Turkey Company.

CHAPTER VII.

THE EAST INDIA COMPANY.
(1600—1702.)

IT was seen (p. 73) that the English not only reached India, but actually made a beginning of trade with that region, first by the overland route. But the attempt to maintain commercial relations with the peninsula through the territories of two powerful Mohammedan empires (Turkey and Persia), constantly at war either with each other or with some of the neighbouring States, must have even at that time seemed premature, and predestined to failure. Yet, on the other hand, the seaward route round the Cape must have seemed still more impracticable before the naval power of Spain (and of Portugal, then absorbed in the Spanish monarchy) was crippled by the destruction of the great Armada.

But after that event (1588) the thoughtful eyes of politicians and political economists were inevitably turned in this direction, and before the close of the sixteenth century the ground had already been cleared for the establishment of the greatest of chartered companies, which was incorporated in 1600, and which within two hundred years from that date had acquired the over-lordship of the whole region from the Himalayas to Cape Comorin.

As if with a presentiment of its future greatness, its foundations were from the first laid on the broadest lines, as clearly appears from the wording of the royal charter granted on December 31, 1599, to George, Earl of Cumberland, and 215 knights, aldermen, and merchants, ' that at their own cost and charges they might set forth one or more voyages to the East Indians in the country and parts of Asia and Africa, and to the islands thereabouts, to be one body politic and corporate by the name of *the Governor and Company of Merchants of London trading to the East Indies*, to have succession, to purchase lands without limitation, to have one Governor and twenty-four persons to be elected annually, who shall be called committees jointly to have the direction of the voyages and the management of all other things belonging to the said company, Sir Thomas Smith, Alderman of London, to be the first Governor, both governors and all the committees to take the oath of fidelity. The company may for fifteen years freely and solely trade by such ways and passages as are already found out, or which shall hereafter be discovered, into the countries and parts of Asia and Africa, and into and from all the islands, ports, towns, and places of Asia, Africa, and

America, beyond the Cape of Bona Speranza (Good Hope) to the Straits of Magellan . . . any statute, usage, diversity of religion or faith, or any matter, to the contrary notwithstanding, so as it be not to any country already possessed by any Christian potentate in amity with her Majesty, who shall declare the same to be against his or their good liking.'

Thus, all the oceanic regions of the globe, with the necessary reservations, are already comprised in the company's charter, while the permission to 'purchase lands without limitation,' and sundry other expressions, seem to anticipate the transformation of this trading association into a powerful State subordinate to the Crown of England, to which all the company's directors are 'bound to take the oath of fidelity.'

Other clauses of the first charter, which with occasional modifications persisted till the year 1708, deal with the export and import of bullion, a problem which to this day remains unsolved; with the company's naval forces, which are fixed at 'six good ships and six pinnaces with 500 mariners, unless the royal navy goes forth'; with the penalties incurred by interlopers; with the licenses which the company is empowered to grant to outsiders 'to trade to the East Indies,' a most important provision too often lost sight of in our estimates of the company's action; with the determination and renewal of the charter for periods of fifteen years, according as it may appear to be profitable or otherwise 'to the Crown and realm,' a notice of two years to the company being allowed whenever it may be deemed advisable for the charter to 'cease and determine.' Later, this last clause was subjected to diverse modifications, the periods of lapse and renewal shifting from fifteen to twenty-one years; and although the charter was made perpetual in 1610, we here see that the periodicity principle was recognised from the first.

It will be noticed that these provisions all tend in the same direction—on the one hand, to strengthen the corporation against foreign aggressors, and enlarge the sphere of its usefulness to the realm; on the other, to enable the State to control its action, thereby making itself directly responsible for the company's policy and proceedings in those distant Eastern lands. So wisely framed was this first charter of rights by the Queen in Council! It may be added that the company started with a modest capital of £72,000, the original shares subscribed being £50 each. It was with such humble beginnings that England—somewhat vicariously, no doubt, but still England—began that career of expansion, which has ended by constituting her the mightiest and most beneficent of Eastern powers.

Even before the issue of the charter, steps were taken to obtain for the company the usual commercial privileges from the Great Moghul, to whom, early in the year 1600, Elizabeth sent her Envoy, John Mildenhall, from Constantinople by the overland route. But owing to the opposition of the Spanish and Portuguese Jesuits at his Court, it was some years before that potentate could be induced to make any concessions in favour of the English.

Meantime, the company began operations by sending a first venture of three armed vessels with a freight of £27,000, not to India proper, but to the Indian Archipelago, whence, after capturing a Portuguese prize and delivering letters from the Queen to the Rajas of Achin and Bantam, and establishing a factory at the latter place, they returned in 1603 with a cargo of pepper and other spices, after a prosperous voyage of two years and seven months.

It is curious to read that the very first objection raised, even before Elizabeth's death, against this budding trade turned on the silver question. It was argued that it would exhaust our supply, to which it was retorted that by this trade as much silver would be drawn from other countries as would be needed for India.

Another curious objection was that our shipping would be ruined by the worms unless sheathed with lead, to which it was replied that, on the contrary, our shipping would be greatly improved in size and efficiency, so that on occasion they would prove of greater service to the nation than all the other shipping of London.

The first factory opened by the company in India proper was in 1603 at Surat, where they at once met with the keenest opposition from the Portuguese, who claimed the exclusive right to trade in those Eastern parts, not against any section of their own people, but, in virtue of Alexander VI.'s famous Bull, against all Christendom. Hence, being at that time the strongest European Power on the west side of India, they attacked both the English and the Dutch, who had arrived soon after on the scene, seizing their ships and merchandise, and murdering their heretical crews.

These hostilities, fomented by material interests and racial and religious animosities, were now prevalent everywhere in the East, and when the English fleet, sent out in 1604, reached Amboyna, in the Banda Group, they found the Portuguese and Dutch at open war about the sovereignty of those important Spice Islands. The Dutch eventually drove out their adversaries, but unfortunately took a lesson from them in cruelty, applying it relentlessly to the English when these also tried later to gain a footing in the Banda Archipelago. But the dark chapter associated with the name of Amboyna is matter of common history, and those unpleasant memories need not here be revived.

As above stated, the charter was made perpetual in 1610, because of 'the profit and honour which this trade brought to the nation,' and, as if to celebrate the event, the company now built 'the largest merchant ship that England ever had, 'which was of 1,100 tons burden, and significantly named the *Trade's Increase.*' These big ships were now sorely needed, for we read that in the same and following years they had to fight the Turks at Mocha (Red Sea), and the Portuguese again at Surat, this time more successfully than on the first occasion. Despite their great superiority, two of the English vessels defeated four of their great galleons and twenty-six frigates sent to their aid from Goa, much to the delight of the Surati people, ' by whom the Portuguese were much hated.' Thus, the English were gradually acquiring that naval supremacy in the Indian waters which later contributed so largely to the successful issue of their struggle with the French for the supremacy on land.

Hitherto the trade had been carried on by several separate stocks, each enjoying its own profits and subject to its own losses. But in 1612 these separate interests were merged in one, and the affairs of the company were henceforth conducted on strict joint stock principles. About this time also (1613) its sphere of action was extended to Japan, whither Captain Saris sailed with letters and presents from James I. to the Mikado, then resident at Meaco. He was well received at Court, and having obtained permission for the company to trade with Japan, established a factory at the port of Firando, where he had first landed. But he had much to complain both of the Dutch and of the Jesuits, then in high favour with some of the great feudal lords. Nevertheless, a regular trade was kept up for a few years, when the religious persecutions broke out, followed by the expulsion of all Europeans except the Dutch, who were permitted to keep open their factory at Nagasaki on ignominious conditions. Thus matters continued till Japan itself was thrown open to the trade of the world in our days.

The year 1614 witnessed another defeat of the Portuguese in the Indian Ocean, and saw also Sir Thomas Rowe appointed the King's and the company's Ambassador to the Great Moghul to watch over the interests of our rapidly growing Indian trade. This able Minister, who resided several years at the Court of Jehanghir, successor (1605) of the great Akbar, kept the company well informed on the political and commercial relations of the empire in the early part of the seventeenth century. At this time the imports consisted chiefly of costly wares, such as found a ready sale amongst the princes and nobles of the land. Amongst them are mentioned rich velvets and satins, fine cutlery, good fowling-pieces, saddles and gay trappings, swords with damascene blades, choice pictures, cloth of gold and silver, flowered silks of gold and silver, precious stones set in enamelled work, fine English and Norwich embroidered stuffs, perfumed gloves, fine Arras hangings, mirrors, drinking and perspective (spy) glasses, fine light armour, porcelain and china ware.

This, taken in connection with the costly silks, shawls, muslins, diamonds, brass or bronze ware, etc., brought back in exchange, gave rise to the still-prevalent impression of the fabulous 'wealth of India.'

In 1620 a step was taken which, although attracting little notice at the time, was pregnant with far-reaching consequences. On the west side of the peninsula, Surat continued to be the chief centre of the company's trade till its removal in 1686-87 to Bombay. But Surat was merely a seaport free to all comers, where they had only a factory, with no jurisdiction beyond its enclosure. Now, however, they acquired a firm footing on the east side, where they obtained leave from the Raja of Golconda not merely to settle, but to erect the afterwards famous Fort St. George at the then obscure town of Madraspatan on the Coromandel Coast. The fort stood on its own ground, with a population of about one hundred thousand in a little district subject to the company, which thus became in a small way a political State as well as a commercial corporation. The time came when its commercial were absorbed in its political functions.

In this very year 1620 some of these political functions were exercised with unwonted vigour. The company's outward-bound fleet not only again fell foul of the Portuguese, capturing several prizes, but, as it is naïvely put by the chronicler, ' found themselves likewise obliged to master some of the Moghul's own ships called junks, and some of the King of Decan's likewise, who had used our people ill.'

Their successes against the Portuguese were followed up by an alliance with Shah Abbas of Persia, who had founded Bandar-Abbas (Port of Abbas) with a view to developing the naval resources of his kingdom. But the object of the present alliance was the recovery of

the city and island of Ormuz (Hormuz), which had long
been held by the Portuguese, greatly to the Persian
monarch's annoyance. This object was now effected
by the aid of the English, who in return for this great
service received half the booty, besides various privileges, and also leave to hold the Castle of Ormuz, and
to enjoy half the Customs of Gombrun, to which place
the trade of Ormuz had been removed. These benefits,
which were enjoyed for about half a century, were
valued at some £40,000 yearly, apart from the prestige
now acquired by the company as the rising naval power
in the Indian Ocean. After their expulsion from Ormuz,
the Portuguese, reluctant to lose their hold on the
Persian Gulf and its pearl fisheries, established themselves at Mascat on the opposite (Arabian) side of the
entrance, whence they were finally driven by the Sultan
of Oman.

Soon after these transactions (1623) the position of
the company as a political State, an *imperium in imperio*,
may be said to have been formally recognised by King
James, who, for the better administration of their Indian
territory, now empowered their presidents and councils
to punish all capital or other crimes committed on land
in India, either by martial or common law, the accused
being in all cases entitled to be tried by a jury of twelve.
Similar powers appear to have been already conferred
on them in respect of offences committed in their ships
on the high seas.

That the company was now doing a very prosperous

business in Eastern produce may be inferred from the subjoined table of prices in India and in England given by Malyns in his 'Centre of the Circle of Commerce':

	Cost in India. Per lb.		Sold in England. Per lb.	
	s.	d.	s.	d.
Pepper - - -	0	2½	1	8
Cloves - - -	0	9	5	0
Nutmegs - - -	0	4	3	0
Mace - - -	0	8	6	0
Indigo - - -	1	2	5	0
Raw silk - - -	8	0	20	0

No mention occurs of cinnamon, because the Portuguese, being still masters of Ceylon, had a monopoly of that commodity, which could be procured only from Lisbon.

Out of the Ormuz affair there now arose a curious incident, which throws a somewhat lurid light on the public morality of the times. When the company's fleet was about to sail for the East in 1624, the Duke of Buckingham extorted £10,000 for the liberty to weigh anchor, he being then Lord High Admiral of England. This high-handed proceeding being included in the articles of impeachment in 1626, the Duke pleaded in his defence that the company had taken many rich prizes from the Portuguese, especially at Ormuz, a large share of which was legally due to the King, as well as to himself, as Lord High Admiral; and further, that the said £10,000 was really 'a blessing in disguise,' the company having compounded for that amount, instead of £15,000, which the law would have compelled them to give; and, moreover, that all but £200 of the said item was applied by the King for the service of the navy. Of course, neither the Crown nor the Admiral had any legal claim to a share in the company's prizes, and as they were keeping up heavy armaments in the Indian seas, it might seem somewhat unreasonable to fleece them also for the maintenance of the Royal Navy at home.

Space will allow no more than an allusion to the famous expedition of Sir Thomas Herbert, one of Britain's many crowded-out worthies, who in the year 1626 sailed with a gallant fleet of six ships on a somewhat roving commission for the East Indies. The two English envoys, Sir Robert Shirley and Sir Dudmore Cotton, with whom he was travelling in Persia, both died at Kasbin, whence he returned by the overland route to England. Herbert's account of his four years' wanderings in the East may still be read with pleasure and profit.

In 1631 a royal proclamation was issued 'for restraining the excess of the private trade carried on to and from the East Indies by the officers and sailors in the company's own ships.' In this document is given a list of the commodities licensed to be exported to and imported from India, from which it would appear that the company itself was restricted in its exclusive dealings with the East.

7

Amongst the imports mention occurs of such curious items as myrabolans, bezoar-stones, blood-stones, aloes sucatrina, worm-seeds, and 'purlane of all sorts.' *Purlane* was merely an eccentric way of writing *porcelain* at a time when English orthography was in the transition state between chaos and a relative degree of order. *Worm-seeds*, 'short' for wormwood-seeds, were the seeds of *Artemisia maritima*, still used in India as a stomachic tonic. *Aloes sucatrina* is what we now call Socotrine aloes (*Aloe socotrina*), still imported from Bombay, but a product of the island of Socotra, whence its name. The *blood-stone* is the heliotrope, a variety of quartz, so called from the small jasper-like reddish spots disseminated through it. More interesting is the bezoar-stone (*Lapis bezoar orient.*), a popular antidote to all poisons, to which miraculous virtues were attributed, and which, consequently, often fetched ten times its weight in gold, being in reality worthless. It is the Persian *pad-zahr*—an antidote (lit., poison-expelling)—with special reference to the ball of undigested food occasionally secreted by the wild goat of Persia, vulgarly supposed to possess this and other virtues, both physical and spiritual, as in Chillingworth : 'The healing bezoartical virtue of grace.'

Soon after this time (1635), Charles I., apparently from sordid motives, intermeddled in the affairs of the company in a way for which even his most devoted partisans could never find a colourable excuse. In the previous year, peace for once prevailing between

England and Spain, with which Portugal was still united, some of their ships touching at Goa were well received, and obtained a free trade not only with that place, but also with all other ports in China and India where the Portuguese were settled.

Thereupon Charles set up a rival association to occupy this new ground, as well as Japan and other parts, all included in Elizabeth's charter. His pretext was that the East Indians 'have neither planted nor settled a trade in those parts, as we expected, nor made such fortifications and places of surety as might encourage any hereafter to adventure thither ; neither have we received any annual benefit from thence, as other princes do, by reason of the said company's neglect to fortify for the good of posterity, and principally by the daily decrease of our Customs for imports from India, owing to the said company's supine neglect of discovery. And as all the attempts for a northward passage to East India hitherto proved unsuccessful, which, however, we believe might be performed from Japan,' therefore a new society is chartered, partly for this, partly for general trading purposes to India, China, Japan, 'or elsewhere,' the old company 'not to molest them in their said East India commerce.'

Their privileges were confirmed for five years in 1637, when it appeared that amongst the founders and shareholders (Sir W. Courten, Sir Paul Pindar, Captain John Weddell, etc.) were also the King himself and Endymion Porter, a groom of his bed-chamber. And so the real motive came out, the above recited plausible pretexts and allegations being stigmatized as 'shamefully mean, and unworthy of a great monarch.'

But the project met with no success, their two rich ships, with cargoes valued at £151,600, being seized in 1640 by the Dutch, who the same year destroyed both their factories in India. The same fate overtook their settlement in Madagascar, but at the hands of the old company, who naturally regarded them as interlopers, and who, during the Civil War, could at that distance afford to defy the royal mandates.

Although their Indian trade had been languishing for some years, partly owing to this arbitrary interference of the King, but still more because of the increasing strength and aggressiveness of the Dutch East India Company, the old association was still energetic enough to occupy the island of St. Helena in the year 1651. As some erroneous statements are still current regarding this historical Atlantic rock, it will be convenient here briefly to give such particulars as concern its relations with the company. Discovered in 1501 by the Portuguese—and by them stocked with swine, poultry, etc., and also planted with lemons, oranges, figs, and other fruit-trees for the use of their outward and homeward bound ships—it was a few years later entirely abandoned by them, being no longer needed after the establishment of their numerous stations on both sides of the African mainland.

The island was then occupied by the Dutch, who in

their turn abandoned it in 1651, when they made their first settlement at the Cape under Jan Anthon van Riebeck. Thereupon our East India Company took possession of the rock, as the only available victualling station for their shipping in those Austral seas. In 1661 their ownership was fully recognised by the renewed charter, which even permitted them to erect fortifications on the island. But it was captured by the Dutch in 1665, and, after changing hands twice in 1672, it was finally recovered by the English in 1673, when it became vested in the Crown, but the same year regranted to the company in absolute possession for ever, reverting to the Crown again, on the determination of all the company's chartered rights.

At, or immediately after, the treaty of peace concluded on April 5, 1654, between the Commonwealth and Holland, various other matters that had long been pending between the English and the Dutch East India Companies were also settled. Frequent reference has above been made to the persistently aggressive action of the Dutch against the English in those Eastern parts, and although the Dutch were undoubtedly the greater offenders, there must naturally have been a good deal of give and take on both sides. In any case, the cumulative claims of the English company, set down at £2,695,990 15s., for injuries sustained between the years 1611 and 1652, were met by counter-claims on the part of the Dutch amounting to £2,918,611 3s. 6d.   But the matter was now finally adjusted and altogether wiped out by the Dutch agreeing to pay the English company £85,000 to restore to them the island of Poleron, and to compensate the heirs of the sufferers at Amboyna with a solatium of £3,625.   These were extremely moderate terms, especially considering that at that time Cromwell had the Dutch in the palm of his hand, and had compelled them to strike their flag and recognise that 'Britannia ruled the waves.'

It was on this occasion that another ground of quarrel, connected with the seizure of some English ships and goods by the Dutch within the dominions of Denmark in 1652, was also adjusted by two arbitrators from each commonwealth, who met for the purpose in the Goldsmiths' Hall, London; here, 'to proceed without respect or relation to either State, for the adjustment of this matter, and unless they agree upon sentence before the 1st of August, 1664, the aforesaid arbitrators shall from that day be shut up in a chamber by themselves, without fire, candle, meat, drink, or any other refreshment, till such time as they shall come to an agreement concerning the matter referred to them.'

'This,' remarks Anderson, 'is perhaps the most singular stipulation that was ever made between two independent nations.'

Anyhow, it was effective, the award being promptly made for £97,973 against the Dutch under these distinctly urgent conditions. It was on this occasion, also, that the Dutch earned their historic reputation of being a nation who never lost anything for want of the asking.

But although ready enough to vindicate their claims and protect them against foreign aggression, Cromwell was at heart no friend of the company. Indeed, the very year following the Dutch treaty, he practically annulled their charter by countenancing and encouraging interlopers in every way, if not actually declaring the navigation and commerce to the East Indies to be free and open to all English subjects, about which point there appears to be some doubt. But, however this be, it is certain that during the years 1653-56 they were reduced to dire straits by the multitude of private adventurers who now swarmed into the Eastern seas, with the result, as asserted by Samuel Lamb, of 'a great lowering of English commodities and advancing of Indian commodities, an increase of presents [bribes] to governors, etc., to such an odious excess that at length the very private traders themselves, being without union or protection, were the forwardest petitioners for a return to a joint stock.'*

The question of free or exclusive trade was by Cromwell's action now brought to the touch in the most practical manner, and there can be but one opinion as to the issue. It might be quite true that a

* 'Seasonable Observations for the Encouraging of Foreign Commerce,' 1657, quoted by Anderson, ii., 586.

momentary revival of trade took place under the open system in those years of peace with the Dutch. But it was not for long, and there can be scarcely a doubt that in the end—that is, in the course of three or four years—the private adventurers were the losers, the reason being their helplessness to contend individually against attacks of the corsairs, and the intrigues of the Portuguese and other jealous rivals at the Courts of the Indian princes.

But the question scarcely bears discussion. Cromwell himself was prompt to discover his mistake, and, seeing the imminent ruin of English commerce and influence in those Eastern regions, he hastened, in 1657, to reinstate the company in all its rights and privileges. They were now re-established with a joint stock of £739,782, in which the separate traders were no doubt glad enough to take shares, and thus revive their waning fortunes.

Out of these troubles arose the famous Skinner incident, which, soon after the Restoration, made a great noise, and for some time even kept Lords and Commons at loggerheads. Thomas Skinner, a private adventurer who persisted in trading on his own account after the renewal of the company's charter, had his ship, cargo, and other effects confiscated in 1655; and, being even refused a passage home, was fain to return overland to England. Here he became the man with a grievance, and, after years of vain appeals to the King, at last petitioned the House of Lords for redress.

The company being then called upon to answer, pleaded their exclusive rights, and also demurred to the jurisdiction of the Peers, even petitioning the Commons against them when the case came on for hearing in 1667. Thereupon the Peers awarded Skinner £5,000 damages, instead of receiving which he was committed to the Tower by the Commons, and, in fact, never had any redress at all. He had, however, the satisfaction of raising his case to the dignity of a constitutional question, on which Parliament was adjourned no less than seven times. The quarrel even broke out again in the session of 1670, when the King contrived *tantas componere lites* by inducing both Houses to erase all their resolutions and drop the subject.

Meanwhile the company, to make matters safe, obtained in 1661 a fresh charter on the lines of those granted by Elizabeth and the first two Stuarts, with additional clauses, securing to them the absolute possession of all their plantations, lands, forts, factories, etc., in the East Indies. They were further empowered to appoint governors and judges with jurisdiction over all persons living under them both in civil and criminal matters. Then came the all-important clause authorizing them to 'make war and peace with any prince or people that are not Christians within their limits, as shall be most to the benefit of their trade, and may recompense themselves on the goods, estates, or people there who shall injure them.' There was, however, a proviso that on three years' notice by the Crown the charter might be revoked, should it hereafter appear to the King or his successors not to be profitable to the Crown or kingdom.

The company was thus constituted a sovereign State, subject only to the supreme authority of the Crown of England.

A first result of these enlarged privileges was the acquisition of the port and island of Bombay, which had been ceded to Charles by Alphonso VI. of Portugal as part of his sister Princess Catherine's dowry, and which Charles granted to the company in perpetuity in 1668 under an annual rent of £10. An attempt had been made by the King to keep this place as part of the royal domain, but he soon found that it did not pay, and as it also brought his soldiers and sailors into collision both with the company's agents and with the natives, he was fain to part with it on these terms to the company. Thus were obtained by peaceful means the two places, which long continued to be the centres of the company's trading operations on the east and west coasts, and which later became the respective capitals of the presidencies of Madras and Bombay. Thanks to its far more convenient position, Bombay has greatly outstripped its eastern rival, and ranks at present as one of the chief emporiums of the world, with a population (1891) of over 820,000 souls.

The island of Poleron, one of the Banda Group, noted for its spices, especially cloves and nutmegs, bulks largely in the history of the English and Dutch wars in Malaysia. But at present it figures on no map under that name, which is a curious corruption of the Malay Pulo Ron (Run)—Island of Ron (or Run). This tiny islet, which lies some fifteen miles west of Great Banda, had changed hands more than once before this time. But it was finally captured by the Dutch in 1664, after which date the English held nothing in the Eastern Archipelago till a much later period, except Bantam in Java (lost in 1682) and Benkulen, with a few other stations in Sumatra. Benkulen was occupied in 1685 for the pepper trade, and held till 1824, when it was ceded to Holland in exchange for Malacca. The present British possessions in the Eastern Archipelago (Labuan, Sarawak, North Borneo) are acquisitions of the nineteenth century, with which the East India Company were not concerned.

But although they lost nearly all the spice trade by their expulsion from the Moluccas, the company continued to develop their general commerce to such an extent that, according to Sir Josiah Child, they were about 1670 employing ' from thirty-five to forty sail of the most warlike merchant ships of the kingdom, with sixty to one hundred mariners in each ship '; while they imported ' pepper, indigo, callicoes and several useful drugs [it is to be hoped that Sir Josiah did not include the bezoar-stone amongst his ' useful drugs '] to the value of £150,000 to £180,000 yearly,' besides other commodities re-exported to the yearly value of £200,000 or £300,000. 'And those goods exported, do produce in foreign parts, to be returned to England, six times the treasure in species which the company exports from England to India.' Hence the general conclusion that, 'although the East India Company's imports greatly exceed its exports of our manufactures, yet, for the above reasons, it is clearly a gainful trade to the nation' (*op. cit.*).

Nevertheless many of the sagacious political economists of those days (Adam Smith was not yet born) continued to clamour against this profitable East India trade, which was undoubtedly enriching England, besides greatly strengthening her naval power and influence in the Eastern seas. Their chief grounds of complaint were twofold. In the first place, it was argued that the country was flooded with manufactured wares 'made in India,' greatly to the detriment of our local industries; to which the answer was that this was not a question of mere exchange, but also of the carrying business and of the profits on the large quantities of Indian goods re-exported abroad.

These profits were, as above shown by Sir Josiah Child, far more than sufficient to compensate for the drain of bullion required to make up the balance against us in the Indian market. This annual exportation of bullion to India, stated now greatly to exceed the former average of £40,000, was the second, and in fact the stock, argument by which it was then and long after sought to be made out that we should be the better were the

Indian market closed altogether.* The logical inference was not drawn quite in this rigid way; hence the *reductio ad absurdum* was perhaps not clearly seen by those philosophers who, so far from desiring to see the Indian market closed, really wanted it thrown wide open to all British subjects. Their shafts were in fact aimed, not at the Indian trade itself, but at the company's exclusive trade, only the battle was now being fought with different weapons.

This was made evident a few years later (1676), when Charles II. granted them a new patent, confirming all his previous concessions, ' notwithstanding any misuser, non-user or abuser whatsoever of their former rights, liberties, etc.' The action was taken because Charles was desirous to reaffirm in the strongest way the royal prerogative against those opponents of the company who were now objecting to their privileges on constitutional grounds.

Meanwhile, instead of being ' overturned and annihilated,' the company was rapidly extending its sphere of operations. Thus, mention is made for the first time

---

* On the question of the circulation of bullion, the anonymous writer of a pamphlet entitled 'The East India Trade a most Profitable Trade to this Kingdom,' etc. (1677), remarks : 'Had we all the gold and silver in the world, if it were absolutely kept and confined within this kingdom, it would neither enlarge our trade nor render us more formidable in strength and power.' And on the import trade from India the same writer (probably Sir Josiah Child) points out that ' our real interest is to buy cheap in India, and to sell dear in Europe.'

in 1680 of the 'South Seas [Pacific Ocean] and China,'
whither were in that year despatched two ships of
430 and 350 tons respectively, and in 1681 'one great
ship for the South Sea and China.' It will be remembered that all these lands and waters were included
within the scope of Elizabeth's world-encompassing
charter, and thus were now laid the foundations of
those commercial relations which have left England
supreme in the Pacific as well as in the other navigable
oceans of the globe. At this time the 'quick stock,'
that is, the trading capital, of our East India Company
was stated to exceed that of the Dutch, its only serious
rival, although 'the stock of the latter sells at 450 per
cent., whilst ours sell not at above 300 per cent.'

Certain sections of the community, whether on this
or other grounds, continued to grumble; and while the
Levantines, as we have seen, complained of their importation of raw silks, the silk-weavers of London petitioned
the House of Commons (1680) against their trade in
Indian wrought silk and other fabrics of all kinds. It
is amusing now to read the speeches of members of
Parliament, such as Mr. Polexfen, who wanted sump-
tuary laws passed against the general wear of East
India silks, 'Bengals,' etc., complaining that 'we at
this time consume to the value of £300,000 yearly in
those East India manufactured goods, including printed
and painted calicoes for clothes, beds, hangings, etc.;
that the company annually export from £200,000 to
£600,000 in bullion; that its trade was now increased

to near one quarter part of the whole trade of the nation,' etc. So now it was made a charge against the company that their business flourished, while other people's languished, owing as much perhaps to their fault as to their misfortune.

It is not surprising to read that the 'collective wisdom of the nation' gave a deaf hearing to such allegations, and refused to check the growing refinement in order to divert trade into other channels. And while no action was taken by Parliament, Charles was easily persuaded to grant them further protection against interlopers by a fifth charter (1683), in which enlarged powers were also conferred on the company as a sovereign State, permitting them to raise, train and muster such military forces as they should judge requisite, and to exercise martial law at their forts, factories, etc.; that is, within the limits of their territory.

The association of interlopers with the company's territory in this charter was not, perhaps, a mere coincidence. In any case, events were now pending, the ultimate issue of which was, partly through the action of the separate traders, a large increase of the company's domain. Owing, as was alleged, to the intrigues of these intruders, the company was brought into direct collision with the Great Moghul for the first time in 1685. The ostensible cause of the quarrel was the murder of some of their people by the natives in the Hugli River (chief branch of the Lower Ganges) during

a local disturbance.   But it was really due to the action
of the Moghul's governors and vassal rajas, who, in
consequence, as was alleged, of the interlopers' mis-
representations, had broken all their engagements and
agreements with the company, depriving them of their
immunities, and even extorting large sums of money
from their agents.

It is specially noteworthy that, after the outbreak
of hostilities, James I. immediately despatched a man-
of - war to India, with instructions to support the
company's action, to seize all interlopers, and order
all loyal English subjects to repair to the company's
territory and submit to their jurisdiction.   That year
(1686) this policy was followed up by the issue of
another royal charter (the sixth since the Restoration),
ratifying all preceding ones to the fullest extent on the
ground that the Indian trade 'cannot be maintained to
national advantage, but by one general joint stock, and
that a loose and general trade will be the ruin of the
whole. . . .

'And further understanding that many of the native
princes and governors of India . . . have of late violated
many of the company's privileges, surprised their servants, ships and goods, besieged their factories, invaded
their liberties, etc., wherefore the King grants full power
to the company to appoint admirals, vice-admirals, rear-
admirals, captains, etc., from time to time, who may
raise seamen and soldiers on board their ships, who
may seize all English interlopers, etc.; also to make

war on such Indian princes as may hurt the company. And in time of open hostility with any Indian nation, etc., they may on the other side of the Cape of Good Hope use the martial law in their ships. The company may also coin in their forts any species of money usually coined by the princes of those countries only,' etc.

We thus see that the Crown not only took occasion to enlarge the company's sovereign powers to the utmost extent when they were engaged in their very first war with the Great Moghul and his vassal princes, but also co-operated in that war by the despatch of a battle-ship, as above.

In a report on their trade in 1689, the company speak of this as 'a most successful war with the Moghul,' which 'brought him to reasonable terms, confirmed by that Prince's own *phirmaund*,* and secured by a strong garrison at Bombay.' No mention is here made of Calcutta, although it was in this very year that they removed to this place from Hugli, on the branch of the Ganges named from this place, where they had first established a factory in Lower Bengal. At Calcutta was also erected the fort named Fort William, in honour of William of Orange, on a piece of land which was later (1700) acquired by purchase, or perhaps as a present from Azim, grandson of Aurengzib, and which included the three villages of Chattanatti, Govindpor

---

* Properly *firmán*, an edict, proclamation or decree of any kind, the final *d* being a Cockneyism, as in *drownd* for *drown*, *sound* for *soun*, the original form of the word, from Fr. *son* (Lat. *sonus*).

8

and Calcutta. At Hugli there was no English fort till much later, although both the Dutch and the French had forts at different times at this place, which was the Moghul's Custom-house for levying dues on the vessels trading in the Lower Ganges.

During the reign of William and Mary various attempts were made by their opponents to induce the Crown to dissolve the company, and in 1692 an address was presented by Parliament to the Crown praying that all their privileges might determine after the three years' notice legally required to be given. But the only results were three new charters, which were chiefly intended to regulate their internal affairs, hence called charters of regulations. In 1694, however, a great outcry was raised against them on the ground of corrupt practices, so that the House of Commons was induced to institute an inquiry into these charges. It then appeared that over £80,000 had been spent ' for secret services,' that is, to obtain the three last charters, to buy off the interlopers, and for similar purposes. There was no doubt a good deal of stock-jobbing carried on at that time, and some of the transactions might be described as a pale anticipation of the ' Panama scandals,' in consequence of which several of the directors were committed to the Tower by the House of Commons in 1695.

Owing to these disclosures prejudice was naturally deepened against the company, which, while throwing off fresh branches abroad, was wellnigh uprooted at home. In 1697 a great clamour was again raised by their old enemy, the London silk-weavers, their grievance still being the great quantities of silks, calicoes, and other Indian manufactured goods, imported and worn by all sorts of people. They stirred up the excitable mob, always ready for a row, tumultuous gatherings were held in the streets, and attempts were even made to storm the East India House and plunder its treasure. These riotous proceedings were scarcely suppressed, when there ensued a fierce war of pamphlets, by which both sides assailed each other, until their energies or the public patience were exhausted. Some of these were very able documents, and Dr. D'Avenant's essay on the 'East India Trade' in defence, with Mr. Polexfen's reply, 'England and East India inconsistent in their Manufactures' (both 1697) may still be read with interest, presenting as they do some vivid pictures of human folly balanced by sound judgment and discretion.

But opinions remained divided, and the irreconcilables were strong enough again to interest the legislature in these squabbles, this time not without results. At first the question assumed the aspect of an undisguised attempt on the part of the rival interests to outbid each other for the favour of Parliament. Thus, with the view of thwarting their opponents, the company offered, in 1698, to advance £700,000 for the public service at 4 per cent. (the Treasury being somewhat depleted by the late war with France), pro-

vided they were secured in their exclusive trade with
India. Thereupon Mr. Samuel Shepherd and others
proposed jointly to advance £2,000,000 at 8 per cent.*
in return for a charter transferring to them the exclusive Indian trade.

This demand for a rival exclusive charter must even
at that time have been regarded as somewhat startling,
seeing that the petitioners were not only the avowed
champions of open trade, but were even now opposing
the company on the very ground that the time had
come for abolishing this Indian monopoly. Their
counsel before the House had, in fact, just pleaded
'that the patents for some trades with joint stocks,
whilst the trades were in their infancy, have been permitted for the settling of a trade, and until the first
adventurers had reaped some reasonable compensation
for their expense and risk, yet afterwards, when such
trades have grown considerable, the wisdom of the
nation has always, or generally, judged it fitting to
open a way for the kingdom to receive a general benefit
therefrom.'

But the discussion degenerated, as often since, into
a party question, the Tories standing by the company,
while the Whigs backed these illogical candidates for a
monopoly in their own favour. Their arguments, aided
by the £2,000,000, eventually prevailed, and in 1698 an
Act of Parliament was passed, establishing a new and

---

* This 8 per cent, as given by Anderson, is probably a misprint
for 3 per cent.

privileged company under the title of the General Society of Traders to the East Indies. They were even empowered to begin operations forthwith, despite the three years' notice to which the old company were legally entitled before their rights could be thus encroached upon. A clause, however, was added, whether designedly or by an oversight, whereby ' corporations having shares herein might trade in proportion to their shares.'

Taking advantage of this clause, the old association took up £315,000 of the new stock of £2,000,000, which, to the astonishment of everybody, was all subscribed for in the course of two days. As the old association were also empowered to continue their business till 1701, that is, for the term of three years above specified, an almost impossible situation was now created, which by the pamphleteers was described as ' a strange jumble of inconsistencies, contradictions, and difficulties, not easily to be accounted for in the conduct of men of judgment, unless they were purposely so intended for the service of the old company.'

It was in particular pointed out that ' three years before one corporation could be dissolved a new one was set up, with power to begin an immediate trade where they had no just right till three years after;' and further, that ' the old company were allowed to subscribe so considerable a part of the new capital, whereby they were enabled to trade separately from the new one, which was in effect the establishing of two rival companies at

once, besides the separate traders, who still continued
to act by themselves.'

It seemed like a reversion from order to chaos, the
only possible escape from which was either the abolition of all privilege, for which the times were not ripe,
or else a fusion of the two bodies in a single corporation, as was fortunately brought about before they had
mutually destroyed each other.

A union of the two societies had become imperative,
especially after 1700, when another insane statute was
passed, which aimed at the total annihilation of the
Indian trade in the supposed interests of the home
industries, by prohibiting the use of all Indian, Persian,
or Chinese silks and calicoes, ' which were to be locked
up in warehouses appointed by the Commissioners of
the Customs till re-exported [bonded, in fact], so as
none of the said goods should be worn or used in
either apparel or furniture in England on forfeiture
thereof, and also of £200 penalty on the person having
or selling any of them.' How often in those days of
rampant stupidity called ' protection,' the student of
history is reminded of the Swedish Chancellor Oxen-
stjerna's exclamation at ' the little wisdom with which
States were governed '!

Peace was at last effected by the so-called tripartite
indenture of July, 1702, between Queen Anne and the
two corporations, providing for a continuance of the
Indian trade for seven years by an equitable readjust-
ment of the two united stocks. After this period a

more thorough fusion was to take place, the old company removing from their offices and warehouses in Leadenhall Street to the new premises at Skinners' Hall on Dowgate Hill (close to where is now the Cannon Street Railway Station). Arrangements were also made for the surrender of their old charter at the same time, the corporation henceforth to be called the United Company of Merchants of England trading to the East Indies.

CHAPTER VIII.

THE EAST INDIA COMPANY—*continued.*
(1702—1858.)

IT was thought desirable, even at the risk of being tedious, to present in some detail the first period of a hundred years in the life of the East India Company. This period is generally neglected, or dealt with in a very summary way, by Indian historians, so that no clear idea is conveyed to the reader of the early growth and development of this great association. Some erroneous impressions have thus also sprung up, and are still prevalent, regarding its inner constitution, and the course of events in subsequent times, impressions which could be removed only by a more careful study of the circumstances by which the company's later career was largely determined.

No great extent of territory was acquired till after the middle of the eighteenth century. Before that time, the energies of the company were mainly engaged in the struggle with the Portuguese and the Dutch, and in holding the command of the seas, which afterwards proved of such vital importance in the more serious conflict with the French for the supremacy in the East Indies. It was the aggressive action of the French that compelled the company in self-defence to become a great territorial power, and it is a pleasure to be entirely in accord with Professor Seeley in this aspect of the question.

In 1708, the two companies having been amalgamated as provided for by the agreement of 1702, a further advance of £1,200,000 was made to the public funds, the whole capital thus invested now being £3,200,000 consolidated at 5 per cent. This is one of the first instances in the financial history of England of the application of the principle, which was afterwards so fruitfully adopted, and out of which has grown the present system of consolidated funds, hence called ' Consols.' In return for this service, the united company received a prolongation of their exclusive Indian trade for fourteen years and a half longer. That is to say, whereas by the law of 1698 they were to be redeemable upon three years' notice after 1711 and repayment of principal and interest, their redemption was now prolonged to three years' notice after Lady Day, 1726.

This extension of their exclusive trade was followed by the usual outcry against privilege. The Legislature was inundated by a deluge of pamphlets urging it to lay open the Indian trade, or at least to allow a proportional share of this profitable traffic to Bristol,

Hull, Liverpool, and other large or rising commercial towns. London was thus regarded as holding a monopoly of the trade, which was, of course, a delusion on the part of the separate adventurers. The essential point was overlooked that the Indian stock, being transferable, every British subject was free to purchase shares therein at their current market value. Although dividends are at present distributed by the Bank of England, no one now pretends to argue that the city of London holds a monopoly of the public funds.

Hence, it is not, perhaps, surprising that the only answer vouchsafed to the pamphleteers was a renewal in 1712 of all the company's immunities by an Act of Parliament specially framed to prevent its dissolution, even should their funded stock be redeemed as above provided for. This favour was granted 'upon the said company's humble petition, and to the intent that the company and their successors may be better encouraged to proceed in their trade, and *to make such lasting settlements for the support and maintenance thereof for the benefit of the British nation.*'

The clause here italicized might be supposed to endow the corporation with a perpetuity which was revoked by the periodicity principle supposed to have been introduced after the year 1748. But it was not so; for in this very Act of 1712 there was added a provision 'that at any time upon three years' notice after Lady Day, 1733, and repayment of the said

£3,200,000, and of the said yearly fund of £160,000 [*i.e.*, the interest on this stock at 5 per cent.], then the said duties and fund shall absolutely cease and determine.' And it is added 'that the company shall be subject to the restrictions, covenants, and agreements of former Acts and charters now in force.' Consequently, the three years' notice clause of all the charters issued after the Restoration is here upheld.

It is interesting to note that about this time (1720) it was computed that between the years 1711 and 1719 the silver bullion exported by the company to India amounted to £3,786,000, being at the annual rate of £420,667. But instead of being impoverished by this 'drain,' the country was greatly enriched, for the reasons set forth in the last chapter. In this very year (1720) the company's funded stock of £3,200,000 was quoted 'on 'Change' at 445 per cent., though, to be sure, the financial pendulum was just then vibrating somewhat wildly over the South Sea, and several other equally mad, if less notorious, schemes.

Still more interesting is the record for 1726, when the three cardinal points of the peninsular 'trilateral' are for the first time brought simultaneously into view. In the renewed charter granted by George I. in this year, full powers were given to establish corporations with Mayor and Aldermen at Fort St. George (Madras), at Bombay, and at Fort William (Calcutta), with perpetual succession to each, and power to make by-laws, as well as to try causes both civil and criminal, high treason only excepted.

At this period the company's annual sales (imports) were calculated to exceed £2,200,000, while the whole trade showed a yearly gain of £800,000 to the nation. It is added that 'the company's trade maintains very many people at home as well as considerable numbers of our people in India, who bring home much wealth to their native country.'* Here it is also estimated that the silver exported between 1602 and 1726 from all Europe to India, 'there buried so as never to return,' amounted to £150,000,000; and a curious calculation is made to show that had that vast sum remained 'to this day in Europe . . . we should not have been richer in such case than we are at present.' In any case, it was already understood that it is not circulation, but stagnation, that impoverishes a nation. India has derived immeasurably less benefit from all this 'buried' bullion than have those countries which have with seeming prodigality poured such a stream of wealth into her lap.

As the period for the redemption of the company's funded capital, and for the determination of their exclusive trade, would expire on three years' notice from Lady Day, 1733 (see above), they obtained in the teeth of strenuous opposition a renewal in 1730 of all their exclusive privileges for a term of thirty-three years—

* Philips' 'State of the Nation,' etc., quoted by Anderson, vol. iii., p. 385.

that is to say, for thirty years from 1736 to 1766, and three years' notice then to be given. This prolongation, however, was not granted by Parliament without a great struggle, and without some considerable concessions on the part of the company, which set apart £200,000 for the public service of that year free of interest, and also consented to an abatement of 1 per cent. (from five to four) on their funded estate of £3,200,000.

Moreover, it was provided that on the repayment of this capital 'their exclusive privileges of trade shall cease and determine. Yet, nevertheless, the company shall continue as a corporation for ever, to enjoy the East India trade *in common with all other subjects*.' The italicized words show that after 1769 their position would be exactly similar to that of the Hudson Bay Company, which, after surrendering its exclusive privileges for £300,000, was not dissolved, but to the present day continues its old peltry trade in its corporate capacity. The trade, no doubt, is thrown open, but the company is in possession of the field, and can well afford to defy the puny efforts of private competition. So it would doubtless also have been with the East India Company, had their exclusive privileges really lapsed in 1769.

But between 1736 and that date many things happened, which gave a new turn to the course of events, for during that period of their history the company, without ceasing to be a trading association were forced into that career of conquest by which after many vicissitudes they became a sovereign State of the first magnitude.

It is significant that just at this time their field of operations received a considerable development in the Far East by the introduction of tea, a commodity to which allusion was for the first time made about a hundred and fifty years previously as 'an herb out of which they (the Chinese) press a delicate juice, which serves them for drink instead of wine ; it also preserves their health, and frees them from all those evils that the immoderate use of wine doth breed unto us' (Botero). Shortly after this it was introduced into England by the Dutch, its price ranging from £6 to £10 per lb., but no mention is made of it in any Act of Parliament before 1660, and it was then still so rare that the East India Company is stated to have purchased 2 lb. 2 oz. for presentation to Charles II.

The company's first importation was for less than 5,000 lb., but despite a duty of 4s. per lb., it had already become almost a necessity amongst the better classes during the first half of the eighteenth century ; and although fifty years later (the very year when they secured their new lease of existence) four of their ships, which were engaged in the China trade, arrived in the Thames with no less than 1,700,000 lb., it scarcely sufficed for the demand, and in an Act passed in 1745 the company were actually threatened with an infringement of their charter should they fail 'at any time to keep the London market supplied with a sufficient quantity of tea [pronounced *tay*] at reasonable prices, to answer the consumption thereof in Great Britain.' It might be supposed that the readiest way to arrive at the 'reasonable prices' would be a lowering of the duty; but our legislators appear to have taken over a hundred years to discover that very obvious truth.

In consideration of a further advance of £1,000,000 at 3 per cent., the company secured from Parliament a prolongation of their exclusive privileges for a further term of fourteen years. On this occasion also it was provided that on repayment of their funded capital, with all arrears of interest, their exclusive trade should then cease, but that they might continue as a corporate body to trade as before, like all other subjects of the Crown. At this time—that is, on the eve of the momentous events now pending—the company had to their credit in the public funds a total sum of £4,200,000, of which £3,200,000 was at 4, and £1,000,000 at 3 per cent. Their exclusive trade was also safe for the next forty years.

This was a tolerably sound position with which to enter on their struggle with the French for the ascendancy in the peninsula, a struggle, however, which began with a disaster.

At the outbreak of the war an English fleet was despatched to the East with a view to the capture of Pondicherry, the headquarters of the French possessions in the peninsula. But partly at the request of the Nabob* of the Carnatic, partly through the fears of the Governor of Madras, no attack was made on that place.

The year after our capture of Cape Breton in the New World, a French squadron under La Bourdonnais avenged the blow by seizing one of the company's largest ships, surprising Fort St. George, and capturing the neighbouring town of Madras, and all the merchandise and treasure accumulated in that important station. The terms of capitulation, however, were not observed by Dupleix, Governor of Pondicherry, who had already aimed at the conquest of India by employing native levies (sepoys) and by fomenting dissensions between the local potentates, who had risen to power after the decline of the Moghul Empire early in the century. His designs, however, were frustrated partly by his failure to capture Fort St. David, the centre of the British administration in the Carnatic after the fall of Madras, partly by the arrival of Admiral Boscawen, who, though repulsed at Pondicherry, anticipated the French designs on the strong position of St. Thomé, near Madras, by occupying that place on behalf of the company. In fact, this first trial of strength between

---

* Properly *nawwáb*, plural of *ná'ib*, a deputy or viceroy, then a ruling prince, especially one who has risen from a state of vassalage to an independent position. It is an Arabic word, consequently applied properly only to Mohammedan princes, and particularly to those viceroys who in various parts of India rose to power during the decadence of the Moghul Empire.

the two rivals was decided mainly by naval tactics, and showed plainly enough that, as Cicero wrote long ago to Atticus, 'qui mare tenet, eum necesse est rerum potiri'—who holds the sea must needs prevail.

But further hostilities were for a short time suspended by the peace of Aix-la-Chapelle, one of the stipulations of which was that Fort St. George should be restored to the company in exchange for Cape Breton given back to the French. The incident is important, as showing that the losses of the company were now, as always, regarded as national losses, and that the country, so far from being indifferent to its prosperity, was willing to surrender strategical points acquired in other parts of the world in return for the restoration of forts and factories wrested from the company in India. Such vicissitudes were, and continued to be, the concern, not of the company alone, but also of the people of England, who were as deeply interested in its progress in the Far East as they were in the progress of their colonies and settlements in the Far West.

It will be convenient here to tabulate the chief forts, factories or lands held in India by European States towards the middle of the eighteenth century, when the struggle for supremacy was resumed by the French and English :

GREAT BRITAIN.

Surat and Bombay on west coast, held in sovereignty; factories at Karwar, Calicut, Tellicherry, and Dabul on

9

same coast; factories at Agra, Ahmedabad, Lahore, and a few other places, in the interior; Forts St. George (with Madras and St. Thomé), St. David, Vizagapatam, Ganjam, etc., on east coast; in Bengal, Fort William (Calcutta); factories at Balasore, Cassimbazaar, Dacca, Patna, etc.

FRANCE.

Pondicherry, fortified town, and some subordinate forts and factories on east coast; factories at Balasore, Chandernagore, and other places in Bengal; factories at Surat and other places on the west coast.

HOLLAND.

Factories and forts at Rajapore, Cochin, Calicut, Tegnapatam, Karnapoli, Tuticorin, Palicat, Negapatam; factories at Balasore, Cassimbazaar, Patna, Dacca, etc.; Ceylon.

PORTUGAL.

Goa, Diu, Daman, Elephanta Island, Mangalore, all fortified.

DENMARK.

Forts at Tranquebar and Danesburg on east coast.

Before the war the company's transferable stock was paying 8 per cent. But this had now to be reduced to 6, although since the peace there was a great expansion of trade, the imports for 1755 being valued at over £2,000,000. This was no doubt partly due to the heavy losses sustained at the capture of Madras, but much more to the necessity of reorganizing the administration on a military footing in preparation for a renewal of hostilities. A permanent force of sepoys as well as of some English troops had now to be kept up, and some of Dupleix's tactics had also to be adopted, involving the payment of large subsidies 'to the nabobs and other great officers in India, for keeping them in our company's interest' (Anderson, iii. 594). In fact, this trading association was now being rapidly transformed to a military, and even an aggressive, power, for it was obviously impossible by adopting defensive measures alone to make a stand against the no longer disguised machinations of the French.

Although France and England were at peace for the next eight years (1748-56), there was no suspension of hostilities in India, and it was during this very period that the most strenuous efforts were made by Dupleix to realize his dreams of conquest. Hence the extraordinary spectacle now witnessed of the English and French East India Companies engaged in a life-and-death struggle, while the two nations were elsewhere enjoying a short interval of repose from the almost incessant warfare of the eighteenth century. At first no doubt the combatants themselves felt the incongruous nature of the situation, as, for instance, when they came into collision over the rival claims of Nazir Jung and Muzaffar Jung to the dominion of the lately deceased Nizam ul-Mulk. It was on this occasion that M. d'Auteuil, before the first battle in the Carnatic, sent a message to Major Lawrence that, although the two companies took opposite sides, he had no intention of shedding any English blood ; but not knowing in what division of Nazir's army the English were posted, he could not be blamed if any stray shot came that way.   To this Lawrence made the retort courteous that he was equally unwilling to spill French blood, but that if any shot came his way it would certainly be returned.   But such scruples were soon laid aside, and both French and English blood flowed copiously enough before the question of ascendancy in the Carnatic was decided in favour of the English by the military genius of Clive.

During these campaigns—that is, down to the time (1756) when hostilities again broke out between the two nations (the Seven Years' War)—the forces of the English and French companies could be regarded as little more than bands of mercenaries taking part for their own purposes on opposite sides in the intestine quarrels of the native potentates.   Hence they considered that international law was sufficiently observed if they abstained from invading each other's recognised territories.   In this way is explained the protest made in 1752 by the French commander Kerjean against a threatened violation of French territory when Major Lawrence, following up his successes, was approaching unpleasantly near Pondicherry. Lawrence fully acknowledged the force of the protest, and satisfied himself with storming an outpost which lay beyond the limits of the Pondicherry district. He also refrained from molesting Kerjean's forces as long as they remained encamped under the walls of Pondicherry, but did not hesitate to attack and utterly rout them as soon as Kerjean, in obedience to Dupleix's peremptory orders, advanced beyond that district. Clive no doubt during the operations against Suraj ud Daulat in Lower Bengal, after the 'Black Hole' atrocity, did attack and capture the French station of Chandernagore, 1757, but at that time intelligence had reached India of the war declared between the two countries in the previous year.

These abnormal relations between peoples at war in the East though at peace in the West were again illustrated when the Dutch, although at that time a friendly Power in Europe, being alarmed at the successes of Clive in Lower Bengal, made their last desperate attempt to restore the balance of power in that region. A formidable armament was despatched from Batavia to the Ganges Delta, troops were landed, an alliance formed with Mir Jaffier, Nabob of Bengal, for avowedly hostile purposes, and preparations were made for the squadron to force the passage of the Hugli, in order to reach the Dutch factories at Chinsura and Cassimbazaar higher up the river. Clive was greatly embarrassed, as prompt action might involve England and Holland in war, while all the fruits of his victory at Plassy might be lost were the ships allowed to pass the English guns at Charnoc's battery and Fort Tannas. Hence his expressed wish 'that the next hour might

bring us news of a declaration of war with Holland.'
All arrangements, however, were made to meet both
the land forces and the squadron, both of which when
hostilities became inevitable were vigorously attacked
and utterly routed. It was on this occasion that Clive,
whilst engaged in a game of whist, received a note from
Colonel Forde, who was in command of the English
troops, asking for an Order of Council to fall on the
Dutch, whom he had a good opportunity of destroying,
and, without interrupting the play, Clive sent the famous
reply in pencil, instructing him to destroy them, and
promising the Order of Council *next day.* After this
event the Dutch retained little in the peninsula beyond
a few dismantled posts and factories, and the stronghold of Negapatam, which they lost in the next war.

After the declaration of war in 1756 the conflict with
France assumes a new and, one might say, a more
legitimate aspect. Henceforth both nations are engaged
in the struggle ; their forces fight side by side with those
of the companies, and the war is carried on with renewed
vigour both by land and sea. But we are not here
specially concerned with these historic events, and it
must suffice to say that in 1761, that is, two years after
their flag was lowered in the New World, the French
were driven out of India by the capture of their great
stronghold, Pondicherry, as well as of every fort and
factory over which their flag had hitherto waved throughout the peninsula.

No doubt the French possessions were restored by

the Treaty of Paris (1763), but under conditions which prevented them from again taking an active part in the affairs of the peninsula, except for a little while as allies of Haider Ali and Tippú Sáhib of Mysore (1782-83). Thus they engaged 'not to erect fortifications, or to keep troops in any parts of the dominions of the Subah [properly, Subahdar, or Nawwab] of Bengal;' and by the Treaty of Versailles, at the conclusion of the next war (1783), a similar provision was made with regard to Pondicherry, and all other places again restored to the French in India. Bonaparte's attempt to renew the struggle by the expedition to Egypt (1798) was thwarted by the Battle of Aboukir, and the subsequent operations, resulting in the capitulation of the French army after the Battle of Alexandria, 1801.

Barras, the famous Member of the Directorate, has left us in his 'Memoirs' an instructive estimate of the situation at this time. 'In vain did Bonaparte amid a mass of sophisms, the children of his lively imagination, assure us that, once master of Egypt, he would establish connection with the potentates of India, and with them attack the English in their possessions ; all that I knew of India from personal experience confirmed me in the belief that the English Government was unassailable in that portion of Asia as long as it remained master of the seas.'[*]

It is important to note that the fall of Pondicherry threatened for a moment to bring the company into

[*] Barras's 'Memoirs,' vol. iii. ; translated by C. E. Roche, 1896.

direct collision with the Home Government, as represented by the British forces at that time serving in
India. The demand of Mr. Pigot, Governor of Madras,
that Pondicherry should be handed over to the presidency, as having now become the property of the
East India Company, was met by a refusal on the part
of Colonel Sir Eyre Coote, speaking for the chief
officers both of the army and navy in council assembled. 'The contest might have occupied considerable time had it not been cut short by a declaration from Mr. Pigot that, if Pondicherry were not
delivered up, the presidency of Madras would not
furnish money for the subsistence either of the King's
troops or of the French prisoners. This stopped all
further argument, and the authority of the presidency
was admitted, under protest.'*

In this incident were foreshadowed the relations that
continued to prevail between the State and the company until its demise, after the Mutiny of 1857. The
inconvenience of a divided rule in the peninsula may
perhaps have already been foreseen, and a *modus vivendi*
between the State and the company was found in the
arrangement already in operation during the late wars,
by which England supplied a contingency of the fight-
ing material at the expense of the company, which
retained the administration and revenues of the acquired territories. Hence even Bombay, originally a

* Edward Thornton, 'History of the British Empire in India,'
vol. i., p. 358.

possession of the Crown, was handed over to them, and so long as they exercised sovereign powers no land was held directly by the Central Government except the adjacent island of Ceylon, finally conquered mainly by the Imperial forces during the Napoleonic wars, and always administered as a Crown colony.

Henceforth the relations between the corporation and the Home Government continue to become more frequent and more intimate, until the outer history of the great trading company merges at last in the general history of the Empire.

There can be no doubt that they profited largely by the frequent changes in the subadarship of the Great Moghul's provinces of Bengal, Orissa, and Behar. Thus, the appointment of Mir Jaffier earned for Clive, amongst other perquisites, a *jaghir* * in perpetuity of the annual value of £30,000 ; and when Mir Jaffier was replaced by his son-in-law, Cossim Ali Khan, Vansittart received five lakhs of rupees, and the other members of the Select Committee one, two, or more lakhs.† Then the deposition of Cossim Ali Khan and restoration of Mir Jaffier (1763), and at his death (1765) the appointment of his son, Nujum ud Daulat, required fresh distributions of lakhs, while the company's treasury was being depleted by the wars with Cossim, with

* A *jaghir* (*ja*=place ; *ghiriftan*=to take) is a landed estate or district, the revenues of which are assigned to anyone by the overlord, generally for services rendered or expected.

† A lakh=100,000 ; a rupee at that time, 2s. ; so five lakhs = £50,000.

the Moghul's Vizier Shuja ud Daulat, and with the Moghul himself, who at this time was merely a 'lay figure,' carried about from place to place in the camps of his ambitious subadars or grasping viziers. After the great victory of Buxar (1764), gained by Major Munro over himself and his Prime Minister, the helpless Emperor actually sent a letter to the English commander congratulating him on his triumph over Shuja ud Daulat, and apologizing or explaining that though he had been in camp with his Vizier, he had decamped on the night before the battle.

Clive returned to England in 1766, after arranging for the transfer of the *diwani,* or financial department, of the Lower Bengal provinces from the Subadar to the company. The effect of this arrangement was to leave the nominal authority to the Subadar, and transfer the real power to the company, whose pensioner that potentate became. As this last stroke was effected by agreement with the Emperor, Clive, on quitting India, left the company absolute masters of a vast domain comprising many millions of inhabitants, and over a hundred and fifty thousand square miles of some of the richest alluvial lands in the world.

But he left behind him and brought back combustible materials enough to set Ganges and Thames simultaneously on fire. The flames were eventually extinguished by the enlightened administration of the much-traduced Warren Hastings, and of his illustrious successors in the East; and in the West by the active

intervention of Parliament, henceforth the true con-
troller of events in the company's dominions. A Parliamentary Committee had been appointed in 1767 to
inquire into the general state of the company's affairs,
to produce copies of their charters, treaties with the
native princes, their correspondence with their servants
in India, the state of the revenues in the provinces
under their jurisdiction, together with an account of
the expenses incurred by Government on the company's behalf in the naval, military, and other departments. Their absolute right to territorial acquisitions,
although not formally included, was frequently discussed, but never seriously questioned in subsequent
deliberations; and this vital point may be said to have
been settled by a tacit agreement between the State
and the company on the principle of accepting 'accomplished facts.' In any case, it was felt that this
ground was sufficiently covered by special clauses in
the early charters, clauses which were never formally
revoked, and which might consequently be held to be
renewed with the successive renewals of the charters
themselves.

But on other matters the company felt that a crisis
was approaching, to stave off which certain offers were
made, such as the payment of £400,000 per annum for
three years in return for certain advantages asked for
with respect to the inland duties on their teas, raw
silks, and Indian textiles. This offer, limited, however,
to two years, was accepted; but measures were at the

same time passed regulating the qualifications of voters in trading corporations, and restraining the company from raising their dividends above 10 per cent. till the next meeting of Parliament.

For the company had come to be regarded as a permanent source of revenue, like some other departments of the public service ; and it may have been feared that, unless their yearly dividends were kept under control, all available profits might be distributed amongst the shareholders, and nothing left for the State. A compromise, however, was made, by which, on condition of continuing the annual payment of £400,000 for five years, they might in that time gradually increase their dividend up to 12½ per cent. But should their profits not permit of such dividends, then the annual douceur, as it might be called, was to be lessened proportionably, and to cease altogether should the dividend fall to 6 per cent. A brief reference to these obscure financial transactions was needed to enable the reader to understand the true inwardness of the relations now being developed between the India House and Parliament.

Dividends having been reduced in 1770 to 6 per cent., owing to the serious state of affairs in the East, a Bill was passed in 1772 appointing a Select Committee to inquire generally into the condition of the company, both as a trading corporation and as a political body exercising sovereign rights. During the now annually-recurring debates in the House, it had been argued on the one hand that they should be restrained from all manner of trade, and on the other that their territorial dominions should be brought under the direct administration of the State. A resolution, however, was carried to the effect that these territories should remain in their possession for a term not exceeding six years, and that an advance of £1,400,000 should be made to the company, then sorely in need of Parliamentary assistance.

In the same year a radical change was made in the constitution of the association by an Act of Parliament, which provided that the original Mayor's Court of Calcutta should be limited to petty civil cases, and that a new Supreme Court should be established, consisting of a Chief Justice and three puisne judges to be appointed by the Crown, the presidency of Bengal being at the same time made supreme over those of Madras and Bombay. Henceforth the company must be regarded as almost entirely in the hands of the Ministers of the Crown, and only so far responsible to Parliament as were the Ministers themselves.

How completely they were looked upon as a department of the central administration was seen in this year (1773) in connection with the permission they now received to export tea free of duty to North America, the concession being made to indemnify them for losses incurred in other directions. But the colonists, now ripe for rebellion, drew no distinction between the company's and other British merchandise,

and the cargoes of tea thrown by the people of Boston
into the harbour were, in fact, the property of the
company, which had thus the distinction of giving the
first direct incentive to the American Revolution.

No more striking illustration could be given of the
extent to which the national interests were henceforth
bound up with those of the company. This great
association might be made the subject of stormy
debates in the House and of stringent legislation—it
might even be threatened with extinction ; but so long
as it existed, all intelligent statesmen felt that its commercial and military successes or reverses were of
public concern, and that the only intelligible policy of
the State—natural heir to all its triumphs—was to
control and not to crush, to encourage, not to paralyze,
its latent energies ; not, indeed, to countenance, but to
deal leniently with errors, from which nothing human
is exempt, and while censuring wrong-doing not to
forget the really preponderating good and brave deeds,
in the credit of which the whole nation might legiti-
mately share.

Discrimination was also a virtue, the exercise of
which was much needed at a time when the Court of
Directors was liable to be involved in the guilt of its
representatives in India, and the local government to
be similarly made responsible for the lawless conduct
of individual members or sections of the presidential
councils. In those days, before the introduction of
steam and telegraphy, the time required to com-

municate with the peninsula was long enough for unscrupulous servants of the company to deeply compromise it before the news of their nefarious transactions could reach England. Thus, the directors were still ignorant of any troubles in Tanjore, when they were startled by the intelligence that their ally, the Raja of that State, had actually been unjustly attacked, overcome and deposed by their other ally, Muhammad Ali, Nabob of Arcot, aided by the forces of the Madras Presidency. There was no shadow of a pretext for a quarrel with the Raja; but the Nabob, then all-powerful in the councils of the presidency, owed him a grudge about some pecuniary squabbles, and also coveted his throne, which he now seized with the co-operation of the Madras Government.

Thus was suddenly raised the famous Tanjore question, but more easily raised than laid. Mindful of his former services, the directors forthwith despatched Mr. (afterwards Lord) Pigot to remedy the evil by reinstating the Raja, and bringing to book the unruly members of Council. But meanwhile the Nabob had made his arrangements, one of which was to borrow largely from several of his friends in Council at the seductive rate of 30 per cent. interest, mortgaging to them the revenues of his newly-acquired Tanjore estate as security for capital and interest. By this stroke he at once identified their interests with his own, and especially made them the warmest partisans for his retention of Tanjore. Nevertheless Pigot succeeded in restoring the Raja (1775-76), and also obtained the suspension of two members of Council, after which on his own authority he put under arrest Sir Robert Fletcher, Commander-in-Chief of the forces. Then he met the fate of the late Prince Alexander of Bulgaria, being spirited away by a secret plot of the fractious members of Council to a place of military confinement, whence Sir Edward Hughes, Commander of a squadron in the roadstead, failed to rescue him.

On receipt of this intelligence a General Court (1777) first approved of Pigot's action, though censuring him on some grounds. Then, through the intrigues of the Nabob and his party, a Court of Directors decided to order Pigot home immediately, in order to inquire into *his* conduct, and to recall both his friends and enemies for the same purpose. Such was the influence of the Nabob, that when the matter was referred to the House, a small majority rejected the resolutions moved by Governor Johnstone, to support Lord Pigot, to condemn the Madras Cabal, and to annul the resolution for Pigot's recall. But meantime the Governor had been relieved by death, and the imbroglio settled by the prosecution and conviction of four of his opponents, who, being all of them men of great wealth, got off with a fine of £1,000 each. For this miscarriage of justice, however, the House, and not the Court of Directors, was responsible.

But these were evil days for Southern India, and for the fair fame of England, tarnished by treason seated in the high places. While the wild Mahratta horse in Haider Ali's pay scoured the plains of the Carnatic, and surged up against the breastworks of Madras, supineness and rank corruption ruled within its walls. Sir Eyre Coote, bent with age and honours, was left with his heroic starvelings to grub for food in the intervals between their hard-fought battles, while the craven officials, gorged with ill-gotten wealth, sneaked back to England, and presented themselves with un-abashed effrontery before the indignant but helpless Court of Directors; nay, bought themselves seats in the Lower House, to vote on the question of supplies when the company with exhausted coffers was fain to appeal for temporary aid to the Parliament of England.

Then were appointed those Secret and Select committees to inquire into their affairs, which pro-voked so much protest, and inspired the eloquence of Burke with fresh shafts of ridicule. ' Sir,' exclaimed the great orator, ' when the company is thus tender of encroaching upon any of our rights, is it not cruel, is it not ungenerous, in administration to harass it with two committees—with a Committee of Secrecy, founded on the principles of the Inquisition ; and with a Select Committee, which is declared by one of its friends to be a mockery of the company? A gentleman who generally votes with the Administration finds the Bill to be illegal, inexpedient, and alarming, and he finds the Secret Committee to be an inquisition, too

10

rapid and violent in its motions. Another friend of
the Ministry declares the Select Committee so slow in
its progress as to be a perfect mockery. What is to
become of the company between both? I protest I
can compare them to nothing but a jack. The Select
Committee is the slow-moving weight, the Secret
Committee is the flyer, and what with the slow motion
of the one and the rapid motion of the other, the
company is effectually roasted.'

But Burke did not know everything; nor was it
suspected till afterwards that Muhammad Ali, who had
his emissaries in London offering 'presents' to the
Duke of Grafton himself, and proposing to advance
money (£700,000 at 2 per cent.) to the British
Government, or to deposit it in the public funds, was
at that very time without men, money or influence,
and utterly unable to render the least assistance to the
presidency against Haider Ali's devastating hordes. It
seemed as if the company's estate had grown too big
and unmanageable for a Court of Directors seated in
London, and unable to communicate under six months
with its servants in the peninsula.

Hence, in 1781 the Ministry actually brought forward for the consideration of the House a series of pro-
positions, amongst which were the following: Whether
it might be advisable for the Crown to take the
company's territorial possessions and revenues entirely
into its own hands, and at the same time throw open
the trade of India, or else grant a monopoly of it to

another company. In any case it was suggested that no new charter should be granted except for a short term, and in return for a large participation of the public in their profits and revenues on the revival of trade and prosperity; and further, that a tribunal should be established in London for the purpose of controlling and inquiring into the management of affairs in India, and punishing such servants of the company as should be convicted of having abused their power. These radical measures were met by counter-propositions on the part of the association, and for the present a compromise was effected by a temporary Act (1781), allowing the company to continue its exclusive trade and the management of its estate for a short time.

Then, after the general peace of 1783, Fox brought forward his two famous Bills for vesting in commissioners the government of the company's territories, which had at that time an estimated population of 30,000,000; and for making such other reforms in the administration and judicial procedure as should henceforth preclude all kinds of arbitrary and despotic proceedings for the government of these territories. These Bills were opposed by Pitt, both on their merits and on the general ground of equity. They were, in fact, denounced as aiming at a confiscation of the property, and a disfranchisement of the members of the East India Company, seeing that they required the directors to deliver up all lands, tenements, houses, books, records, charters, instruments, vessels, money, securities and property of every description. And all this was to be done without any trial or conviction whatsoever on the charges urged against the company, as was pointed out in the petitions presented to the Commons against the Bills by the directors, the body of proprietors, and the City of London. Nevertheless, they were passed by a very large majority (208 to 102), but thrown out by the Lords, their rejection involving the fall of the Fox Administration, and the assumption of office by Pitt.

But Pitt was no blind champion of abuses, nor was he one of those who favoured the still prevalent doctrine that foreign possessions were to be administered rather for the benefit of the State than for the welfare of the natives. Hence he lost no time in bringing forward two measures (1784), the first rejected, the second adopted, for the better government of the company's vast domain, and the regulation of the company's exclusive trade. Of the first Bill, the fate of which involved a dissolution of Parliament, it will suffice to say that it provided for the appointment of commissioners by the Crown to check, superintend and control all matters connected with the civil or military government or revenue of the company's estate, and also for the appointment of the commanders-in-chief to be vested in the Crown. When Pitt, on appeal to the country, was returned with a strong majority, he easily carried his second Bill, under which the company's affairs were henceforth conducted till the cessation of their exclusive trade (1813 and 1833), and their final dissolution in 1858.

As amended in committee, this Act (August 9, 1784) constituted a Board of Control, somewhat similar to that contemplated in the previous Bill, but with power in urgent cases to originate measures, and also in matters of peace and war, where secrecy was important, to send its orders directly to the commanders-in-chief over the heads of the Court of Directors and of the several presidencies. Absolute power was given to the Governor-General and Council of Bengal to originate orders to the Bombay and Madras presidencies, while the Supreme Council was, on the other hand, forbidden, without orders from home, to form offensive treaties, or to declare war against any Indian rulers unless they first began or contemplated hostilities against our possessions. Inquiry was ordered to be made into the dealings of the High Court with the zamindars,* or hereditary farmers, the op-

---

* Zamindar (*zamin*=land, *dar*=holder), a landowner, landlord, and especially the hereditary middlemen who collected or farmed the Government land taxes under the system of tenure created by the Moghul emperors. This position naturally led to great abuse and oppression of the ryots (peasantry holding under the old Hindu village tenure); but these relations of the zamindars to the communes and the Crown being misunderstood, and not recognised by English law, the zamindars were often treated with great injustice by the High Court of Calcutta as at first constituted. The bailiffs charged with the execution of writs forcibly entered their premises, and even violated the sanctity of the zenanas (women's apartments), while the zamindars were being advised by prominent legal

pressive rents and contributions that had been extorted from them, and measures were directed to be
taken for their relief and future protection. Crimes
committed by English subjects in any part of India
were to be cognizable by all British courts of justice
in the same manner as if they had been committed in
the possessions of the Crown. Presents other than
ceremonial were forbidden except to lawyers, chap-
lains, physicians and surgeons; and still further, to
prevent malversation, all servants of the company
were required to give an estimate on oath to the
Court of Exchequer of their property within two months
after their arrival. Other provisions were made for the
effective administration of justice and control of the
company's affairs; but the clauses vesting the nomina-
tion of the several commanders-in-chief at Bengal,
Bombay and Madras, and the appointment of directors,
in the King, were withdrawn in committee.

A certain friction could scarcely fail to arise between
the Board of Control thus constituted and the Court
of Directors, as was seen the very next year in connection with the entangled question of the Nabob of Arcot's
debts and the exclusive power claimed by the company

---

authority that they were not amenable at all to the jurisdiction of
the High Court. Here were abundant elements of confusion and
disorder for later and more enlightened legislation to deal with. At
present the Bengali zamindar enjoys the status of an English landed
proprietor, subject to the payment of the land-tax and to a certain
ill-defined tenant-right conceded to ryots long in possession of their
holdings.

to nominate the Governor-General and Council of the
Bengal Presidency. Hence further measures were passed
in 1786, by which the respective functions of these
bodies were more clearly defined. Another measure,
passed in 1788, had for its object the removal of all
doubts respecting the power of the Board of Control
'to direct that the expense of raising, transporting, and
maintaining such troops as may be judged necessary
for the security of the British territories and possessions in the East Indies should be defrayed out of the
revenues arising from the said territories and possessions.'

It is clear from all these transactions that the con-
quests and annexations of the company in the peninsula
were regarded as British possessions in the strictest
sense of the term, and that the civil and military affairs
of those territories were henceforth placed under the
supreme control of the Central Government.

' From the time of Pitt's India Bill (1784) the supreme
management of Indian affairs passed out of the hands
of the company. Thenceforth, therefore, an enterprise
begun for purposes of trade fell under the management
of men who had no concern with trade. Thenceforth
two English statesmen divided between themselves the
decision of the leading Indian questions, the President
of the Board of Control and the Governor-General, and
as long as the company lasted, the leading position
belonged rather to the Governor-General than to the
President of the Board. Now, it was under this system

that the conquest of India for the most part was made.'
—'Expansion of England,' p. 314.

No one will feel disposed to question this view,
although elsewhere Professor Seeley speaks of 'the
conquest of India by English merchants' (p. 35). But
it is more important to note that at this time was
introduced the more regular periodicity period, during
which the charter was uniformly renewed for a term
of twenty years—1773, 1793, 1813, 1833, and 1853, this
last (1853 to 1873) lapsing in 1858, when the corporation ceased to exist. Each renewal was marked by
some changes or modifications of its constitution, all
of which tended in the same direction towards final
extinction. Thus, in 1773 began the rule of the governors-
general, and then also was created the Supreme Court
of Calcutta, while the proprietors, that is, the shareholders, were disfranchised, that is, excluded from all
further interference in the affairs of the corporation.
The next renewal of 1793, when an effort was made
to shut out all individual English enterprise, including
even missionary work, coincides with the permanent
settlement of Bengal, 'one of the most memorable
acts of legislation in the history of the world.'—*Ibid.*,
p. 310.

Then came in 1813 the first serious encroachment
on the company's exclusive trade, a monopoly which
was at last absolutely abolished in 1833. With this
Act the company ceased to exist as a privileged trading
corporation, while the extensive patronage which it still

enjoyed was swept away by the system of appointments by competition introduced at the last renewal of the charter in 1853. Then came the *débâcle* of the Indian Mutiny in 1857, and next year a somewhat inglorious extinction. The company had outlived its time, and should have expired at the beginning of the nineteenth century, when England became undisputed mistress of the seas, and when the Indian trade should consequently have been thrown open to the world. Whether the inheritance bequeathed by it to the nation of an Empire held by military tenure, comprising in 1896 (with Ceylon) nearly 2,000,000 square miles, and over 290,000,000 inhabitants, should be regarded as a blessing or a *damnosa hereditas* is a purely academic question, the discussion of which could lead to no profitable results. The point most worthy of consideration is, not so much the inheritance itself, as the discipline and great qualities developed in its acquisition, and the inspiring memories which must survive even should the 'pageant' itself dissolve, and 'leave not a rack behind.'

CHAPTER IX.

THE HUDSON BAY COMPANY.

HERE is a sudden change of scene, effected as by the magic wand of Prospero, from the 'cloud-capped towers, the gorgeous palaces and solemn temples' of tropical India to the glacial waters, the gloomy woodlands and storm-swept steppes of Arctic North America. But though the contrast could scarcely be greater between the two environments, the human, or at least the politico-commercial, relations remain much the same. For here again the battle for supremacy has to be fought out between the everlasting French and English rivalries; here again the same national qualities of courage, endurance, and enterprise find ample scope for their exercise; and the outcome of the struggle is still the same, a vast imperial domain of some million square miles bequeathed in perpetuity by a trading company to the Anglo-Saxon race.

But in its first inception this trading association is to be compared rather with the Russia than with the East India Company. As the one was founded partly with the view of discovering a North-East Passage, so the other had for a chief object the finding of a North-West Route, the ultimate goal of both being the rich China and India trade at that time monopolized by the Hispano-Lusitanian nations. It was long supposed that the icy tundras and lacustrine regions of the Far North were capable but of a feeble commercial development, and that consequently any trading relations that might be established with the scattered tribes of Algonquian or Athabascan aborigines could be regarded only as a means to an end, that end being the silks and spices and other treasures of the Far East. But as the hopes of finding a clear northwestern route where none existed grew fainter and fainter, all the stronger became the prospects of developing the local resources to profitable results. There were not only the deep-sea and teeming freshwater fisheries, but also a boundless wealth of timber, even now far from exhausted, and the costly furs of fox, bear, marten, beaver, and many other richly-clad denizens of those trackless Northern forests.

The first attempts to open a North-West Passage are associated with the names of Frobisher (1576-78), Davis (1585-87), Hudson (1607-10), Batton (1611-12), and Baffin (1616). But when the last-mentioned announced on his return to England that 'there is no North-West Passage,' all efforts in this direction were suspended till the year 1631, when the attempt was twice renewed for the avowed purpose of reaching

China by sea. The first voyage, ordered by the King himself, was made by Captain Luke Fox, who penetrated to Port Nelson, and here restored the cross and inscription formerly set up by Sir Thomas Batton in the King's name. Fox was followed by Captain Thomas James, who was despatched by the Bristol merchants, and who greatly enlarged our knowledge of those inland waters, but nevertheless returned only to confirm Baffin's negative verdict.

But these heroic efforts, foredoomed to failure, none the less bore fruit in other and unexpected directions. They led indirectly to the formation of a chartered corporation, which in the seventeenth century was rightly considered the most effective instrument for securing to England the possession of those boundless regions which her mariners had first discovered, but which must else have fallen a prey to the French, at that time strengthening their hold of the Laurentian lands, and even encircling the English settlements on the sea-board by a chain of posts, which extended from the St. Lawrence down the Mississippi to their later colony of Louisiana on the Gulf of Mexico. The course of events will show that, if by this far-seeing policy the New England and Virginia colonies were being surrounded by a French 'hinterland,' the French possessions in the St. Lawrence basin were themselves being wedged in between the English settlements south of the St. Lawrence and the Hudson Bay territories north of that river. This balancing of the situation, though little attended to by historians, had much to do with the final issue, and was almost from the first clearly perceived by the French, as shown by their persistent efforts to break down the barriers which threatened to enclose their Laurentian settlements towards the north. Those barriers were, in a sense, later burst through by the hardy Franco-Canadian traders and trappers; but the efforts of this energetic race of half-breeds were for the most part expended in the service of the English Hudson Bay Company.

This company was first incorporated in 1670, the immediate events leading up to its formation being the happy issue of two expeditions sent out the previous year by Prince Rupert 'and seventeen other persons of quality and distinction.' The first, in command of Captain Newland, formed a settlement at Port Nelson, the first station founded by the English north of the St. Lawrence; the second, under Captain Gilham, brought back some prospects of opening a profitable trade with the native tribes thinly scattered round the shores of Hudson Bay.

Even in those days of lavish royal dispensations the charter of incorporation, dated May 2, 1670,* was regarded as of an extremely liberal character. It set forth in the preamble 'that those adventurers had at their

---

* The date usually given is 1669, but this is probably due to a confusion between the year of Prince Rupert's two preliminary expeditions, and that when the charter was actually granted.

own great cost undertaken an expedition for Hudson's
Bay, in order for the discovery of a new passage into
the South Sea, and for the finding of some trade for
furs, minerals, etc., and having already made such discoveries as encourage them to proceed further in their
said design, by means whereof there may probably
arise great advantage to us and our kingdoms; and we
being desirous to promote all endeavours for the public
good, do by these presents grant for us, our heirs and
successors, unto them, and such others as shall be
hereafter admitted into the said society, to be for ever
one corporate body and politic, by the name of *The
Governor and Company of Adventurers of England trading
into Hudson's Bay*, with perpetual succession, and to be
capable of holding, receiving, and possessing lands,
rents, etc.' (without limiting the value or extent thereof),
' and to alienate the same at pleasure.'

Then it is provided that ' they are to have the sole
trade and commerce of and to all the seas, bays,
streights, creeks, lakes, rivers, and sounds, in whatsoever latitude they shall be, that lie within the entrance
of the Streight commonly called Hudson's Streights;
together with all the lands, countries and territories
upon the coasts and confines of the said seas, etc.,
which are now actually possessed by any of our
subjects, or by the subjects of any other Christian
Prince or State, together with the fishing of all sorts
of fish, of whales, sturgeons, and all other royal fishes
in the said seas, bays, etc., together with the royalty

of the sea within their limits aforesaid, as also all
mines royal of gold, silver, gems, and precious stones,
and that the land be from henceforward reckoned and
reputed as one of our plantations or colonies in
America, and to be called Rupert's Land; the Company to be deemed the true and absolute Lords and
Proprietors of the same territories (saving always the
faith, allegiance, and sovereign dominion to us, our
heirs and successors), to be holden as of our manor of
East Greenwich in free and common socage, yielding
and paying yearly to us, our heirs, etc., for the same
two elks and two black beavers, etc.

'The Company may make bye-laws, etc., for the
good government of their forts, plantations, and
factories, and may impose fines, etc., on offenders.'
Their exclusive domain is also extended to 'all
havens, bays, creeks, etc., into which they shall find
entrance or passage by water or land out of the
territories, limits, and places aforesaid, and to and
with all other nations inhabiting any of the Coasts
adjacent to the said territories, etc., which are not
already possessed by any Christian potentates, or
whereof the sole liberty or privilege of trade is not
granted to any other of our subjects.

'The Company may send ships of war, ammunition,
etc., and may erect forts in their territories, as well as
towns; may make peace and war with any Prince or
people not Christian; also may make reprisals on any
others interrupting or wronging them; may seize on or

send home all such English or other subjects sailing into Hudson's Bay without their licence, etc.'

Commenting on this very ample patent of privileges, Anderson remarks (iii. 27) that if the constitution, and especially the Declaration of Rights, ' had not limited the prerogative in the case of exclusive charters, this company would undoubtedly be absolute in those immense territories. But the case, to our great happiness, is now quite otherwise; and since that great establishment of our liberties, neither the Hudson Bay nor any other company not confirmed by Act of Parliament has any exclusive rights at all. Therefore any British subject may as freely sail into Hudson's Bay, fish and traffic with the native Indians there; may travel into and make discoveries therein, either by land or water, as freely as the said company can do, as will be shown has since been practised frequently in our own days.'

Such, undoubtedly, was the law after 1689; but meantime the association, starting with a capital of about £110,000, held by a small number of proprietors, had taken such firm hold of the ground that for a long time no serious attempt was made by private traders to encroach on their domain. As remarked by the same authority, the company possessed in any case the great advantage over other adventurers of their forts and stations, ' by which their agents can reside in so inhospitable a country during the winter, preparatory to their trading with the savages against the arrival of their ships in summer, and that thereby they have not only more safety and protection, but also more experience in trading with the native Indians thereabouts than any private adventurers can have, whose ships cannot with safety remain in that vast bay above a part only of our summer, lest they should be shut in by the ice which fills the bay with heaps of it, like mountains. And, indeed, these advantages alone on the company's side are so considerable that they are not likely to be rivalled successfully in haste by any private adventurers' (*ibid.*, p. 28).

These proved to be prophetic words, and, as will be seen when much later another powerful association attempted to enter into competition with the chartered body, they were ultimately compelled either to retire or to save themselves by amalgamation. Yet their progress was slow at first, and towards the middle of the eighteenth century they had not more than about 120 persons in their employment, 'who for nine months of the year live in a manner shut up within those forts in low houses, for defending them from the piercing cold, snow, and rains. In summer they go out and shoot, hunt and fish, and meet with deer and wild-fowl, and they have some few wild fruits, as strawberries, dewberries, and gooseberries. From England they send annually three or four ships laden with coarse woollen goods, guns, powder and shot, spirits, edge-tools, and various other utensils, in return for which the natives sell them all kinds of furs

or peltry, goose-quills, castorum,* whale-fins, and oil,
bed-feathers, etc., and they make handsome annual
dividends to their proprietors' (*ibid.*, p. 28).

These 'handsome dividends' are readily accounted
for when we read further that the trade for a long time
was carried on by barter with the natives, one beaver's
skin being procured for half a pound of gunpowder, or
four pounds' weight of lead shot, or two hatchets, half
a pound of glass beads, one pound weight of tobacco,
eight small or six large knives; twelve good winter
beaver-skins for a gun of the best sort; six ditto for a
good laced coat; five ditto for a plain red coat; four
ditto for a woman's coat, 'and so on in proportion for
kettles, looking-glasses, combs, etc.' (p. 29).

At first the corporation lived on friendly terms with
their French neighbours, as appears from the 'General
Collection of Treaties of Peace and Commerce' (1732)
prepared for the use of the English plenipotentiaries
at the Treaty of Utrecht, where it is stated that 'Mr.
Bailey, the Company's first Governor of their factories
and settlements in that Bay, entertained a friendly
correspondence by letters and otherwise with Monsieur
Frontenac, then Governor of Canada, not in the least
complaining, in several years, of any pretended injury
done to France by the said Company's settling a trade
and building forts at the bottom of Hudson's Bay;

* Properly *castoreum*—that is, the mucilaginous substance found
in the two inguinal sacs of the castor (beaver), of pungent smell and
acrid taste, formerly much used in the European Pharmacopœia.

nor making pretensions to any right of France to that
Bay, or to the countries bordering on it, till long after
this time.'

One reason why the company was for a long time
left to itself was the general impression, at first
commonly believed in, afterwards sedulously propagated
by those who knew better, that the whole region was
useless, except as a hunting and fishing ground, pro-
ducing nothing but brambles and beaver-skins, worthless for tillage, too cold and inhospitable for European
settlement. Hence the British public are assured
that 'in so wretched a country there can be no plantations properly so called, and much less any towns or
villages. Our people must, of course, be supplied from
England with bread, beef, pork, flour, pease, and other
necessaries.'* Now the tables are reversed, and from
many parts of the Hudson Bay Company's domains
England draws considerable quantities of these very
supplies. Some of the western tracts comprise several
hundred thousand square miles of the finest wheat-
growing land in the world. But even in the eighteenth
century the truth began to leak out, and we are told
how 'some of its later voyagers relate that some
barley, oats, and pease have been tried with success'
(*ibid.*).

The amicable relations with their French neighbours

* Anderson, vol. iii., p. 28. At that time by 'plantations' were
understood any strictly agricultural settlements, whether worked
by free or slave (black) labour.

did not last long, and, as in India, the French were
again the aggressors. In 1682, while the two countries
were at peace, two ships fitted out in the St. Lawrence
sailed into Hudson Bay, and suddenly appeared before
Port Nelson, where a fort was in course of erection.
But, no attack being expected, no preparations of any
kind had been made to defend the place. It had
accordingly to capitulate unconditionally, and all the
company's servants were carried prisoners to Canada.
Such an unprovoked attack in profound peace naturally
raised a great outcry in England, and the piratical
expedition had to be disowned by the French King,
who even promised satisfaction to the company. But
no adequate indemnity appears to have ever been
made beyond restoring the station to its lawful
owners.

With a view to preventing the recurrence of such
unpleasant surprises, the company afterwards erected
a very strong fort at the mouth of the Churchill River
higher up the same side of the bay. This stronghold,
the ruins of which are still standing, formed a square
of three hundred feet, with walls no less than seventeen
feet thick, faced with dressed stone imported from
England, and originally mounting forty guns. The
total cost was £24,000; yet, for all its strength, we
shall see that it shared the fate of its neighbour before
the close of the next century. Another stronghold was
also erected on Charlton Island, in the shallow inlet of
James Bay, and this was now made the general depot

for the peltries and other produce collected from the surrounding districts, and here shipped for England.

There were also at this time (1682) forts and factories on Albany River, which flows from the west to James Bay; on Hayes River (Fort York), close to Port Nelson; at the mouth of the Severn (New Severn), some distance farther south; and on Rupert's River, near Charlton Island. Thus the whole of the south-west coast of the great basin, from the head of James Bay to the mouth of the Churchill River, was occupied in a little over two decades after the establishment of the association.

There can be no doubt that the French were already greatly alarmed at the rapid progress of the company's affairs in ' Rupert's land.' Hence in 1686, peace still prevailing between the two nations, another raiding expedition was sent from Canada, this time overland —that is, across the low water-parting between the Laurentian and Hudson basins, into the company's territory. Its success was even more complete than on the previous occasion, for it took by surprise no less than four of the newly-erected forts, leaving nothing in the hands of the company on the mainland except the fort at Port Nelson.

The outcome was even worse than before. The company petitions for redress; King James vows and protests, demands restitution and full compensation; the wily Louis XIV., 'being sure of our king,' as Anderson quaintly remarks, restores all the forts but one (Fort Charles), and breaks his promise to indemnify the company for its losses, which, as afterwards appeared, were nicely estimated at £108,514 19s. 8d. In fact, no satisfaction was ever made, while the retention of Fort Charles enabled the French in subsequent negotiations to put in a claim for sovereign rights over this territory on the favourite diplomatic maxim of 'accomplished facts.' It served, in any case, as an excellent set-off against the report of the commissioners who were appointed by King James to treat with those of the French for the restitution of the captured forts, and who stated that they had clearly made out James's 'absolute right to the whole bay and streight of Hudson, and to the lands adjoining, as well as to the forts taken by France and the sole trade to all parts within the said streight and bay.'

During the general war of 1689-97 the Hudson Bay forts changed hands more than once, and at the Peace of Ryswick some of them had to be abandoned to the French, although all had been recovered the previous year (1696) by an expedition of two ships with some land forces, despatched thither by King William. During the war of the Spanish Succession (1701-13) the French arms were again successful, at least at first, and at the close of the war they were still in possession of several of the company's stations at the mouths of the rivers flowing into Hudson Bay and its southern inlet.

But matters were to some extent set straight at the

Treaty of Utrecht (1713), by which the French sur-rendered to Great Britain in full right for ever the whole of the Hudson Bay territory, including all such parts thereof as were still held by them, whether by conquest or otherwise. Commissioners were also ap-pointed to determine the boundaries between that territory and the conterminous parts of Canada, and to settle this matter within a year. But these boundaries never were determined, though this did not matter much, because within the next half-century the French had retired from the scene, and left their English rivals in possession of the northern continent. Commissioners were further appointed to ascertain the amount of damages fairly due to the company for their hostile incursions and depredations in time of peace, which losses, as above seen, were found to exceed £108,000: but this also did not matter, as no adequate satisfaction was ever given.

Justice, however, requires it to be stated that the French claims to the sovereignty of the Hudson Bay territory were not based solely or exclusively on the fruits of these depredations. So early as 1656, that is, four years before the company was incorporated, an expedition was conducted from Quebec to Hudson Bay by Jean Bourdon, who, with the usual formalities, took possession of the lands encircling the southern shores of the great inland basin—that is to say, the inlet dis-covered by Captain James (1631), and still bearing his name. So at least it is stated by Charlevoix in his

generally accurate 'Histoire de la Nouvelle-France'
(i. 476). But this writer is not always to be trusted
in his account of the relations between the French and
English settlers north of the St. Lawrence during the
second half of the seventeenth century. Thus, he
gives quite a different complexion to the above-related
piratical expedition of 1682, telling us that the Franco-
Canadians fitted out an expedition, which explored the
west coast of Hudson Bay as far north as the fifty-seventh
parallel of latitude, where the two large rivers which
here converge in a common estuary were surveyed and
respectively named the Sainte-Thérèse and the Bourbon.
Here also was erected Fort Bourbon on the island which
is formed by the two rivers at their mouth (p. 478).

All this is supplemented by M. Vivien de Saint-Martin,
who adds ('Hudson Territory,' p. 750) that these two
rivers are those that *now* bear the names of Hayes or
Hill and Nelson 'on our maps,' and that Fort Bourbon
'has been replaced by that founded a little later by the
English under the name of Fort York.' This is a good
specimen of the way in which history may be written
backwards. The fort in question, as above seen, was
already in course of erection when the Quebec filibusters
captured and renamed it Bourbon, and at the same time
brought its English defenders prisoners back to Canada,
about which incident the French writers are silent. In
fact, one might suppose from their accounts that the
Quebec filibusters were the first Europeans to visit this
part of the coast, and to name the two great rivers

which had already been named the Hayes and the Nelson* by their precursors, the English pioneers and discoverers of those inland waters.

But, apart from these details, a sufficiently valid claim to priority of possession might have otherwise been based on the Quebec expedition of 1656, but for another circumstance also overlooked by the French writers. Not only were all the first explorers of the Hudson basin English navigators, but, as above seen, two of them (Button and Fox) had taken formal possession of the whole region long before the French found their way into those waters under Jean Bourbon. Hence the article of the Treaty of Utrecht providing for the surrender of all these lands to the English was but an act of restitution, returning the stolen property to its lawful owners.

During the unusually long interval of peace between the two nations (1713-44), the company were left in undisturbed possession of their vast domain, the resources of which they continued somewhat slowly to develop. The era of serious geographical exploration in the interior of the 'great lone land' had not begun, and commercial intercourse with the natives

---

* Thus, on the banks of the common estuary 'were interred, in 1612, the remains of the navigator Nelson, whose name is perpetuated by the river' (Reclus, vol. xv., English edition, p. 216). It should be stated, however, that Nelson was not the 'navigator,' but the owner of the vessel, which was in command of Captain (Sir) Thomas Button, discoverer of the river seventy years before any Frenchman was ever seen in those parts.

was consequently confined mainly to the coast tribes. At least, if any important discoveries were made, the information was carefully buried in the archives of the association, whose policy it was to throw every obstruction in the way of private adventurers.

In their trading relations they also continued to maintain a somewhat passive attitude—that is to say, instead of themselves employing trappers and 'voyageurs' to search the forests for local produce, they restricted their operations chiefly to the purchase by barter of such commodities as were brought by the Indians down to their stations round the coast.

The Franco-Canadian *coureurs des bois* could not, of course, be employed until they had become British subjects, after the Peace of Paris (1763). Nor, on the other hand, were there any English or Scotch settlers available for this purpose until colonists from Great Britain began to take possession of the provinces of Upper Canada. It thus became evident that by their narrow exclusive policy the company were crippling their own resources, and preventing the natural development of their territory.

Some light is thrown on the extent and character of their barter trade by a return made in the year 1730 of the company's importations into England. These comprised : Coat and parchment beaver skins 11,040 ; ditto of cubs 4,404 ; damaged and stags' parchment 3,830 ; ditto cubs 990 ; martens 1,648 ; damaged ditto 3,130 ; otter skins 380 ; cat skins 890 ; fox skins 260 ;

wolferins 540 ; black bear skins 410 ; wolves skins 190 ;
wood shocks 30. The last item seems to point at a
humble beginning of the lumber trade, which later
received such an immense development. ' Shock' is
technically a lot or bundle of sixty pieces of loose
articles, such especially as staves or shingles.

The peltry business, although scarcely exceeding
thirty thousand skins altogether in average years, was
still at the time regarded as satisfactory. On this
point Anderson remarks that ' by this trade we now
save much money which we formerly sent to Russia for
this kind of useful peltry, now entirely purchased with
our own coarse woollen and other manufactures and
produce' (iii. 419). An anonymous pamphlet was
issued about this time, entitled ' The Importance of
the British Plantations in America to this Kingdom,'
etc. (London, 1731), in which the subjoined reference
is made to the operations of the Hudson Bay Company :

' The Hudson's Bay trade employs generally three
ships from London, carrying thither coarse duffle cloth
or blanketing, powder and shot, spirits, etc., and
in return brings home vast quantities of peltry of many
kinds—bed-feathers, whale pins, etc. And as that
small company [' small' in respect of the number of
its shareholders] makes a large dividend of eight, or
formerly ten, per cent. on their capital of about
£100,000, beside the employment they give to our
people in fitting out and loading those ships, it may

truly be said to be an advantageous commerce, pro-
portioned to its bulk.'

The curious word *duffle* (properly *duffel*) is of Dutch
origin. It has reference to the town of Duffel, near
Antwerp, which was long noted for the manufacture of
a thick, coarse kind of woollen cloth with a close nap
or frieze, thus referred to in Wordsworth's 'Alice
Fell':

> 'And let it be of duffel gray,
> As warm a cloak as man can sell.'

This material was much fancied by the natives, who
easily converted a strip of it into a loose, flowing toga,
in which they stalked about like lords of creation in the
vicinity of the company's stations.

These braves, however, did not confine their pur-
chases to duffel. We are told by Mr. Arthur Dobbs
that about 1742-43 they were taking in exchange for
their peltries a great variety of other wares, such
as glass beads, broadcloth, brandy, sugar, thread,
vermilion, buttons, fish-hooks, fire steels, files, guns,
flints, mittens, hats, finger-rings, runlets (rundlets—
little barrels of varying capacity from three to twenty
gallons), knives, ice-chisels, looking-glasses, sashes,
tobacco, and finery for their squaws. But the whole
business did not amount to much—apparently at this
time about £4,000 more or less. Yet Mr. Dobbs, who
had a fierce quarrel with the company, or their
champion—Captain Middleton—over the North-West
Passage and other fine-spun speculations, brought a

charge against them of retailing these goods at two thousand per cent. profit. How he made this out is not clear, because he tells us that beaver-skins were in his time the local currency, and that one such skin fetched a pound weight of brass kettles, or a pound and a half of gunpowder, or five pounds of lead shot, or six pounds of Brazil tobacco, or two yards of gartering, or one pair of breeches, or one pistol, or two hatchets, etc. Here there seems no room for such a margin of profits, even if the beaver-skin sold for its weight in silver in England, which was far from being the case. In 1743 furs of all kinds—some much more costly than beaver—were exported from Canada to Rochelle to the number of 311,000, and these were valued at not more than £120,000 altogether, or an average of about 8s. per skin.

But Mr. Dobbs' main grievance was that there really existed a North-West Passage from Hudson Bay (he had never been there himself), but that Captain Middleton, acting in the interest of the company, would not find it, although despatched thither for that express purpose by the Admiralty Board in 1741. He found, indeed, the inlet, which he named Wager Bay in honour of Sir Charles Wager, at that time head of the Admiralty. But this did not satisfy Mr. Dobbs, who insisted that the said inlet, of which he had never before heard, if followed up would certainly lead right across the continent to the Pacific Ocean. As a matter of fact, the bay runs a very little way inland from the channel known as Rowes Welcome, and consequently stops short of the Pacific some fifteen hundred miles. But Mr. Dobbs knew better, and protested that Captain Middleton was blindfold and favoured the company, who, as he alleged, 'had no sort of inclination to forward this discovery, as believing it would be the means of laying open their trade, as they certainly have no legal exclusive right by Act of Parliament, but merely by King Charles II.'s charter.'

On the other hand, Captain Middleton, who had been over twenty years in the company's service, urged that, were the corporation dissolved and the trade laid open, compensation would have to be made for the Hudson Bay forts, which would still have to be kept up against the French and their native allies by a rate or tax on private traders. It might no doubt be desirable to extend the trade farther inland from the shores of the great bay ; but it could not reach all the way to China in the absence of a clear waterway across the continent. Nor would it be wise to throw open the trade so long as the French were masters of the St. Lawrence basin, whence the territory might easily be invaded both overland and by sea, as repeatedly shown in previous wars, as well as in times of peace. And so the paper warfare died down after being vigorously waged for fully three years, from 1741 to 1743.

But the North-West passage fever broke out again in 1745, when an Act of Parliament was actually passed offering a reward of £20,000 to the finder of what had

no-existence, or, rather, had no existence as the problem
was stated. By this time it ought to have been well
known that Hudson Bay was an almost completely
land-locked basin, accessible only from the east—that
is, from Europe—and from the north—that is, from the
North Pole. Nevertheless, the Act insisted upon the
passage being found westwards or southwards—that
is, precisely in the two directions where it had no
existence, as Captain Middleton had been trying to
convince the public from his own personal knowledge
ever since his expedition of 1741. As, however, this
statement may seem to be incredible, let the Act speak
for itself.

'That if any ship of His Majesty's subjects shall
find out and sail through *any passage by sea between
Hudson's Bay and the western and southern oceans of
America,* the owner shall receive a reward of twenty
thousand pounds . . . provided, however, that nothing
in this Act shall any ways extend to the prejudice of
any part of the estate, rights or privileges belonging to
the Governor and Company of Adventurers of England
trading to Hudson's Bay.'

Let the reader glance at the map, and see for himself how safe the company's interests were under this
sapient measure. In 1746 two ships, fitted out at a
cost of £10,000, were sent in search of the passage;
but after wintering at Port Nelson, and making several
futile attempts to pierce the continent, they returned
next year ' quite disheartened and unsuccessful.' And

thus much good money was thrown after bad, as, indeed, happened again more than once before the hopeless quest was finally abandoned.

The fall of Quebec, followed by the reduction of Canada, was the turning-point in the history of the Hudson Bay Company. Had France remained in possession of the St. Lawrence, it is doubtful whether they could have ever developed the resources of their magnificent domain. Their right to the greater part of this domain itself would assuredly have been contested by their restless and unscrupulous neighbours, for it will be remembered that the Commission appointed at the Peace of Utrecht to settle the frontiers between the French and English possessions came to nothing. This meant that the French had no intention of disposing of the boundary question, until it suited their convenience to do so in their own way— that is, by asserting their claim to all the lands north of the Laurentian basin, and thus confining the company by a narrow conventional line to their few scattered forts and factories round the shores of the bay.

Here they might have for some time continued to carry on a languid barter trade with the few surrounding coast tribes. But they could never have hoped to establish solid commercial relations with the interior, still less to compete for any great share of the peltry trade with the splendid race of Franco-Canadian trappers and hunters, who were already ranging the boundless north-western prairies, penetrating into the recesses of the trackless forests, crossing the portages and navigating every lake and stream in the vast lacustrine region stretching westwards to the Saskatchewan and Upper Missouri affluents, and northwards to the head-waters of the Mackenzie. They had even built a fort at the eastern base of the Rocky Mountains so early as the year 1752.*

But by the withdrawal of the French all was changed. There were no more boundary questions, and the Franco-Canadian trappers, the finest hunting material in the world, passed into the service of the company, which was thus enabled at once to effectively establish its claim to the immense territory of millions of square miles covered by the ample provisions of its Caroline charter. Roughly speaking, this territory extended from Hudson Bay westwards to and even beyond the Rocky Mountains; in fact, practically from the Atlantic to the Pacific, and from the Laurentian 'height of land' northwards to the Frozen Ocean.

Now came their answer to the carpers and snarlers, who were continually complaining in and out of Parliament that the company had done nothing, were doing nothing, to open up an inland trade, and should consequently forfeit their privileges to give private adventurers a chance of showing what they could do.

---

* H. H. Bancroft, 'History of the Pacific States of North America,' vol. xxii., p. 28.

These complaints were made at a time when it was as wellnigh impossible to extend their operations into the interior as it was to discover that North-West Passage, for concealing which they were also censured. But when the opportunity came with the Peace of Paris (1763), the trading relations both round the coast and in the interior developed at such a rapid rate that during the next French war (1778-83), the company could afford to lose £500,000, when their factories were visited and again surprised by a French squadron under the famous navigator Lapérouse in 1782.

Amid the stirring events of the present war, when England was battling in 'splendid isolation' against a world in arms, this expedition of Lapérouse generally escapes the attention of the historian. Yet it was not a little remarkable, if only because it was planned, and carried to a successful issue, immediately after the crushing defeat of the French West India fleet by Admiral Rodney. It was on this occasion that the great stronghold of Port Prince of Wales, at the mouth of the Churchill River (see above), was surrendered by Governor Samuel Hearne on the French captain's first summons.

In consequence of this incident, much obloquy has been heaped on the memory of Hearne by writers blindly copying each other, and profoundly ignorant of the circumstances. These are correctly set forth by Anderson's continuator, Coombe, who was living at the time, and who tells us that the company 'possess six of those buildings, which are called forts, in Hudson's Bay, being in reality factories, created at the mouths of the principal rivers. The buildings are necessarily strong, as well to guard against the climate as against other dangers, and are furnished with artillery to command respect from the different nations of the savages who come from the remotest parts to dispose of their furs and peltry. But they had not a single soldier in all these forts, and the whole number of storekeepers, clerks, and servants of every denomination, which the company maintain at so many stations, does not exceed one hundred and twenty persons. The enemy, therefore, landed without opposition, and destroyed the settlements, forts, merchandise, etc., to the amount of about £500,000 sterling. Having committed this commercial mischief, the French commanders, in the beginning of September, set sail for Europe' (vi., p. 560). Elsewhere this writer describes the expedition as 'merely predatory,' its sole object being havoc and plunder, in which it was eminently successful. No attempt was made to seize territory or to permanently hold those stations, which would have been impossible after the naval supremacy of England had been established in the American waters by the brilliant victories of Rodney, Hood, and Drake in the West Indies.

This was the last time that a hostile French fleet was seen in the Hudson basin, and henceforth the company's troubles were chiefly with our own people.

With the natives they never had any quarrels, and their dealings with these aborigines, extending over a period of exactly two hundred years (1670-1870), present a picture of harmony and mutual goodfellowship absolutely unique in the records of international relations. The picture is all the more striking when contrasted with the scenes of incessant strife and bloodshed which prevailed till quite recently between the British settlers and the Indians south of the St. Lawrence. Over £100,000,000 has been spent by the United States on its Indian wars, and in the vast territory stretching from ocean to ocean there is scarcely a square mile of ground that has not been reddened with the blood of whites and redskins. But north of the Canadian line there never have been any hostile encounters between the Athabascan or Algonquin tribes and the 'King George's men,' as the company's people were familiarly called in contradistinction to the 'Boston men'—that is, the enterprising traders and speculators from the New England States on the Pacific coast. Nor was the company's territory held by military tenure, for no money was ever spent, either by the association or by the British Government, to keep these multitudinous tribes in peaceful subjection.

How, then, was the miracle achieved? It would be absurd to attribute the contrast to any marked differences of a moral order between the two great branches of the Anglo-Saxon race respectively occupying the regions south of the St. Lawrence and north of the old Canadian frontier. There were differences, however, between the northern and southern aboriginal populations, the latter being, on the whole, more fierce and warlike than the former, and undoubtedly to such differences may be attributed some of the corresponding results.

But these results are in far greater measure to be explained by the different policies pursued in the north and south, nor would it be fair to forget that these policies themselves were largely determined by the different conditions prevailing in the States and in the Hudson Bay territory. The attitude assumed by the United States Government towards its Indian subjects need not here be discussed, being matter of common knowledge. We are more concerned with the policy adopted from the first both by the company and by the Crown towards 'Our American Subjects,' as the natives were called in official documents. The very expression showed that they were regarded as human beings, entitled to be treated with justice, and it was soon found that such treatment brought its own reward. During the first period of its existence (1670-1763), the company was in a measure at the mercy of the natives, for its own people could not hunt or range the forests to any distance from the seabord without coming into collision with the much more skilful and expert Franco-Canadian *voyageurs* (boatmen) and *coureurs des bois* (forest rangers).

Hence they had to depend on the Indians for their supply of furs, and this could not be effected except on the base of kind treatment and just dealings.

The same policy, which had now become a tradition, continued to be pursued after the withdrawal of the French, when the company's operations were extended far and wide in the interior. It was the practice to train white hands for the administrative part of the service, and these were duly impressed with the standing orders, that the Indians were not to be cheated or harmed in any way, but, on the contrary, relieved in their distress, even when there were no great prospects of returns. In case of misdeeds they were to be treated leniently, and not shot down indiscriminately for every petty theft or act of violence. Other much more effective means were adopted to maintain order and foster a feeling of confidence amongst the natives. All stolen articles had to be restored, and criminals delivered up to the company's agents for punishment, else the tribes harbouring them were cut off from commercial intercourse, and the fort-gates closed against them. Rewards were also offered for the capture of delinquents, and numberless instances might be cited where ' criminals were tracked for thousands of miles, and where an officer of the company would enter a hostile camp alone, and, shooting to death a murderer, walk away unharmed. This certainty of punishment acted upon the savage mind with all the power of a superstition. Felons trembled before the white man's justice as in the presence of the Almighty.'*

Alliances were even encouraged between the company's men and the native women, and in this way there sprang up a generation of half-breeds of English speech, who presented some curious points of contrast with the older and more numerous Canadian half-breeds of French speech. On the father's side they were descended mainly from Scotchmen (Highlanders), Orkney Islanders, and Irishmen, but very few English, and amongst them were some very able men who rose to positions of great responsibility in the company's service. As a rule, all the half-castes inherited the deep-seated passions of their Indian mothers; but 'while those of the French fathers are frivolous and extravagant, the sons of Scotchmen are often found to be staid, plodding, and economical. Though swarthy, the half-breeds are usually large, handsome men, proud of their parentage and nationality, and quite hardy. They are a sharp-sighted, sharp-tempered race, yet too often uniting savage sluggishness of mind with civilized proclivities to drink and disease; yet I have seen many beautiful and intelligent ladies who were daughters of Indian mothers. The half-breeds have large families, and, though their instincts are Indian, they are generally kind-hearted and hospitable. The women are better than the men; they make good wives, and are quite thrifty.'†

* H. H. Bancroft, vol. xxii., p. 538.   † *Ibid.*, p. 544.

It was above remarked that after the disappearance of the French the company's troubles were mainly with our own people. These troubles, which gradually assumed the aspect of an extremely embittered internecine warfare, began almost immediately after the Treaty of Paris (1763), when Montreal and the surrounding districts of Upper Canada were rapidly occupied by settlers from the British Isles. These new arrivals soon discovered that the speediest road to wealth was the fur trade; hence, disregardful of the company's real or pretended claims to an exclusive monopoly of this trade throughout the boundless regions north of the old Canadian frontier, they began as early as 1766 to swarm into the northern 'game preserves' of the Hudson Bay territory.

At first they appeared as private traders and trappers acting on their own account, but soon found it necessary to combine for mutual self-protection against the 'high - handed proceedings' of the company, who peremptorily warned all such intruders off the premises. Such was the origin in 1783 of the famous North-West Company, which never had or asked for a charter, being established from the first on the principle of free and open trade, in accordance with the privilege of all British subjects formulated in the Declaration of Rights (1689).

The headquarters of the Canada Company, as it was also called, was at Montreal, where it was organized by a few Scotch settlers avowedly for the purpose of continuing the peltry business which had already been developed by the French colonists, and in which many Frenchmen, now become British subjects, still took part.

Through the influence of these associates, the new company had little difficulty in securing the invaluable services of many Franco-Canadian agents, *voyageurs,* and *coureurs de bois,* and this, combined with the shrewdness and capital invested in the undertaking by its long-headed Scotch founders, explains the astonishing rapidity with which its operations were developed throughout the western provinces of British North America. So early as 1766 a small band of Scotchmen, aided by the Canadian boatmen and guides, had founded a first inland station at Michilimackinac (Mackinaw) in the Great Lake region; a little later Thomas Curry had followed the old Franco-Canadian track across the Laurentian water-parting all the way to Fort Bourbon; while James Finlay penetrated westwards to Nipawee, the farthest French station on the Saskatchewan River; and Joseph Frobisher pushed northwards beyond the Churchill River in the very heart of the Hudson Bay territory (1775).

Thus was the ground prepared for amalgamating all these tentative efforts under the new association formed in the winter of 1783-84 by Simon McTavish, Benjamin and Joseph Frobisher, McGillivray, Rechéblave, Thain, and a few other wealthy and influential Scotch mer-

chants of Montreal. But an opposition was immediately started by Peter Pond and Peter Pangman, two
men with a grievance, and when Pond was conciliated,
Pangman held out, and founded the rival X. Y. Company in association with Gregory and the famous
explorer, Alexander Mackenzie. A bitter feud, accompanied by bloodshed, prevailed between these two
bodies till the year 1787, when a temporary reconciliation was effected, and the opposition admitted on
equal terms into the original society. But the X. Y.
Company was revived in 1790 by some of the original
partners, who established themselves at the Grand
Portage, on the north-west side of Lake Superior, and
maintained an unfriendly attitude till the year 1805,
when a final fusion was effected. Then the old fort of
Grand Portage, which was found by the Boundary
Commission to lie within United States territory, was
demolished, and replaced by Fort William, which still
stands on a bluff at the point where the Kanimistiquia
River flows into Thunder Bay, on the north side of
Lake Superior. This fort was named in honour of
William McGillivray, who introduced the co-operative
system, in virtue of which efficient clerks became in
due course partners or shareholders.

With the foundation of this famous trysting-place of
the Canada Company's people with the Ojibways, Crees,
and the other Indian tribes of the surrounding regions,
began the series of open conflicts between the free
association and the chartered Hudson Bay corporation,

which lasted with little interruption till the fusion of the rival companies in a single body by the interposition of the Crown in 1821. Matters were brought to a head by the intrusion (1812) of the Earl of Selkirk's Scotch settlers in the Red River Valley, which was regarded by the chartered people as a westward extension of Rupert Land, and consequently a part of their domain.

At first the antagonism took the form of a policy of reckless competition, in which the monopolists tried to drive the Canadians out of the field by the usual devices of outbidding and underselling them at the stations, for which purpose a mandate was issued, that wherever the enemy planted a post, another was to be set up beside it. Such a policy could not fail to provoke reprisals, and thus bring about a state of open warfare, attended at times by surprises, murderous attacks, and even pitched battles.

Some personal encounters had taken place at various points even before Lord Selkirk's colonists made their appearance in the Red River district, which had been purchased from the Hudson Bay Company for the purpose of clearing the land, and founding an agricultural settlement in the Far West. But the scheme was fiercely opposed by the 'Grays,' as the North-Westers were called in contradistinction to the 'Blues,' or Hudson Bay people, being so named in reference to the uniforms of those colours respectively worn by the officers of the two associations. The claims of the

'Blues' to the land were questioned, as lying so far to the west of their exclusive domain ; and in any case it was held that they had no right to alienate such a large portion of the common game preserve. If the process were continued, the fur-bearing animals must rapidly disappear, and with them the resources both of the chartered and free companies.

Hence open hostilities now broke out, and the strange spectacle was witnessed of two sections of the community waging fierce war against each other in times of profound peace.   Lord Selkirk's people were everywhere attacked and driven from their holdings, while farmsteads, stations, forts, and factories were all alike involved in ruin.   The conflict was carried on with relentless fury throughout all the western regions as far north as Lake Athabasca, where Mr. Clarke was besieged and compelled to capitulate after losing seventeen of his faithful 'Blues' by starvation. Despite the proclamations issued by the Governor-General of Canada, threatening all disturbers of the peace with the vengeance of the law, the hostilities were continued with unabated vigour for several years, during which forts were stormed, men killed, and the affairs of both companies threatened with imminent ruin.   But a crisis was reached in 1816, when a party of the 'Grays,' under Alexander Fraser and Cuthbert Grant, descending the Qu'appelle River, were challenged by Governor Semple of Fort Douglas, and responded by slaying nearly all his men, amongst the killed being the Governor himself, Dr. White, McLean, Rogers, Holt, Wilkinson, and eighteen others of less note.

Then followed four years of almost equally disastrous lawsuits, prosecutions, inquiries into title-deeds, and other costly proceedings, which, after an expenditure of over £50,000 on both sides, left things exactly as they were at the outset. The 'Blues' still held Rupert Land, the 'Grays' still disputed their right to exclusive trade, and still carried off the lion's share of the traffic. At last both parties began to realize the fact that it was time to put a stop to this life-and-death struggle. More peaceful councils gradually prevailed, and the war was brought to a close by the deed-poll statute of March 26, 1821, by which 'Blues' and 'Grays' were merged in one body, which was authorized to carry on the exclusive trade as before under the name of *The Adventurers of England trading into Hudson Bay*. The union was consummated by the Act of Parliament passed on July 2 of the same year for regulating the fur trade, and establishing a civil and criminal juris-diction in those still unsettled parts of British North America, which now practically constituted the united company's domain.

Despite the civil strife that had so long prevailed, this domain had gradually been extended by one or other, often by both of the rival associations, north-wards to the Arctic Ocean, and westwards beyond the Rocky Mountains to the shores of the Pacific. Thus it happened that both the original Hudson Bay and the North-West Company had stations not only in what is now British Columbia and Vancouver Island, but also throughout the whole of the Oregon region, which was later assigned by other Boundary Commissions to the United States. They were thus conterminous in the extreme north with the Russians, at that time owners of Alaska, while maintaining in the extreme south-west a hot struggle for supremacy with the ' Boston men,' who had founded Astoria and other trading - stations in the Columbia region. Astoria, around which the struggle chiefly raged, took its name from its founder, the German adventurer, who laid the foundations of the colossal fortune still enjoyed by his descendants of New York and the Thames Valley. This place, which dates from the year 1811, was sold by the Astor Company to the North-Westers for £16,000 in 1813, and eventually passed to the Americans, its original owners, by the treaty of 1818.

Amongst the arrangements of 1821 was a fresh charter, by which the united company obtained an extension of their exclusive trade throughout their vast domain for a further period of twenty-one years. In fact, the monopoly, which by the Declaration of Rights had been invalidated, was now made absolute, at least till the year 1842, and was, moreover, confirmed by another Act passed in 1834 for further regulating the fur trade throughout the company's estate.

Thus the company's privileges remained unchallenged till the year 1859, when the monopoly was declared illegal. But there still remained certain rights, or at least claims and vested interests, which, however, were all surrendered in 1869 to the newly constituted Dominion of Canada. On this occasion a very profit-able arrangement was made, by which the company gave up all its shadowy privileges in return for an indemnity of about £300,000, and an absolute grant of 7,000,000 acres in the most fertile part of the territory. It was also agreed that they should retain possession of all their 'forts,' or trading-stations, with a space of sixty acres round each enclosure. By these negotiations all danger of future litigation was avoided, while hundreds of millions of acres of magnificent arable land (Manitoba, Assiniboia, etc.) were imme-diately thrown open for free trade and settlement, and are now traversed by the Canadian Pacific trunk line of railway.

On the other hand, the company, as a powerful free-trading association, lost little or nothing by the abandonment of its exclusive privileges. Their richest game preserves lay farther north, and these lands, being little suitable for settlement, remain a practical monopoly of the association. Here they continue to hold the stations, so indispensable to a profitable peltry business; here also their system of operations is thoroughly organized, while their influence with the trappers, guides, boatmen, interpreters, and surround-ing Indian tribes is unlimited, based, in fact, on their traditional just and humane treatment of their servants and native 'American subjects.' Thus, 'although all restrictions have been removed, the theoretical right of freely trading with the Athabasca-Mackenzie Indians has hitherto tempted no outside speculators, who could scarcely hope to compete successfully with an association of capitalists who have for generations controlled all the trappers throughout a region six times the size of France. . . . The official suppression of the monopoly in British territory has in no way disturbed the trading relations in these northern regions, and the natives themselves may possibly have remained ignorant of the changed condition of things.'*

In the 'Great Lone Land' of the Far North, the commercial supremacy of the disfranchised company has scarcely yet been threatened by private traders or speculators. Here they are still looked upon by the native tribes as the masters of the land, while their interests are sedulously promoted by a loyal and well-trained corps of considerably over a thousand servants and agents (1895), comprising many English, Scotch, and French Canadians, besides the half-breeds or English and French speech, who still constitute the dominant element.

Thus, of all the great historical chartered bodies, the Hudson Bay Company alone has not only survived the surrender of its privileges, but has continued to prosper as a private trading association down to the

* Reclus, vol. xv., p. 198.

present time. The great game preserves of the Mackenzie basin are, however, being slowly encroached upon, and the vast mineral resources of the northern regions cannot fail ere long to attract numerous miners and settlers, and thus create other interests fatal to the preservation of the fur-bearing animals in that almost uninhabited wilderness.

CHAPTER X.

THE claim made by England to the rightful possession
of the East Atlantic seabord from Labrador to Florida
was based on priority of discovery, and it is now
generally admitted that the whole of these coastlands
were first sighted and roughly surveyed by the two
Cabots. The father, Giovanni (John), was no doubt
of Venetian birth, but he was a naturalized English
subject and a merchant of the city of Bristol. The
son, Sebastian, was a native of that place, although it
must be allowed that several of his later expeditions
were made in the service of Spain.

The first concession granted by the Crown of England
for the purpose of discovery, trade and settlement in
the New World was issued in favour of the Cabots in
1496, before any of those lands had yet been visited, or
were even known to exist. In fact, it appears from the
tenor of the charter, which was of a very comprehensive
though necessarily somewhat vague character, that its

main object was the discovery of that western route to Asia which the Spaniards had failed to find in lower latitudes.

Hence Henry VII. gives these Bristol merchant adventurers ' all power and authority to navigate all the ports, countries and bays of the eastern, western and northern seas, under our banners, flags and ensigns, with five ships and such and so many mariners and men as they shall judge proper, at their own sole cost and charges, to find out, discover, and investigate whatsoever islands, countries, regions, or provinces of Gentiles or infidels in whatever part of the world they may be situated which have hitherto been unknown to all Christians, with power to them to set up our said banners in any town, castle, island, or continent of the countries so to be discovered by them. And most of the said towns, castles or islands so found out and subdued by them to occupy and possess as our vassals, governors, lieutenants and deputies, the dominion, title and jurisdiction thereof, and of the *terra firma* or continent so found out, remaining to us, provided that of all the profits, emoluments, advantages, gains, and produce arising from this navigation or expedition the said Cabot and sons [Lewis, Sebastian, and Sancio] shall be obliged to pay us for each voyage they shall so make, on their return to our port of Bristol, to which port they are hereby absolutely bound to steer, after all needful costs and charges are deducted, one-fifth part of the whole capital gain, either in merchandise or in money; the said Cabots to be free from all customs on the goods they shall so import; the lands they shall so discover and subdue shall not be frequented nor visited by any others of our subjects without the license of Cabot and sons, under forfeiture,' etc. ('Fœdera,' xiii. 595).

In their very first voyage (1496), with three ships 'laden with gross and slight wares,' these pioneers reached the north side of Labrador, whence they sailed 'southward along the shores of America as far as the isle of Cuba, and so returned back to England.'* Thus, instead of finding their way to 'Cathay and the Spice Islands,' they discovered, like Columbus himself, a large section of the American seabord, naming it Prima Vista, or First Sighted. It is pleasant to read that, after over half a century of exploring voyages in the Atlantic waters, Sebastian retired on a pension of £166 13s. 4d. granted him by Edward VI. in 1549.

Far different was the fate of his two illustrious successors, Sir Humphrey Gilbert and his half-brother Sir Walter Raleigh, both of whom were prematurely cut off while engaged in laying the foundations of the English Empire beyond the sea. Ever since the discovery of Newfoundland (1496?), its banks had been frequented by the Western maritime peoples, English, French, Spaniards, Basques, and Portuguese, and it is curious to learn from Hakluyt that 'the English had the best ships, and therefore gave the law to the rest,

---

* Captain Fox, quoted by Anderson, vol. i., 724.

being in the bays the protectors of others, for which it was then, and had been of old, a custom to make them some sort of acknowledgment as Admirals, such as a boatload of salt, for guarding them from pirates and other violent intruders, who often drive them from the good harbours,' etc.

This was in 1578, and in the same year Sir Humphrey Gilbert received a charter from Elizabeth for new discoveries and to settle a colony in those parts. But he did not sail till 1583, when by the aid of those English 'Admirals' he took possession of Newfoundland for himself under the Crown of England. But not liking the nebulous prospect, he sailed thence to the mainland, and after losing all his fleet except one ship and a little pinnace of ten tons, had to return homeward without founding a settlement on any part of the coast. Then being 'unwilling that the humblest of his men should risk more danger than himself, he chose to sail in the boat rather than in the larger and safer vessel. A terrible storm arose; he sat calmly reading a book, and, to encourage those in the other vessel, he was heard to cry to them, "We are as near to heaven on sea as on land." That night those on the larger vessel saw the lights of the little boat suddenly disappear.'*

THE VIRGINIA COMPANY.

Nothing daunted by this failure, in which he was deeply involved, Walter Raleigh obtained the very

* J. H. Patton, ' History of the United States,' etc., p. 39.

next year (1584) a charter from Elizabeth to found a colony on the continent of North America, whither he despatched his friends, Arthur Barlow and the Huguenot Philip Amidas, to make a preliminary survey. Having explored Albemarle and Pamlico Sounds, they returned with such a favourable report that the Queen, perhaps on Raleigh's suggestion, named the whole region Virginia, and immediately constituted it a colony of unknown limits, appointing Ralph Lane its first Governor (1585).

At first this colony was understood to comprise the whole seabord from Florida to the St. Lawrence, or even to Labrador. But it was soon found convenient to divide it into two sections, respectively named South and North Virginia, the parting-line being a neutral zone corresponding to the present states of Delaware, New York, and New Jersey. Bearing this in mind, the reader will have the less difficulty in understanding the somewhat intricate relations of the Crown and of the settlers themselves to the various chartered companies that were now formed in rapid succession for the purpose of colonizing and developing the resources of the Atlantic coastlands. With the history of the colonies themselves we are not here concerned, except so far as may be necessary to show to what an extent their progress may have been furthered or retarded by those corporate bodies.

And here a distinction should be drawn between charters granted to English trading companies, which on the whole were injurious, and charters granted to the settlers themselves, which were often beneficial and highly prized as legal instruments affording protection against the oppressive or unconstitutional measures of the Crown and the provincial Governors. In general it may be said that charters of this second category should alone have been granted, or at least the others should have been withdrawn as soon as the colonists felt themselves strong enough for self-government. Indeed, there was a natural tendency in this direction, and the control of the trading associations was ultimately everywhere replaced by representative assemblies.

But the change was not always effected without considerable friction, which was due to the fact that the Home Government was slow to recognise the true relations that ought to have prevailed from the first between the colonies and the mother country. Those colonies were, and should have been regarded as, mere extensions of England beyond the seas, as Professor Seeley has clearly shown in his 'Expansion of England,' and had this patent fact been grasped by the ruling classes in the eighteenth century, there need, perhaps, never have been an American Revolution.

THE LONDON COMPANY.

Of the early English seafarers in the north-west Atlantic waters, the most successful was Captain Bartholomew Gosnold,* who, after several prosperous voyages about the beginning of the seventeenth century, obtained from King James a double charter for exclusive trade in those parts in the year 1606. The first, called the South Virginia Company, and later the London Adventurers' Company, comprised the region answering to the present Southern States of the Carolinas, Georgia, Virginia, and Maryland, the principal patentees being Sir Thomas Gates, Sir George Somers, Edward Kingfield, and the famous Mr. Hakluyt, Prebendary of Westminster. To the Plymouth Adventurers, as the second was named, was assigned the seabord thence northwards to 45° north latitude, thus including the present States of Pennsylvania, New Jersey, New York, and the whole of New England.

Although settlement was to be promoted, both charters were essentially of the exclusive trade class, because no permanent colonies had yet been anywhere founded on the seabord. In fact, the first was that of Jamestown, established by the London Company in this very year (1606), near the mouth of the Powhatan

---

* This now almost forgotten pioneer should be remembered as the navigator who first successfully attempted the short passage across the Atlantic, the route hitherto followed having been round by the Canaries and the West Indies to the north-west Atlantic seabord. In 1602 he sailed directly for the New England coast, arriving at a point near Nahant in seven weeks, afterwards discovering Cape Cod, Martha's Vineyard, and other neighbouring islands.

(James) River in Chesapeake Bay. Associated with this enterprise were some memorable names, such as those of Captain John Smith, Sir Thomas Dale (the first Governor), the Earl of Southampton (Shakespeare's friend, the Right Hon. Henry Wriothesley), Sir Edwin Sandys, Sir John Danvers, Sir Maurice Abbott, Alderman Abdy, Mr. Percy (brother of the Earl of Northumberland), and even the great Lord Chancellor, Sir Francis Bacon, who on this occasion wrote his essay on ' New Colonies.'

Sir Walter Raleigh does not appear in this goodly fellowship, because he had already been committed to the Tower by the ignoble first Stuart. It should, however, be stated that the charter of 1606 was in substance a confirmation of that granted in 1584 to Raleigh for the ill-starred Roanoke expedition (1587-88), and which he had now transferred with all its privileges on very liberal terms to the London Company. Thus, although continuity of settlement was broken by the total disappearance of the hapless Roanoke settlers, a certain continuity in the efforts at colonization was effected by this transfer of Raleigh's patent to the new association.

How exclusive that first charter was may be seen from those clauses which granted to Sir Walter and others the possession of ' such remote heathen lands as they should discover in six years, of which they thereby had the property granted to them for ever, reserving to the Crown the fifth part of all gold and silver ore found therein, with power to seize to their proper use all ships, with their merchandise, that shall without leave plant within two hundred leagues of this intended settlement, excepting, however, the Queen's subjects and allies fishing at Newfoundland.'* Free 'denization' (domicile), however, is granted to all 'planters' (settlers), and their posterity residing in the country, though no mention is yet made of a representative government, or even of municipal rights; while the chartered association is empowered to make by-laws 'not repugnant to those of England.' No doubt mention is made of two governing 'councils,' one resident in England, the other in the colony; but both were to be appointed by the King, so that the first settlers had no vote in choosing their own magistrates. In religious matters, also, they were not allowed to indulge in any theological differences, but to conform absolutely to the tenets of the Church of England. In a word, the future colonists were to be treated as free Englishmen so far as might be consistent with the royal prerogative and the monopolies of the company.

With regard to the neutral ground between North and South Virginia—that is to say, the tract extending from the Potomac to the mouth of the Hudson—it was arranged in the double charter that the two companies were to be at liberty to found settlements within fifty miles of their respective boundaries. It may be stated

* Anderson, vol. ii., p. 210.

that this zone was later detached from both Virginias, and separate charters granted to Maryland and Delaware, but not to New York. When this province was wrested from the Dutch, by whom it had been first planted, the time had passed for issuing charters either to trading associations or to settlers already strong enough to look after their own affairs.

In 1609 the London Company's charter, being found somewhat unworkable, was so far modified that the council was henceforth to be chosen by the stockholders, and was, moreover, to have the appointment of the Governor, who, however, still retained almost absolute authority. No privileges were yet granted to the settlers, who were thus left at the mercy of the Governor, himself the agent of a soulless corporation whose main object was gain. Their action at this period, especially in sending over a worthless class of settlers, 'vagabond gentlemen, idlers, and gold-hunters,' instead of respectable citizens, farmers, and mechanics, had certainly the effect of retarding the natural development of the colony. Much, however, was done to mitigate the resultant evils by the appointment in 1609 of the wise and enlightened Lord Delaware to the governorship, when the colony was on the very verge of ruin.

He was succeeded in 1619 by the no less able Governor, George Yeardley, who was commissioned by the company to grant the colonists a large measure of representative government. The House of Burgesses, consisting of twenty-two members chosen by the people, met for the first time in July, 1619, and it may be remarked that this was absolutely the first legislative assembly constituted in any part of the New World. The House was to assemble once a year 'to ordain whatsoever laws and orders would be thought good and profitable for our subsistence,' though at first both Governor and council took part in the deliberations. Moreover, the laws passed by the colonial legislature had to be sanctioned by the company in England ; while, on the other hand, the interference of the Crown was restricted by the provision that no measures emanating from the King should be valid unless ratified by the House of Burgesses. Thus matters continued until James dissolved the London Company itself by arbitrarily depriving it of its charter in 1624.

The direct result of this high-handed proceeding was to transform South Virginia to a Royal or Crown colony, retaining, however, its Assembly, as appears from the subjoined interesting extract from the proclamation of a new settlement issued in 1625 by Charles I.: 'That whereas in his royal father's time the charter of the Virginia [London] Company was by a *quo warranto* annulled, and whereas his said father was, and he himself also is, of opinion that the government of that colony by a company incorporated, consisting of a multitude of persons of various dispositions, amongst whom affairs of the greatest moment are ruled by a majority of votes, was not so proper for carrying on prosperously the affairs of the colony; wherefore, to reduce the government thereof to such a course as might best agree with that form which was held in his royal monarchy, and considering also that we hold those territories of Virginia and the Somer Isles [Bermuda], as also that of New England lately planted, with the limits thereof, to be a part of our royal empire; we ordain that the government of the Colony of Virginia shall immediately depend on ourselves, and not be committed to any company or corporation, to whom it may be proper to trust matters of trade and commerce, but cannot be fit to commit the ordering of State affairs. Wherefore our Commissioners for those affairs shall proceed as directed till we establish a council here for that colony, to be subordinate to our Privy Council; and that we will also establish another council, to be resident in Virginia, who shall be subordinate to our council for that colony. And at our own charge we will maintain those public officers and ministers, and that strength of men, munition, and fortification, which shall be necessary for the defence of that plantation. And we will also settle and assure the particular rights and interests of every planter and adventurer.'

Provision was further made for the regular meeting of the House of Burgesses by authority of the Crown for legislative purposes, with the consent of the King's Governor and council, this last body henceforth acting separately as an Upper House, the last appeal in all legal matters being to the Assembly. Thus closed the connection of South Virginia with the London Company, and with all exclusive trading associations, but not with charters of the second category, as will be seen.

THE PLYMOUTH COMPANY.

After failing to form a settlement in 1607 at the mouth of the Kennebec in the present State of Maine, the Plymouth Company appear to have remained inoperative till the year 1614, when an expedition sent out under Captain John Smith effected the first permanent settlement in North Virginia, partly by force, but mainly by agreement with the 'Sachems,' or chiefs of the surrounding Algonquian tribes. Having surveyed the inland district, Smith, on his return, presented a map of it to Charles, Prince of Wales, who thereupon gave the country the name of New England.

Thus was prepared the way for the Pilgrim Fathers, the true settlers of this region, who, however, had originally intended to emigrate to South Virginia, and had even obtained the consent of the London Company to settle there in 1617. But dissension having broken out in the company itself, owing to the opposition of the Church party, they obtained through Sir Robert Naunton, Secretary of State, the King's consent and patent to establish themselves in North Virginia. Here was founded their first settlement of New Plymouth in 1620, when 'they associated themselves into a society by a formal instrument, in which they declared themselves subjects of the Crown of England, and solemnly engaged themselves to an absolute submission to such laws and rules as should be established for the good of the colony; and they elected their own Governor for one year only.'*

But this region being within the limits of the Plymouth Company, they obtained from the council of that association two patents, granted in 1627-28 to Sir John Rowsel, Sir John Young, and several other persons of distinction, for the purpose of extending their territory to the Massachusetts Bay district. The object of this step was to find room for their Puritan brethren, who were now streaming into the country in ever-increasing numbers. Under these patents a stimulus was given to the emigration by the remarkable agreement that the money was to be furnished by the company, while the emigrants were in return to give their entire services for seven years, these services at the same time to constitute their stock in the association.

Much difficulty, however, was experienced in determining the respective rights of the Crown, of the chartered company, and of the settlers, some under contract service, some in the enjoyment of their self-framed constitution, which had actually been drafted

* Anderson, vol. ii., p. 383.

in the cabin of the *Mayflower* before they landed.   The confusion was increased by the concession of privileges to other societies for exclusive trading purposes within the limits of the Plymouth Company.   Thus, so early as 1622 Thomas Weston, a London merchant interested in the New Plymouth colony, obtained a charter for trading with the natives in a small district near the present Weymouth on Boston Harbour, and sent over a number of indented servants and others to develop this trade.   But their idea of trading with the aborigines was to ill-treat them, steal their corn and furs, and thus excite their hostility against all the settlers, being naturally unable to distinguish between the evil deeds of 'Weston's men' and the pious aspirations of the Pilgrims.   Hence the disorders that ensued should be laid to the account, not of chartered trading corporations in general, but of the abuse of the royal prerogative in granting charters to all applicants, irrespective of the prior rights of other patentees.

Another source of trouble was the unjustifiable action of the English merchants, who sought to indemnify themselves for the small profits derived from their investments by charging exorbitant prices for the goods needed by the settlers, and also by trading over their heads directly with the natives.   But by thrift and industry the pilgrims not only triumphed over all their difficulties, but in the course of a few years found themselves wealthy enough to buy up the whole stock of the Plymouth Company.   This stock and the land were equitably divided amongst all the settlers in such a way that every member of the community became the owner of a freehold plot of ground. Being thus released from control in local matters, the colonists formed a government on liberal principles, at least in civil affairs, and down to the year 1640 the whole adult male population elected their Governor, whose power was limited by a council of five.

THE MASSACHUSETTS BAY COMPANY.

Of the numerous overlapping charters issued either by the Crown or by the Plymouth Council, which had taken the place of the Plymouth Company, the first in time and importance was that granted in 1628 by the Council to some gentlemen of Dorchester for the settlement of Massachusetts Bay. By this was understood a strip of territory extending from three miles south of the bay to three miles north of any part of Merrimac River, with a 'hinterland' reaching, as was then customary, to the Pacific Ocean, which, for anything that was known to the contrary, might be a few hundred or many thousand miles away to the west. Meanwhile operations were begun at Salem on the bay itself under the leadership of John Endicott, many influential persons, such as Thomas Dudley, John Winthrop, Saltonstall, Bellingham, Johnson, Simon Bradstreet, and William Coddington, being associated with the enterprise. The action of the council was really limited to the sale of land, but the purchase was confirmed by

14

a royal charter issued in 1629 by Charles I., who regarded the colony rather as a trading association than as a civil community. By the terms of this charter, which controlled the administration of Massachusetts for over half a century, the royal signature was not needed to give validity to its enactments.

No provision, however, was made for popular rights, so that as long as the charter remained in England the colonists could take no part in the management of their own affairs. But by one of the articles the governing council was allowed to choose the place of meeting for the transaction of business, and advantage was taken of this clause to establish a large measure of ' Home Rule.' By the simple expedient of choosing the colony itself as the place of meeting, the governing council, with its charter, was transferred from London to Boston, and virtual independence thus established.

When Charles II. arbitrarily compelled the City of London to surrender all its charters in 1684, the Massachusetts Bay Company had to go with the rest. But in 1691 the province was again incorporated by William and Mary under its old name. The Crown, however, now reserved to itself the appointment of the Governor, Deputy-Governor, Secretary, and ' Judge Admiral,' the other officers, civil and military, to be nominated by the House of Representatives, who were also to elect the council. And thus matters continued with little change till the Revolution. The chief alterations were of a territorial character, New Hampshire being detached from North Virginia as a Crown or Royal colony, while Connecticut and Rhode Island, with 'Providence Plantation,' were constituted charter colonies.

THE CONNECTICUT AND RHODE ISLAND CHARTERS.

Connecticut received its first 'charter of rights' from Charles II. on April 23, 1662. The river which gives its name to this State had already been explored in 1614 by the Dutch, who erected a fortified factory near where Hartford now stands. But not having hands enough to hold the territory, they invited some of the Pilgrims over from New Plymouth to come and live under their protection, the ultimate result being that the Dutch were fain to live under the protection of the English.

After Captain William Holmes had forced the passage of the river in 1633, a compromise was effected by which the Dutch of New Amsterdam (later New York) surrendered the Connecticut Valley to the Pilgrims. But the Council of Plymouth had already, in 1630, granted the district to the Earl of Warwick, who next year transferred his patent to Lords Say and Brooke, John Hampden, and others, the eastern boundary of the grant being the Narraganset River, and the western, as usual, the Pacific Ocean. Hence the fort built by John Winthrop junior, in 1535, at the mouth of the Connecticut River, was named Saybrooke, a precedent followed later by the Boers of Natal, who named their capital Pietermaritzburg in honour of their leaders, Pieter Retief and Gevrit Maritz.

After the great fight with the Pequod Indians, a convention held at Hartford in 1639 framed a constitution on liberal principles, maintaining the right of self-government, and denying any jurisdiction to the Crown in local affairs. They would not even recognise the right of the King to inquire into the validity of the Say-Brooke charter, and when they feared an attempt to change the colony into a royal province, preparations were made to defend their liberties, if necessary, by force of arms.

When Plymouth, Massachusetts, Connecticut, and New Haven joined themselves together for mutual protection under the title of the United Colonies of New England, Rhode Island was excluded, because the settlers in Narraganset Bay refused to acknowledge the jurisdiction of Plymouth. Hence the Rhodians sent the Rev. Roger Williams to England for a charter of their own, and this he obtained in 1644 from Parliament, then at war with Charles I., through the influence of his friend, Harry Vane. This was the so-called 'Providence Plantations' charter, which was confirmed or superseded by the charter granted in 1663 by Charles II. to Rhode Island and Providence Plantation.

As above stated, Connecticut had received its first royal charter in 1662, and both of these patents were framed on such a democratic base that in a report of the Board of Trade to the House of Lords for 1733-34, on the two colonies of Connecticut and Rhode Island, it is stated that 'almost the whole power of the Crown is delegated to the people; and, as their charters are worded, they can and do make laws even without their governors' consent, and directly contrary to their opinions, no negative voice being reserved to them, as governors, in the said charters.'

Universal consternation was naturally caused when the news came, in 1686, that James II. had resolved to take away the charters of all the colonies and make them royal provinces. Under the administration of Sir Edmund Andros, appointed Governor of the whole of New England in that year, efforts were made to give effect to this insane policy. Even the title-deeds of landed estates were declared to be invalid because obtained under a charter which was now said to be forfeited.

Andros went personally to Rhode Island and Connecticut to seize their charters and dissolve their constitutions. He failed in both places, and in Connecticut under circumstances worth recording. He was received by the Assembly with a show of respect, and the discussion on the surrender of their patent was protracted till the evening and continued by candlelight. Then the highly-valued document was laid on the table, but when Andros attempted to seize it, the lights suddenly went out, and with them the charter, which, on the candles being relighted, was nowhere to be found. It had been carried off by Captain William Wadsworth, and hidden in the hollow of the now historical " Charter Oak." Andros, in a rage, wrote in the Assembly's record-book the word *Finis*, which proved indeed prophetic, for the end, not of the people's rights, but of the last of the Stuarts, was at hand. Thus was preserved the Connecticut Magna Charta, which, after the American Revolution, found an honoured resting-place in the national archives.

How had New England fared under her various systems of government by charters? In his 'Summary, Historical and Political, of the First Planting' (Boston, 1751), Dr. William Douglas tells us that Massachusetts contained at that time 200,000 white inhabitants, its government being in the Crown, but the property in the representatives of the people ; Connecticut and Rhode Island had respectively 100,000 and 30,000 white inhabitants, the government and property of both being in the representatives of the people ; New Hampshire had 24,000 white inhabitants, both government and property being in the Crown ; total of New England as then constituted, 354,000.

The history of Maine and Vermont as separate provinces or States had not yet begun. Nor need we here be detained by the settlement of Maryland and Pennsylvania under Lord Baltimore's and William Penn's charters, these being matters of general history with few points of special relevance to privileged corporations, exclusive trade, and monopolies. But it is otherwise with the Carolinas and Georgia, whose early records present many features of great interest to the student of history.

THE CAROLINA CHARTERS.

That section of South Virginia which corresponds to the present States of North and South Carolina and Georgia was first constituted a separate province under the name of Carolana (later Carolina) in 1629, when it was granted by Charles I. to Sir Robert Heath and his heirs for ever. This may be seen from ' Fœdera,' xix., p. 128, where also the King confirms Sir Robert's appointment of Hugh Lamy to the office of Receiver-General of the revenue of 'Carolana,' in which was, moreover, theoretically comprised all the territory westwards to the Mississippi claimed and later settled by the French under the name of Louisiana. In fact, Carolana itself had been first to some extent surveyed and so named by the French in honour of their King, Charles IX., and this title was merely adopted from them by the English as equally suitable to their King Charles I.

Then the whole province was surrendered by Sir Robert Heath (the King's Attorney-General) to the Earl of Arundel, who had even begun to plant several parts of it, when further progress was arrested by the Civil War. Thus was delayed the issue of a proper charter, which was at last granted in 1663 by Charles II.

'to the Lord Chancellor Clarendon, the Duke of Albemarle, the Lord Craven, the Lord Berkley, the Lord Ashley (Chancellor of the Exchequer), Sir George Carteret (Vice-Chamberlain), Sir William Berkley, and Sir John Colleton,' names which still survive in the geographical nomenclature and topography (rivers and counties) of that region.

The limits of this first charter ran from 36° north latitude, being the south end of the present Virginia, to 31° north latitude, being the south end of the present Georgia, but stretched from the Atlantic without limitation westwards to the Pacific Ocean. This boundless domain is assigned to those eight patentees 'in absolute propriety, with all royal mines, fisheries, etc., paying a quit-rent of twenty marks yearly.'

But even with this magnificent domain they were not satisfied, and in the year 1665 they obtained from Charles a second charter extending its southern limits to 29° north latitude. The object of the extension was, no doubt, partly to include the Mississippi Delta, and thus anticipate the French, who were already harbouring designs on that region.* But the main object appears to have been to get at some of the silver-mines away to the west, a report having got abroad that

---

* They did not actually occupy the Lower Mississippi Valley till 1698, when Louis XIV. granted his famous patent to the Sieur Antoine Crozat for a good slice of the North American continent, encroaching on all the hinterland of Carolina, and usurping many hundred thousand square miles of the Spanish main.

none of these rich deposits in Mexico or elsewhere extended farther north than 29° north latitude.

Even the northern limits were advanced half a degree, so that their territory now extended about four hundred and fifty miles along the coast, and for an unknown distance westward to the South Sea. In this second charter the holders are described as 'the true and absolute lords, proprietors of the province and territory of Carolina, saving always the faith, allegiance, and sovereign dominion due to us, our heirs and successors for the same, to be held in free and common soccage, as of our manor of East Greenwich in Kent, yielding and paying to us and our successors for the same the fourth part of all gold and silver ore found within their limits, besides the yearly rent of twenty marks.'

A curious provision was also introduced, absolutely unique of its kind, having for its object to empower the patentees to confer peculiar titles of honour on the great planters in Carolina, so that such titles might be different from any corresponding titles of the nobility and landed gentry in England. The result was exceedingly strange, and even comical, for such new distinctions granted by the company to the first great landowners of Carolina were drawn not only from Germany (landgraves, counts palatine, etc.), but even from the aborigines themselves, so that some of these Anglo-Saxon landed gentry assumed the grotesque title of Indian 'caciques.'

Another somewhat whimsical element was introduced when the famous philosophers, Lord Shaftes-
bury and John Locke, were invited to frame a constitution for the new settlers, based in theory on the
most just and liberal principles, with a view to encouraging men of all persuasions to take part in the
general colonization of the country.   In this scheme
of government the Palatine—that is, the eldest of the
lords proprietors—was assisted in his executive functions by three other proprietors, these four constituting
the Palatine Court, with deputies in Carolina to carry
out their directions.   There was also a representative
body of two chambers, the Upper House consisting of
the proprietors themselves or their deputies, with the
Governor, council, and whole body of caciques and
landgraves ; while the Assembly or Lower House,
comprising untitled settlers, was elected as in other
colonies.

The enactments of the Assembly, however, were
entirely controlled by the Upper House, and the general
tendency of the ' Grand Model,' or ' Fundamental Constitutions,' as the scheme was called, was to place all
power in the hands of the aristocracy ; while the bulk
of the colonists were to be attached to the soil as perpetual tenants.   The freemen—that is, all owners of
fifty acres of land—enjoyed the franchise, but only for
the Lower House ; while all the rest were simply
adscripti glebæ.   Even the parade of religious tolerance
was more or less of a mockery, care having been taken

to declare the Church of England alone the orthodox faith.

But the Grand Model was soon found to be un-workable. The small farmers could not be induced to accept a position differing little from a state of villenage for ever. Many of them even refused to pay quit-rents to the feudal lords, because they regarded themselves as freeholders, having purchased their lands from the natives. And when trade began to be developed, they objected to pay duties or taxes in any form, holding themselves independent alike of King and proprietors. This brought matters to a head, for when the Governor, James Colleton, attempted to collect rents and taxes in 1671, the settlers captured his secretary, impounded the provincial records, and openly defied his authority.

To these troubles were added religious dissensions, over two-thirds of the people being Nonconformists (Presbyterians, Quakers, Huguenots), who deeply resented the tyranny of the licentious ' Cavaliers and ill-livers,' as the ruling party were called. But these, having in 1694 secured a majority of one in the Assembly, forthwith disfranchised all the Dissenters, made the Church of England the established religion, to be supported at the public expense, and divided the colony into parishes, to which the Society for the Propagation of the Gospel was to appoint pastors. An appeal to the House of Lords, however, restored the Dissenters to their political privileges in 1704, although the Church of England maintained its status till the Revolution.

Not so the charter itself, which came to an end in the year 1715 through the direct action of the settlers. After the Indian wars (1712-15), they raised a great outcry against the corporation on the ground that it had done nothing to protect the colonists or to share in the expense of the wars. They therefore resolved, having had to stand the brunt of the battle, that they would henceforth manage their own affairs, and have nothing more to do with the proprietors or their officials. Mutual bickerings and recriminations naturally resulted from this attitude of the people, and when the whole question was brought before Parliament, the proprietors were declared to have forfeited their charter. Most of them sold their claims to the British Government, which in 1729 divided Carolina into two Crown provinces, appointing a royal Governor for each.

It should be stated that this conversion of the Carolinas to a regal government was made on the petition of the people themselves, and not by any arbitrary action of the King. Moreover, the majority of the proprietors (seven out of eight) willingly surrendered their privileges for the small sum of £17,500 (£2,500 each) rather than make themselves liable for the cost of the late Indian wars. This was effected by an Act of Parliament passed in the year 1728, which awarded the said sum to the Duke of Beaufort, the Lord Craven, Sir John Colleton, James Bertie, Dodington Greville, Henry Bertie, John Cotton, Joseph Blakes, Mary Dawson, and Elizabeth Moore, these being at that time the representatives of the original proprietors of seven out of eight parts of the province of Carolina, a province since worth many more millions than the thousands for which it was then surrendered.

Lord Carteret (afterwards Earl of Granville), being the eighth proprietor, declined to part with his share, in consequence of which a special clause was introduced into the Act of 1729 reserving 'to his lordship, his heirs, executors, administrators, and assigns all such estate, right, title, etc., to one undivided eighth part or share of the said provinces, and one-eighth part of all arrears of quit-rents, etc., thereof; notwithstanding which the government of the whole is hereby made entirely regal.' In other words, Lord Carteret's pecuniary interests were respected, while the provinces were reorganized as a Crown colony. The case would appear to be unique in the records of politico-commercial chartered rights.

THE GEORGIA CHARTER.

In one important respect the settlement of Georgia under a royal charter differs from those of all the other chartered colonies. It was a purely philanthropic undertaking, which has had a few more or less successful imitators in later times, but which stands almost alone both for the undoubted nobility of purpose by which its promoters were inspired, and for the disinterested zeal and devotion with which it was carried to a triumphant issue. The scheme, which originated with James Edward Oglethorpe, 'the poor man's friend,' and 'a Christian gentleman of the Cavalier school,' had for its direct object the planting of the still-unoccupied southern parts of Carolina by persons confined for debt in the loathsome prisons of the eighteenth century, and also by Protestants of all denominations who were at that time suffering persecution for conscience' sake in Great Britain and other parts of Europe.

Being aided by many others, chiefly members of Parliament, Oglethorpe easily obtained numerous signatures of men of family and influence to a petition asking George II. for a charter to colonize the territory south of the Savannah River with unfortunate debtors and Protestants from various European countries. The charter, which was issued on June 9, 1732, covered the whole region lying between the Savannah and the Altamaha Rivers, and extending from their head-waters to the Pacific Ocean. This territory, henceforth to be named Georgia, was assigned in trust for the poor to twenty-one original trustees, with power to add to their number, for a period of twenty-one years absolutely.

The trustees 'were thereby empowered to receive and manage the contributions of all persons and corporations inclined to give money for the transporting of people to and settling them in the said country. This corporation was made capable in law to hold and purchase land, etc., in Great Britain, to the value of £1,000 yearly, and in America to an unlimited value, for the said charitable purpose; their Common Council to consist of fifteen persons, with power to make them up to twenty-four (as they afterwards were).

' This corporation might issue commissions to others for collecting contributions, yielding annually to the Crown four shillings for every one hundred acres of land which they shall grant to any planter, which quit-rent to begin to be paid ten years from and after the respective dates of such grants; Georgia to remain for ever an independent province, save only that the government of its militia shall remain in the Governor of South Carolina; but the government of the colony in other respects to be in the trustees for twenty-one years, when it was to be vested in the Crown. Liberty of conscience and freedom of worship allowed to all its inhabitants, Papists alone excepted; lands to be granted to any persons, not exceeding five hundred acres, on such terms as to the Common Council should seem proper; no trustee to hold lands nor office in Georgia; the granting of lands to be registered here in the office of the auditor of the plantations.'

Anderson, who was living at the time, has left us an interesting account of the development of the colony under its first Governor, Oglethorpe. 'The trustees,' he writes, 'took all possible pains for executing the

trust; they erected two good towns, Savannah and
Frederica, at the north and south extremities of the
province, beside several villages and small forts, and
one more famous among the Indians, called Augusta,
with a small garrison for the protection of the Indian
trade 240 miles west from the sea, up the river Savannah,
a common nursery-garden for white mulberry-trees, for
the production of silk. They procured foreign vine-
dressers for improving the native vines, which in great
abundance run up the tallest trees and bear small
grapes; and they have also sent thither many sorts
of vines from Europe, as also some Piedmontese skilled
in the winding of silk and tending the silk-worms. For
several years also they and other lords and gentlemen,
by subscription, maintained a travelling professor of
botany, for collecting the most precious plants and
seeds in various American climates, to be transplanted
to Georgia.

'Yet by having several idle drones, drunkards, and
determined rogues, the prosperity of this colony was at
first much retarded, as it was also by frequent alarms
from the Spaniards [of Florida, who looked on the
settlers as intruders in their domain, and waged a
fierce though unsuccessful war against them to destroy
the colony and recover the territory]; and it must be
confessed in part also by an ill-judged though well-
meant Utopian scheme for limiting the tenure of lands
and for the exclusion of negro slaves, both which mis-
takes have since been rectified. By the planting of

Georgia, Carolina has felt the benefit of being able to run out (as they term it) much land, which, till that new frontier barrier was established, they had no inclination to do, in consequence of which those lands have been raised to five times their former value about Port Royal and toward the river Savannah.'

It should be mentioned that what is here called ' a mistake' was not 'rectified' till after the surrender of the charter, when the period of twenty-one years expired in 1753. Hence the philanthropists were not responsible for the introduction of the plantation system, by which several holdings of moderate size were merged in a single large estate worked by slave labour. At first the slaves were hired from the Carolinas for a short time, and then for a hundred years; but no negroes were introduced direct from Africa for seven years after the final return of Oglethorpe to England.

The first settlers were generally well received by all the surrounding Indian tribes, and it is recorded that Tomochechi, the aged chief of the little Uchee tribe in the neighbourhood of Savannah, presented Oglethorpe with a buffalo-skin, on the inside of which was painted an eagle. ' The eagle,' he explained, 'means speed, and the buffalo strength. The English are swift as the eagle, for they have flown over vast seas; they are strong as the buffalo, for nothing can withstand them. The feathers of the eagle are soft, and signify love;

15

the buffalo's skin is warm, and signifies protection. Therefore I hope the English will love and protect our little families.' The 'love and protection' were proffered, but, truth to say, did not long outlive the charter.

Then came messengers and chiefs from other more famous and warlike nations—Creeks (Muscoghees), Cherokees, and Choktaws—all of whom have long since been removed to reservations in Indian Territory. The Choktaw chief thus addressed the English Governor: 'I have come a long way; I belong to a great nation. The French (of Louisiana) are among us; we do not like them. They build forts and trade with us; their goods are poor, and we wish to trade with you.' Thus was prepared the way for a lucrative traffic with the numerous tribes of the Muscoghee Confederation, who at that time occupied the whole region round the shores of the Gulf of Mexico from Florida to the Mississippi, and inland to the Apallachian hills.

From Europe came the German Moravians with their Bibles and books of mysticism, and zeal for the conversion of the heathen, and they founded their station of Ebenezer a short distance above Savannah. These were followed by a party of Scotch Highlanders with their minister, John McLeod. Other zealous evangelists also flocked to this 'earthly paradise,' amongst others the afterwards famous John Wesley with his brother Charles, and a little later the already famous George Whitefield. Wesley was not a success, or, at least, the people were not prepared for his Gospel of religious asperity, and after two years' preaching in the wilderness, he returned to sow the seed of Methodism in the more receptive soil of England.

But these religious velleities were rudely interrupted by the shock of arms, and the Spanish war (1739-43) had the effect of turning men's minds from theological discussions to mundane matters. To resist the Spaniard, firmly entrenched in his stronghold of St. Augustine, all had to flock to the standards, and the farmers were soon transformed to soldiers. But the Moravians and their adherents, being opposed on principle to bearing arms, quitted the colony in large numbers. Thus Georgia became secularized, and, even before the surrender of the charter, had advanced considerably on the road to material wealth. Hence, when the term expired in 1753, the trustees found it unnecessary to apply for a renewal of their privileges, and the 'colony of the poor' became a flourishing royal province.

CHAPTER XI.

SUMMARY ACCOUNT OF THE GUINEA (ROYAL AFRICAN) AND MINOR CHARTERED COMPANIES.

I.

THE FIRST GUINEA COMPANY.

A LONDON ship and pinnace having made a prosperous voyage to Benin in 1588, Elizabeth granted in that year a patent for ten years to two London merchants and to others of Exeter and other towns of Devonshire for an exclusive trade to the rivers Senegal and Gambia in Guinea, as all that region of West Africa was then called, ' because,' says the charter, ' the adventuring of a new trade cannot be a matter of small charge and hazard to the adventurers in the beginning. Provided, however, that at any time after the date hereof the Queen or six Privy Councillors may in writing revoke this patent upon six months' notice.'

Despite this precarious tenure, the association flourished for some time, and mention is made of a very lucrative venture in 1590, in which ivory, palm-oil, cotton cloth, and 'cloth made of the bark of trees,' were taken in exchange for linen and woollen cloths, ironware, copper bracelets, glass beads, coral, hawks' bells, horses' tails, hats, and the like. But the tremendous expansion of the Guinea trade in the next century was caused by the development of the sugar industry in the West Indies, where the plantations were worked by slave labour. Henceforth the chief exports from the West Coast were slaves, until the traffic was declared illegal and suppressed in the early part of the nineteenth century, mainly by the efforts of Great Britain.

II.

The Second Guinea Company.

Although the original charter has disappeared, there can be no doubt that a concession was granted by Charles I. in 1631 for an exclusive trade to West Africa in favour of Sir Richard Young, Sir Kenelm Digby, and sundry merchants. They were to enjoy 'the sole trade to the coast of Guinea, Binny [Benin], and Angola, between Cape Blanco in 20° of N. latitude and the Cape of Good Hope, together with the isles adjacent, for thirty-one years to come; which charter prohibits not only the King's subjects other than the patentees, but likewise the subjects of every other prince and state, to trade or resort to or within the said limits on any pretence whatsoever; neither were any but those patentees to import into his dominions

any red wood, skins, wax, gums, dyers' grains, nor any
other merchandise, upon forfeiture of ships and cargo ;
and the patentees were empowered to seize on all ships
and merchandise they should find within their bounds,
contrary to this charter; and might also search into
the inner parts of Africa' (' Fœdera,' 1632).

It was certainly a bold assumption of authority to
exclude the subjects of other States from the trade of
the West African seabord, where the Portuguese as
well as the Dutch had already been firmly established.
Nevertheless, in the next year (1632) 'the King granted
his protection to a fleet of ships now fitted out by the
above-named patentees for the said coast of Africa, for
commencing of commerce there within the said limits '
(*ibid.*).

But the attempt to monopolize the trade of this
region ended in disaster, as might well have been
expected. After vast sums had been squandered in
the erection of forts, factories, and warehouses at
various points along the coast, the separate traders of
all nations swarmed into those waters, eager to share
in the profits of the growing traffic in slaves for the
American plantations. Thus the trade was again to a
great extent forced open, and so it remained till after
the Restoration. Under the Commonwealth, however,
a charter was granted for five years to the East India
Company to use the abandoned forts and stations on
the Gold Coast, as lying conveniently on their route to
the East Indies. They even erected two new forts,

and made large profits by licensing ships to trade to Guinea for 10 per cent. of their cargoes, or £3 per ton on the ships.

III.

THE THIRD GUINEA COMPANY.

A third Guinea or African Company was incorporated in the year 1662, for the express purpose of meeting the rapidly-increasing demand for slave labour on the West Indian sugar plantations. At the head of the association was the pious Duke of York, and one of the conditions of the charter was that they should undertake to supply those plantations with not less than three thousand negroes annually. Another more legitimate object was the recovery of the English forts and factories on the Guinea coast, which during the disorders of the Civil War had been captured or destroyed both by the Dutch and Danes. The previous company's stock had thereby been ruined; while their ships and goods, together with those of the separate traders or interlopers, had been taken to the total value of £300,000.

To repair their losses, the new company, being supported by the Duke of York and other influential persons, induced the Government to send thither Sir Robert Holmes with a powerful squadron of fourteen ships for the purpose of surprising the Dutch forts in anticipation of the war then pending between England and the United Provinces. In 1664 Admiral Holmes captured several of the Dutch forts (which, however, were soon recovered by De Ruyter), and he also built a new fort at the mouth of the river Gambia, naming it James Fort in honour of the Duke of York. Thanks to the erection of this stronghold, the English secured and still retain possession of the Gambia, although this territory is now hemmed in on all sides by the French colony of Senegambia.

But the resources of this third company were so exhausted by their constant struggles with the Dutch and with the interlopers, that they were glad to surrender their charter, and sell their three forts of Cape Coast Castle, Sierra Leone, and James Fort for £34,000 worth of shares in the association by which they were succeeded soon after the peace with Holland.

IV.

THE FOURTH GUINEA (AFRICAN) COMPANY.

This powerful association was incorporated in the year 1672 with a capital of £111,000, still under the patronage of the Duke of York. By their energetic action trade was rapidly revived, several new forts were erected, and the traffic in gold developed to such an extent that in 1673 some fifty thousand 'guineas' were first coined, being so named from the country whence the precious metal was imported.* The com-

* Although proclaimed to go for 20s., this coin never went for less than 21s., which was made its legal value in 1717, its intrinsic value being about 20s. 8d.

pany continued to flourish till 1789, when they lost their exclusive trade by the Declaration of Rights.

But even after that time they still continued to trade as an unprivileged association, and to derive a profit from independent adventurers, who were required to pay the company 10 per cent., not for the right of trading, but for the use and maintenance of their forts and stations. This charge, however, which was fixed in 1698, afterwards caused much dissatisfaction, the separate traders complaining of the company's bad faith in exacting the fees, and not giving fair value in return. The forts, which should have been kept in good repair, appear to have been much neglected, so that in 1711 the House of Commons petitioned the Queen to take charge of them pending further provisions.

In fact, about this time the company were practically insolvent, and in 1712 an Act was passed to effect an agreement between them and their creditors. On this occasion several resolutions were agreed to affirming the great importance of the trade for the American plantations, 'which should be supplied with a sufficient number of negroes at reasonable rates.'

Meanwhile the affairs of the company were going from bad to worse, and as they were no longer able to keep up the forts, Parliament voted in 1730 a sum of £10,000 for that purpose. This grant was annually continued till the year 1744, when it was doubled, in consequence of the war with France and Spain, but

later again reduced to £10,000. The grant itself had
the effect of throwing the trade completely open, and of
thus ruining the company, who were unable to compete with the private adventurers in the slave traffic.
Even though efforts were now made to open up an
inland trade in gold, ivory, wax, drugs, dye-woods and
the like, they were still unable to pay any dividend on
a reduced capital of about £200,000, or even to meet
current expenses out of profits.

In 1748 an abortive attempt was made to merge the
now moribund company in a new joint-stock concern,
their debts, due mostly to themselves, to be paid out
of a sum of £150,000, for which they offered to hand
over the forts to the Government. Practical effect,
however, was given to this project by the Act of Parliament passed in 1750, throwing the African trade
open, but declaring that all British subjects taking
part in this trade shall be 'deemed a body corporate
and politic by the name of the Company of Merchants
trading to Africa, with perpetual succession and a
common seal, and may sue and be sued, etc., as other
corporations.'

All the territories of the old company were to be
taken over by the new corporation, which, however,
was not to trade in its corporate capacity, but to take
charge of the forts, factories, etc., for the common
benefit. For this purpose, an annual committee of
nine persons (three for London, Bristol, and Liverpool
respectively) was to be chosen by all those who should

purchase the freedom of the company by a payment of £2, the money thus raised being available for the maintenance of the forts and settlements, for the salaries of the clerks, and such-like working expenses. Lastly, the Court of Chancery was to examine and settle the claims of the creditors of the old company, which was then to be dissolved.

The dissolution took place in 1752, when £112,142 3s. 3d. were voted out of the year's supplies for compensation, etc., to the old company and their creditors. It was at the same time enacted that the new company be 'empowered to arm and train military forces at their forts, and to punish offences, so as not to extend to life or limb ; and to erect courts of judicature for mercantile and maritime bargains, etc.'

Thus was regulated the African trade, the export branch of which consisted largely of slaves, and this arrangement continued in force till the abolition of the traffic in 1833. It may here be stated that in 1788— that is, long before the development of the philanthropic movement which brought about the total suppression of the traffic—an Act was passed by which the horrors of the 'middle passage' were somewhat mitigated. The slave trade was, in fact, already considered as 'disgraceful to an enlightened age, and in this country a spirit is arisen which seems bent on annihilating it altogether, or so changing the nature of it as to blend humanity with the policy.' So wrote Mr. Coombe about the year 1790 (vol. vi., p. 905).

V.

THE MAROCCO OR BARBARY COMPANY.

Patent granted in 1585 by Elizabeth to the Earls of Warwick and Leicester, and to forty others, for an exclusive trade to the territory of Marocco for a period of twelve years. To the Emperor, Muley Hamed, the Queen sent her Minister (Roberts), who remained in the country three years, and obtained some privileges for the English, particularly that in future none of the English should be made slaves in his dominions. By the treaty signed at Mequinez in 1728, these privileges were extended, it being stipulated that British subjects taken on board of foreign ships by the Maroccans should be immediately released and sent to Gibraltar; that provisions and other supplies for his Britannic Majesty's fleets and for Gibraltar might be freely bought at the market prices in any of the Maroccan seaports; and that Moors, Jews, and other natives of Marocco in the service of British subjects there should be exempt from taxes of all kinds. Thus considerable benefits accrued to the nation through this chartered company, whose exclusive trade does not appear to have been long maintained.

VI.

THE CANARY COMPANY.

Created in 1665 by Charles II., who granted a royal patent to sixty persons therein named, and to all others

of his subjects who had within seven years past traded
to the Canary Islands to the value of £6,000 yearly.
The company was to enjoy the exclusive trade to the
Canary Islands, under a Governor, Deputy-Governor,
and twelve assistants.

In the preamble the reasons for granting this charter
are stated to be ' that the trade of the Canary Isles
was formerly of greater advantage to the King's subjects
than at this time; that by reason of the too much
access and trading of subjects thither our merchandise
was decreased in its value, and the Canary wines, on
the other hand, were increased to double their former
value ; so that the King's subjects were forced to carry
silver and bullion thither to get wines ; and that this
was owing to want of regulation in trade.'

Of all the historical corporate bodies, this company
had the briefest existence, its charter having been withdrawn on a suit brought against it before Parliament
in the year 1667. On that occasion both Houses, in
an address to the King, thanked him for revoking its
patent, which would appear to have been obtained by
unlawful means. In fact, in the third article of the
House of Commons' impeachment of the Lord Chancellor Clarendon, that nobleman is directly charged
with having received large sums of money for procuring
this and sundry other illegal patents.

VII.

The Guiana Company.

The first English settlement in Guiana was effected by Captain Ley in 1605. But no charter was issued till about the year 1609, when letters patent were granted to Mr. Harcourt, of Stanton-Harcourt, and sixty others, who had founded a station on the river Weapoco. On Mr. Harcourt's return to England, he obtained through Prince Henry's influence this deed of incorporation for all that coast, together with the Amazons estuary, for himself and his heirs. But the enterprise came to nothing, because, as stated in the second volume of Captain John Smith's 'Voyages,' 'that colony could not exist for want of being duly supported from home, which had likewise been the case of Captain Ley's settlement four years before.'

Then followed the fatal concession in 1616 'to Sir Walter Raleigh and such as he shall join with him to undertake a voyage unto the south parts of America, or elsewhere in America, possessed and inhabited by heathen and savage people, to discover some commodities in those countries that be necessary and profitable for the subjects of these our kingdoms; we being credibly informed that there are divers merchants and owners of ships, and others well disposed to assist the said Sir Walter Raleigh in his enterprise, had they sufficient assurance to enjoy their parts of the profits returned, in respect of the peril of law wherein the said Sir Walter Raleigh now standeth. . . . We have granted full power to him and free liberty to carry and lead out of this realm, or elsewhere, all such of our loving subjects as shall willingly accompany him, together with ships, arms, and ammunition, wares, merchandise, etc. ; and he to be the sole Governor and Commander of the said people, with power of martial law, etc. ; and also power to appoint under him such captains, officers, etc., as he shall judge proper; and to bring home gold and silver, precious stones, and other merchandise, and to dispose thereof at his and his partners' pleasure, paying to us one-fifth part of the gold, silver, and precious stones, and also the usual duties for the other merchandise. And we do grant unto the said Sir Walter Raleigh that these our letters patent shall be firm and sufficient in law, etc.'

The disastrous result of this venture, followed in 1618 by the arrest and execution of Sir Walter under a previous sentence, form a painful episode in the inglorious reign of the first Stuart. The above-quoted passages from the letters patent will, however, show that he had not been sent out, as is popularly supposed, on a roving commission in quest of gold in the Spanish main, but, if possible, to establish a trade for gold and other commodities in those parts of the continent that were 'possessed and inhabited by heathen and savage people.'

It should further be stated, this point not being

generally known, that on his return without gold the
King denied having given him authority to sail to
Guiana, the denial being made to please the Spanish
monarch pending the then projected marriage of Prince
Charles (Charles I.) with the Infanta of Spain. But
despite the disavowal, it is a fact that before sailing
Raleigh had a private interview with James, at which
he explained his whole plan of operations, with a
detailed description of the Orinoco region previously
visited by him.

Moreover, a company had about that very time been
incorporated 'for an intended plantation and settlement of a trade and commerce in those parts of the
continent of America near and about the river of
Amazons, which were presupposed not to be under
the obedience and government of any other Prince or
State.' But in order to conciliate the Spaniard, the
King again disavowed and thwarted the expedition
undertaken in 1620 to Guiana by Captain Roger North
and others 'as members of the company and corporation intended for that plantation.'

Of this corporation nothing further appears to be
known, but in 1628 a fresh charter was granted to the
same Captain North for the purpose of opening a trade
with Guiana. Under the protection of this charter a
footing was even obtained in the lower Amazons
region, where settlements were made and fortifications erected. Although it ultimately disappeared, the
colony appears to have flourished for some years, as it

is recorded in Sir William Monson's 'Naval Tracts' that in 1635 'there was then actually an English colony in Guiana, which yielded the best tobacco, and that the natives were the most tractable of any in our settlements.'

It has been suggested that this was the English colony of Surinam about the river Moroni, which had been first founded in 1640 by the French, and abandoned by them in 1641. The English settlement was made in the same year 1641 at the expense of Lord Willoughby, and although this nobleman ruined his paternal estate in the enterprise, the colony was held by the English till the year 1674, when it was wrested from them by the Dutch. These dates, however, show that this colony of Surinam could not have been the same as that founded by Captain North many years previously.

VIII.

THE BERMUDA OR SOMERS ISLES COMPANY.

This company of about one hundred and twenty members was incorporated by royal charter in 1612, when they purchased the islands from the Virginia Company, who, as first discoverers, claimed possession of them. The discovery, which, however, had been anticipated in the sixteenth century by the Spanish navigator Bermudez, was unwillingly made during the expedition of 1609 by Sir George Somers and Sir Thomas Gates, who were shipwrecked and detained

16

for nine months in the archipelago. By building a ship of the indigenous cedar-wood they got away to Virginia, leaving two men in the largest island. These were found still alive in 1612, when the newly-formed company made its first settlement of one hundred and sixty persons in St. George's Island. Having been joined by five hundred others in 1619, the settlers instituted an Assembly with a Governor and council, to which was later added a chamber of thirty-six deputies. This form of administration still persists, the islands having been retained by Great Britain chiefly for strategical purposes. At present, considerably more than half of the inhabitants are negroes or mulattoes, mainly introduced as free labourers since the abolition of slavery. When the chartered company surrendered such exclusive privileges as it may have originally possessed does not appear. In any case, these privileges would have lapsed after the Declaration of Rights in 1689.

IX.

THE CHINA OR CATHAY COMPANY.

Charter granted in 1635 by Charles I. to Sir William Courten, Sir Paul Pindar, Captain John Weddel, and Endymion Porter to trade to China and Japan, as well as to any parts of India where the East India Company had not established themselves before December 12, 1635, but without prejudice to that company in other respects. A condition was that the grantees should, from the sea of China, Japan, or elsewhere, send one well-furnished ship to attempt the discovery of the North-West Passage. They were granted a common seal, and to all intents they were made a separate corporation from the East India Company, whose rights were thereby infringed. But the venture came to nothing, their factories and 'two rich ships' having been captured by the Dutch East India Company in 1640, with a loss of £51,612. In the treaty between Charles II. and the Dutch in 1662, satisfaction was stipulated to be made for this loss ; but no redress appears to have ever been obtained, and nothing further is heard of this abortive company, whose charter was granted only for a term of five years.

APPENDIX I.

THE NAMES OF NOBLEMEN AND PERSONS OF HONOUR

WHO WERE ADMITTED IN HAMBURG TO THE FREEDOM OF THE FELLOWSHIP OF THE MERCHANT ADVENTURERS OF ENGLAND.

1621. Sir ROBERT ANSTRUTHER, Knight, Ambassador to Denmark.

1631. Sir HENRY VAINE, Knight, Ambassador Extraordinary to Denmark.

1632. The Right Hon. ROBERT SIDNEY, Earl of Leicester, Ambassador to Denmark.

1638. Sir THOMAS ROWE, Knight, Ambassador Extraordinary to Denmark.

1650. RICHARD BRADSHAW, Resident to the Hanse Towns.

1654. BULSTROD WHITLOCK, Ambassador Extraordinary to Sweden.

1658. Sir PHILIP MEDOWS, Envoye to Denmark.

1664. The Hon. Sir WILLIAM SWANNE, Knight, Resident to the Hanse Towns.

1664. The Right Hon. CHARLES HOWARD, Earle of Carlisle, Envoye Extraordinary to Moscow.

1664. The Hon. EDWARD HOWARD, Lord Morpeth.

1666. The Hon. Sir GILBERT TALBOT, Knight, Envoye Extraordinary to Denmark.

1668. The Hon. THOMAS TYNNE, Esq., Envoye Extraordinary to Sweden.

1668. The Hon. Sir PETER WYCHE, Knight, Envoye Extraordinary to Moscow.

1669. The Hon. Sir THOMAS HIGGONS, Knight, Envoye Extraordinary to Saxony.

1670. The Right Hon. ARTHUR CAPELL, Earle of Essex, Ambassador Extraordinary to Denmark.

1670. The Hon. HILDEBRAND ALLINGTON, son of the Lord Allington.

1670. The Hon. CHARLES BERTHIE, son of the Earle of Lindsey.

1670. The Hon. GEORGE RUSSELL, son of the Earle of Bedford.

1672. The Right Hon. HENRY COVENTRY, Ambassador Extraordinary to Sweden.

1672. The Hon. CHARLES FANSHAW, son of the Lord Thomas Fanshaw.

1674. The Hon. THOMAS HENSHAW, Esq., Envoye Extraordinary to Denmark.

1676. Sir EDWARD DERING, Knight, made free in London, being chosen Governor.

1680. The Hon. Sir ROBERT SOUTHWELL, Knight, Envoye Extraordinary to Brandenburg.

1680. The Hon. BEVILL SKELTON, Esq., Envoye Extraordinary to the Emperor.

1681. The Right Hon. CHARLES, EARL OF MIDDLETON, Envoye Extraordinary to the Emperor.

1682. The Hon. PHILIP WARWICK, Esq., Envoye Extraordinary to Sweden.

1693. The Right Hon. the Lord CHURCHILL, Envoy Extraordinary to Denmark.

1684. The Right Hon. LAWRENCE, EARL OF ROCHESTER, made free in London, being chosen Governor.

1685. The Hon. Sir GABRIEL DE SYLVIUS, Knight, Envoy Extraordinary to Denmark.

1687. The Hon. EDMOND POLEY, Esq., Envoy Extraordinary to Sweden.

1689. The Right Hon. the Lord ASHLEY.

1689. The Hon. St. PAUL RYCAUT, Knight, Resident to the Hanse Towns.

1689. The Right Hon. St. WILLIAM DUTTON COLT, Knight, Envoy Extraordinary to the Princes of Brunswick-Luneburg.

1690. The Right Hon. the Lord HIDE.

1691. The Hon. ROBERT MOLSWORTH, Esq., Envoy Extraordinary to Denmark.

1692. The Hon. WILLIAM DUNCAN, Esq., Envoy Extraordinary to Sweden.

1693. The Right Hon. the Lord LUXINGTON, Envoy Extraordinary to Denmark and to the Princes of Brunswick-Luneburg.

1693. The Right Hon. the Lord DARTMOUTH.

1693. The Hon. JAMES CRESSET, Esq., Envoy Extraordinary to the Elector and Princes of Brunswick-Luneburg.

1694. The Right Hon. the Lord GUILFORD.

1696. The Hon. THOMAS ROBINSON, Esq., Resident to Sweden.

1696. The Right Hon. Mr. BERCLAY, son of the Lord Dursley.

1698. The Hon. GEORGE STEPNEY, Esq., Envoy Extraordinary to Brandenburg.

1698. The Right Hon. the MARQUIS OF TAVISTOCK.

1699. The Right Hon. Mr. HOWARD, son of the Earle of Carlisle.

1701. The Hon. Hugo Gregg, Esq., Resident to Denmark.

1701. The Hon. Colonel William Cadagon, Commissary for receiving the Duch troops.

1702. The Hon. James Vernon, Esq., Envoy Extraordinary to Denmark.

1702. The Hon. John Wich, Esq., Resident to the Hanse Towns.

1702. The Right Hon. the Earl of Bridgwater.

1703. The Hon. the Lord Scudemore.

1703. The Right Hon. the Lord Villars.

1705. The Right Hon. Algernon, Lord Marquis of Hartford.

1706. The Right Hon. the Earl of Lincoln.

1706. The Hon. Emanuell Scroop How, Esq., Her Majesty's Envoy Extraordinary to the Elector and Princes of Brunswick-Luneburg.

1706. The Hon. Daniel Poltney, Esq., Envoy Extraordinary to Denmark.

1707. The Right Hon. the Lord Compton, son of the Earl of Northampton.

1710. The Right Hon. the Lord of Danby, son of the Right Hon. the Marquis of Carmarthen.

1710. The Right Hon. the Lord Peregin, son of the Right Hon. the Marquis of Carmarthen.

APPENDIX II.

CHARTER TEXTS.

I.—SPECIMEN OF EARLY TUDOR CHARTER (HENRY VII.).

PATENT OF HEN. VII. TO THE MERCHANT ADVENTURERS AT CALAIS.

HENRIE by the Grace of God King of England and France and Lord of Ireland. To all manner our Officers, Ministers, true Liegemen and subjects as well within this our Realme as elsewhere under our obeysance and rule unto whom these our letters shall be shewed or come and to every of them greeting. Wee let you witt That whereas we have been credibly informed by way of complaint by divers and many of the most sadd, discreet and substantiall Merchants adv^{trs} that for default of good saad and politique Rule and Governance divers harmes dissensions and greeves between the said Merchants Adventurers repairing conversant and abedeing at our Towne of Calays and in the parts of Holland, Zeland, Brabant, Flanders and other places abroad beyond the seas being in Amity with us, oftentymes before these dayes have been moved and grown to the great hurt, destruction and decay of many of the said Merchants and the subversion of the Comonweale of the whole

Fellowship of the same and greater inconveniences in time to come being likely to grow and ensue unless then for the better rate and governance between our said Merchants due remedy be had in their behalfe.

For Reformation whereof and for their relief in the Premises Wee at the humble request and pursuit of our said Merchants to us made at Sundrie and divers tymes greatly desireing the utility and profitt of our said Merchants and the Advancement of their commonweale of their Feate and exercise in the same Will and by the tenor of these presents Give and graunt unto our said Merchants Adventurers Power, Licence, Libertie, and Authority That they as often and whensoever it shall please them shall meete freely and lawfully in places convenient and honest within our said Towne of Calais and Marches of the same when it shall please them; Assemble themselves and then elect and choose a Governor or Governors of themself at their Libertie and pleasure; And also at the election of such said Governor or Governours to choose name and appoint Four and Twenty of the most sadd discreet and honest Persons of divers Fellowships of the said Merchants Adv^{trs}, and the same Foure and Twentie to be called and named foure and twenty Assistants to the said Governor or Governours.

And furthermore we will and graunt unto the same our Merchants Adventurers that such said Governor or Governours or their Deputies and Fouer and Twentie Persons by the said Fellowship of Merchants so from tyme to tyme to be chosen named and appointed or the more part of them, And if any of the said Fouer and Twentie persons be absent then the more part of them that shall be present so that there be thirteen at least wholle agreed have use and exercise full power and authority to Rule and Governe All and Singular our said Merchants and to doe full and speedy Justice to them in all their Causes, quarrells and complaints among them in our said

Towne and Marches, moved and to be moved, and to reforme
decide and pacify all manner of questions, discords, debates,
and variances between themself and between them and other
Strangers in our said Towne of Calais moved and to be moved
and all manner Trespasses hurts misprisons excesses violences
injuries to Merchants Strangers done by the said Merchants
our Subjects to repaire restore and amend, and like restitutions
reparations and amends of other Merchants Strangers or of their
Deputies to require aske and receave. Moreover we give and
graunt by these presents unto our said Merchants Adv^trs That
the Governor or Governours or their Deputies and the said
Assistants in manner forme and number afore rehersed shall
have full power and authority. To make, Ordeyne, and establish all such Statutes, Ordinances, and Customes, as the said
Governor or Governors or their Deputies, and the said
Assistants in manner forme and number before specified for
the better Governance good condition and Rule of our said
Merchants in this behalf shall make and Ordeyne. And for
the better observation of the same to have power to set and
Ordeyne all manner penalties as well by Fines, Forfeitures and
imprisonments as otherwise. And all other Acts and Ordinances by them or their Predecessors made in tymes past or
hereafter by them or their Successors to be made as they shall
think not necessary or prejudiciall to them to revoke, breake,
Admde and Dissolve at their Pleasure and Liberty all and
singular our said Merchants found Contrarious, rebells, or dis-
obedient to the said Governor or Governors their Deputies and
the said Assistants for the tyme being or to any Statutes, Acts,
or Ordinances by them made or to be made after the effect or
importance of the same Acts, Statutes, and Ordinances to
mulct and punish as the quality of the offence requireth without declyning from the power of the said Governor or Governors
their Deputies and the said Assistants for the tyme being and

without any further appeale or provocation. Furthermore, we will and graunt by these presents unto the said Merchants Adv^{trs} That the said Governor or Governors their Deputies and Assistants in manner, forme and number above rehearsed shall have full power and authority to assigne, constitute and Ordeyne one Officer or Divers Officers as well within our Realme, as within our Towne and Marches of Calais, which Officer or Officers we will have power and authority in our behalf to take, receave, levie, and gather all manner fines, Forfeitures, penalties and mulcts of every Merchant our subject convict upon or for breaking and violation of the Statutes, Acts, and Ordinances, made or to be made by the Governors and Assistants afore-named which officer or Officers also we will have power and authority on our behalf for default of payment or for Disobedience in this behalf if need be to sett hands and arrest upon Bodies and Goods of the Offenders as well within this our Realme as at our said Towne and Marches of Calais and if it shall fortune any of the said Fouer and Twentie Assistants to decease or may not for sickness or age or will not of their wilfulness give their attendance, and it be thought to such of the said Assistants in manner, forme and number before rehearsed their being present expedient and necessary to choose other in the places of them so deceased or that may not or will not give their attendance for the causes above said.

It shall be then Lawfull to the said Governor or Governors and the said Assistants in manner, forme, and number, as before rehearsed them to remove and discharge and to choose other in their places in manner and forme afore specified. Provided always that if there be any fewer or lesser number of the said Assistants there present then thirteen that then any act or statute made by the whole Agreement of them be of no force or effect : And in likewise if there be any Act or Statute

made by the same Thirteen or by the said Governor or
Governors or their Deputies and the said Fouer and Twentie
or by any other number of them that shall be or may be
contrary to us our Crowne, Honor, Dignity Royall or Prerogative or to the deminution of the Commonweale of our Realme
be of no force or effect ; And if any Person being Merchant
Adventurers chosen into the said number of Assistants refuse
and will not take upon him, then every such Person so refusing
to pay Twenty pounds sterling halfe thereof to be to our use
and the other half to be to the use ot the said ffellowshippe.
Moreover we streightly charge and command that all and every
Merchant our subject intromitting exercising or in any wise
useing the Acts, Medlings or Feats of Merchant Adv^{trs} to be
in all things contributory and obedient to all manner Acts,
Statutes, Ordinances and Penalties, as a Merchant Adv^{trs} in
that behalf doth and is bound to doe and that every such
Merchant or subject useing as is aforesaid be obedient unto
the said Governor or Governors and Assistants in manner,
forme, and number above rehearsed and come into the said
Fellowship of Merch^{ts} Adv^{trs} and be free of them paying the
Haunse of ten marks stg. according to a certain Act of our
High Court of Parl. made within the tyme of our Raigne, as
by the same Act it may appeare more at large. Alsoe we will
and strictly command our Lieutenant Deputee and other
Counsails of Calais and all other our officers there for the tyme
being as often as by the said Governor or Governors their
Deputies and the said Assistants in manner, forme, and number
above rehearsed they shall be thereunto required they doe
make indilate proclamations openly and solemnly for the
incomeing and outgoeing of every Mart to be holden at our
said Towne from tyme to tyme without tarrying or looking for
any other commandment from us by writeings or otherwise.
Moreover we will and Graunt by these presents unto our said

Merchants Adventurers power and authority that it be lawfull
to the said Governor or Governors their Deputies and the said
Assistants in manner, forme, and number above rehearsed to
prorogue and prolonge every Marte to be holden at our said
Towne of Calais by the space of Fourteen dayes after the end
and expiration of every Mart there holden at their Libertie.
Alsoe we Give and Graunt unto the said Fellowship of our
Merchants Adv^trs power and Authority that the said Governor
or Governors their Deputies and the said Assistants in manner,
forme, and number above rehearsed shall choose, Ordeyne and
Assigne within our said Towne of Calais, Wayers, Porters,
measures, Ployers, Packers at their Liberty and pleasure to
serve onely for their Merchandizes without any Lett or impediment of any of our Officers or any other Persons whatsoever
they be; and if it shall at any tyme hereafter ruin fortune the
said Merchants to make pursuit and request unto to us to
resort and repaire to the said Countries being in Amity with
us, and thereupon have and obteyne our Agreements and
Lycence soe to doe.   That then the said Merchants Adventurers have and enjoy all and every of our said Grauntes as
freely and plenarily in the same Countries by this our Present
Graunt they may doe in our said Towne of Calais.   In witness
whereof to these our Letters Patents we have caused our
Greate Seale to be put, Given at Oxford the Eight and
Twentieth day of September in the One and twentieth yeare of
our Reigne.

II.—SPECIMEN OF A LATE TUDOR CHARTER (ELIZABETH).

CHAR. OF Q. ELIZ: 18TH JULY. 1564.

ELIZABETH by the Grace of God Queene of England,
France, & Ireland, Defender of the Faith &c.   To all &

singular Justices, Mayors, Sheriffs, & Bayliffs, Constables, Customers, Searchers, Surveyors, Comptrollers, & keepers of our Forts, Passages, Havens & Creakes and to all and every our Officers true and Liege men & subjects these our Letters reading, hearing or seeing and to every of them Greeting. Where our Right Noble Grandfather of worthy memory Henry late King of England the Seventh by his Letters Pattents bearing date the Eight & Twentieth day of September in the One and Twentieth year of his Reigne. Hath given & Granted to the Merchants Adv^{ters} of this Realme of England lately tradeing to the Countries of Holland, Zealand, Brabant, Flanders, and other places nigh adjoining for Merchandize by the name of Merchants Adv^{trs}, subjects to the said late King, repayring, conversant and abideing at his Towne of Calais & in the parts of Holland, Zealand, Brabant, & Flanders and in other places beyond the seas being in Amity with the said late King, power, License, Liberty, & Authority that they the said Merchants Adventurers as often and whensoever it should please them should and might freely and lawfully in places convenient and honest within the said Towne of Calais, & Marches of the same where it should please them, assemble themselves and then elect & choose a Gov. or Gov^{rs} of themselves at their Libertie and pleasure and also at the elections each said Govr or Gov^{rs} to choose, name and appoint Four & Twenty of the most sad, discreet, and honest persons of divers fellowships of the said Merchants Adventurers. And that the same Four & Twenty should be called and named Four & Twenty Assist^s to the said Govr or Gov^{rs}.

And have also at this present for their Gov^t our Trusty & Well-beloved John Marth Esquire and to the Senegall Merchants Deputies to the said John Marth now Govr and Fower

& Twenty Assists to the said Govr and Deps duly elected and chosen of se by vertue of the same graunts made unto them by our said Noble Grandfather King Henry the 7th and other our said Noble Progenitors & according to the intent and meaning of the same, wh. said Elections of the John Marth to be Govr and of the Two severall Deps and of the said Fower & Twenty Assists yet remaine and be in full effect.   And where also now of late the said Merchts Advtrs by diverse Streints, Edicts & Proclamations made and sett forth by the Govr & Magistrates of the said Countries of Holland, Zealand, Brabant, & Flanders have been prohibited, Letted & forbidden to traffique & Trade into their said Countries with their wares, Goods & Merchandizes, contrary to the Auncient Priveleges & entercourses thereof heretofore graunted and of long tyme used so that our said Merchts are thereby occasioned for the uttering of the wares, Commodityes & Merchandizes of this our Realme and for their maintenance and continuance of the State and trade of Merchandize to traffique and Trade with their Wares, Goods, Commodityes & Merchandizes in East Friezland, Hamborough, Lübeck, and other Countries or Places by reason whereof divers questions doubts and ambiguityes may arise and be moved, whether the said merchants Advtrs by force of the said former Charters & Graunts to them heretofore made by our said Grandfather and other our noble Progenitors wh. have speciall Relation and doe make expres mention of Calais and of the Marches of the same.   And of Holland, Zealand, Brabant, Flanders, and other Places neare adjoyning, and not of East Friezland, Hambrough, Lübeck & other countries or Places be sufficiently incorporated and inabled to traffique and Trade with their said wares, Commodityes, Goods, & Merchandizes to East Friezland & Hambrough & Lübeck aforesaid or to any other countries or Places then to Calais or to the

Marches of the same or to the said Countries of Holland, Zealand, Brabant & Flanders. We therefore having as tender Zeale & Affection and as careful regard to the continuance weale, profit and Commodity of our said Merch^ts and their Successors shall from henceforth by our speciall Grace and favour prosper and growe in their Exercise and Feate of Merchandize in as great wealth and increase or Greater than their Predecessors have heretofore done at the humble suite and Petition of the said Govr & Merch^ts adventurers in consideration of the faithful and acceptable service of sundrie tymes done by the said Mer. Ad. unto us siththence we came to our Crowne in divers the Great & Mighty affaires of us and our Realme and for the more quietnes and surety of our said Merch^ts in avoyding and takeing away of the said doubts, questions, and ambiguityes and for other good Causes and considerations us specially moveing are pleased and contented, and of our speciall Grace certain knowledg and mere motion Doe by these Presents, for us our heirs & Successors will Ordayne and Graunt that the Fellowship or Co. of the said Mer^s Ad^s by whatsoever name or names they be or at any tyme or tymes hereafter have beene incorporated, united, established, named, called, or knowne, in or by any Charters Letters Patents or Graunts of our said Grandfather or of any other our Noble Progenitors or by force of any Custome, wage, or prescription shall be from henceforth by force and authority of these presents, made, ordeyned, Incorporated united and established one perpetual fellowship & Cominalty & Body Politick & Corporate in name and in deed and shall have perpetuall Succession and a Continuance for ever and shall be named, called, and knowne and incorporated by the name of Govr Assist^s & Fellowship of Mer^s Ad^s of England, and that the said JOHN MARTH, EMANUEL LUCAS,

17

Sir Thos: Leigh K^nt
Sir Wm: Gerrard K^nt
Sir Wm: Chester K^nt
Richard Mallorie
Rich^D Champion
Tho: Rowe
Roger Martin
Ric^D Chamberlain
Rowland Hayward
Edward Jackman,
Ric^D Lambert
Ald: Sir Thos: Gresham K^nt
Laurence Withers
Rich^D Fowlkes
Lionel Duckett
Wm: Gifford
Wm: Beswick
Rich^D Springham
Nicholas Wheeler.
George Balford or Basford
John Gresham
John Traves
Thos: Heton
Thos: Rivett
Matthew Field
Henry Viner
Edward Castlynne
John Rivers
Frances Robinson
John Quarles
John Bodeley
William Gravener
John Violet
Thos: Turnbull
Henrie Beechar
Thos: Blancke
Wm: Peterson
Jeffry Walkden
Thos: Starkey
Rich^D Hills.
John Milner
Wm: Eaton
Edw^D Bright
Edm^D Burton
Rich^D Pipe
Thos: Walker and
Wm: Hewett

And all and every other person or persons, our Subj^s wh. heretofore have or hath been admitted and allowed and now remaine and be free of the Fellowship or Co. of the said Mer^s Adv^rs lately trading at the said Countries of Holland, Zealand, Brabant, Flanders and other Places nigh adjoyning any of them for merchandize and all and every other Person or Persons wh. at any tyme hereafter by reason of patrimony or apprenticeship should or ought to have been admitted received or made free of the said Fellowship or Co.

by the orders and Rules of the same bee and shall be in such sort free of the said fellowship of Govr. Assist^s and Fellowship of Merchants Adv^{trs} of England, and with such diversity and distinction and freedome and in such manner forme and condition to all intents respects, and purposes as they be should or might have beene free of the said Fellowship of Mer. Adv^{trs} lately tradeing the said Countries of Holland, Zealand, Brabant, Flanders and other Places nigh adjoyning or any of them commonly called the Mer. Adv^{trs} by and according to the Rules and Ordinances of the same Fellowship and in no other manner forme sort quallity or condition.

* * * * *

(Here follows repetition of the above names and same persons as already given their Act following.)

And further we by these Presents doe ordeyne Create, and make the said John Marth the first & present Govr of the same Fellowship of Merch : Adv^{trs} of England We untill such tyme as the said Mer^s Adv^{trs} of England shall elect and choose any other of the said F-ship or Corporation to be Govr of the same   In manner & Forme hereafter men^d And alsoe We by these presents doe ordeyne create and make the said

SIR WM : GERRARD Knt.	THOS : HETON
RICH^D CHAMPION	THOS : RIVETT
THOS : ROE	MATT FIELD
RICH^D LAMBERT	HEN. VINER
JOHN RIVERS	FRANCIS ROBINSON
JOHN QUARLES	JEFFRY WALKDEN
WM : GRAVENER	THOS : STARKEY
THO : TURNBULL	RICH^D HILLS
HEN BEACHER	JOHN MILLNER
THOS : BLANCKE	EDW^D BURTON
WM : PETERSON	RICH^D PIPE and
ED : BRIGHT	THOS : WALKER and

every of them the first and present Assist^s to the said Govr and his Dep. and Dep^s To have and continue the same office, Roome, or Stead of Assit^s to the said Govr and his Dep & Deps untill such tyme as the said Fellowship of Merch^ts Adv^trs of England shall elect and choose others of themselves to have and exercise the said office, Roome, and Stead of Assist^s in manner and forme hereafter mentioned.

And moreover We of our said Grace especiall certayne knowledge and mere motion for us our heirs and successors, will, Graunt, Ordeyne, and establish by these Presents That the said Govr Assist^s & Fellowship of Merch^ts Adv^trs of England and their successors by the name of Govr Assist^s & Fellowship of Merch^ts Adv^trs of England, be and shall from henceforth One Body-Politique & Perpetuall Fellowship & Commonalty of themselves Incorporated both in Deed & Name and them and their Successors by the name of Gov. Assist^s & Fellowship of Merch^ts Adv^trs of England.

Wee for us our heirs & Successors Doe really fully and perfectly Incorporate name, Create, Establish and declare by these presents, And also doe graunt for us our heirs and Successors by these presents unto the said Govr Assist^s and Fellowship of Merch^ts Adventurers of England and to their successors That they and their Successors by the same name of Govr Assist^s & Fellowship of Merch^ts Adv^trs of England shall and may have perpetuall succession & a Common Seale, which shall perpetually Serve for the affaires and business of the said Govr Assist^s & Fellowship of Merchants Adventurers of England and their Successors and that they their Successors by the name of Govr Assist^s & Fellowship of Merch^ts of England shall & may from henceforth for evermore be able and have full lawfull and perfect power, ability and capacity in the Lande to sue and implead and to be sued and impleaded to answer and to be answered to Defend and be Defended, to Demand

and to be demanded, before whatsoever Judges Justices, Judg
& Justice, as well spirituall as temporall or other Person or
Persons whatsoever, and in whatsoever Court or Courts place
or places, and in all Actions, Reall Personall and Mixt,
Assizes & Plaints of Nowell Disseisen and alsoe in all other
Plaints, Writs, Bills, suits, quarrells, businesses, Affaires and
demaunds whatsoever they be which shall touch or in any
wise concerne the said Govr Assist^s Fellowship, of Merchants
Adventurers of England or other successors or the Rights,
Priveleges, Liberties, Franchises, Affaires, lands, tenements,
hereditaments, Goods, Chattells, Debts, or businesses of them
or their successors and by the same name shall and may at
all tymes hereafter receive, take, and purchase as well of us
our heirs & Successors as of any other Person or persons, Body
Politique or Corporate whatsoever all and all manner Goods,
Chattells Lands, Tenements, heriditaments, Lycenses, Liberties,
Franchises, profits, Commodityes, discharges, or other benefits
or things whatsoever.   And moreover we for us our heirs and
Successors doe by these presents graunt to the said Govr
Assist^s & Fellowship of Mercht^s Ad^{trs} of England, and to their
Successors, that they and their successors and every of them
or so many of them as can or will shall and may from tyme to
tyme for ever hereafter quietly, freely and lawfully in places
Convenient and honest assemble themselves together beyond
the seas in the Countries and Townes of Holland, Zealand,
Brabant, Flanders, East Friezland, West Friezland and Ham-
burgh and the Territoryes to the same belonging or in any
part thereof in such part of the same where the said Fellowship of Merch^{ts} Adv^{trs} of England shall repayre and be resident
and abideing for the sale of their merchandizes, and that then
and there the said Fellowship of Mer. Adv^s of England or the
greatest part of them there then being shall and may at their
Liberty and pleasures name, choose and elect of the said

Fellowship or Company one Person to be Govr of the same
fellowship of Merch^{ts} Adv^{trs} of England and one or more
person or persons to be Dep. or Dep^s to the said Govr so from
tyme to tyme to be elected the same Govr Dep. and Dep^s to be
and continue in the said office and officers to be removed from
the same by the Assent of the said Fellowship or of the more
part of the same Fellowship so residant as is aforesaid at their
will and pleasure.   And that the same Fellowship of the
Merch^{ts} Adv^{trs} of England and their Successors or the greatest
part of them which shall repayre and shall be residant and
abideing for the sale of their merchandizes at any of the said
places beyond the seas shall and may from henceforth for ever
from tyme to tyme choose and elect Fower & Twenty discreet
and honest persons, of the same Fellowship or Corporation to
be assistants to the same Govr and to his Dep & Dep^s and to
their Successors for the tyme being and same fower & Twenty
persons so chosen and hereafter to be chosen shall be called
Assistants and shall be chosen from tyme to tyme in manner
and forme before declared and that as well the said Fower &
Twenty Assist^s now being made and created by these presents
as such other persons which hereafter shall be chosen to be
Assist^s shall continue in the same place, Roome, Office & Stead
of Assist^s until such tyme as by our the said Fellowship of
Merch^{ts} Adv^{trs} of England so residant as is aforesaid or by the
more part of them they shall be moved put out and displaced
of and from the said Office Roome, and Stead of Assist^s And
if it shall fortune any of the Fower & Twenty Assistants to
decease or that they or any of them may not for sickness age
and otherwise or will not of their wilfullness give their
attendance in the said Roome, Office, or Place of Assistants
that then if for the said Causes or any cause whatsoever it shall
be thought by the said Fellowship of Merchants Adventurers
of England reseant as is aforesaid or by the more part of them

expedient & necessary to choose others in the Places of them so deceased, or that may not or will not give their attendance or shall be thought meet to be displaced for the causes aforesaid or any other whatsoever, It shall be then and so often tymes Lawfull to the said Fellow-ship of Mer. Adventurers of England so resiant as is aforesaid or to the more part of them then present them to amove, displace, and discharge & to choose others in their Places or Roomes as is aforesaid And further we for us our heirs and Successors doe by these presents graunt to the said Govr Assist^s & Fellowship of Mer. Adventurers of England that the said Fellowship of M. As. of England and their Successors or the more part of them so resiant as is aforesaid by and with the Assent of the said Govr or his Dep. or Dep^s and of the said Assist^s for the tyme being or of Thirteen of the said Assistants at the least shall and may forever at all and every tyme and tymes and from tyme to tyme hereafter admit, receive, and take into the said Fellowship or Body Corporate and make free of the same all and every such person and persons as they by their discretions shall thinke meet and convenient and in such manner and forme and with such conditions and distinctions and diversity in Freedome as by them shall be thought from tyme to tyme most expedient and necessary. And that every person hereafter shall be so admitted received or taken into the same Fellowship or Body Corporate of Mer^s Adv^{rs} of England and made free of the same as is aforesaid shall be one of the same Fellowship of the said Mers. Adv^{rs} of England and a Lawfull Member or part of the said Body Corporate and free of the same in such manner and with such conditions and distinction in freedome as shall be, as is aforesaid from tyme to tyme thought convenient until such tyme as by the Fellowship of Mers. Adv^{trs} of England and their Successors or the more part of them so resiant as is aforesaid by and with the consent of

the said Govr or his Dep or Dep^s and of the said Assistants
for the tyme being or of Twenty of them at the least they
for their offences or demerit shall be amoved, put out, displaced and defranchised of and from the same.   And that the
said Govr or his Dep. or Deps and the said Fower & Twentie
Assist^s or the more part of them for the tyme being shall from
henceforth for ever have use and exercise full Jurisdiction,
power, and Authority Lawfully to Rule and Governe the same
Fellowship of Mers. Adv^{trs} of England and their successors and
all and every Merchant & Member of the same in all their
Private Causes, Suits, quarrells, misdemeanours, offences &
Complaints amongst them in the same Countryes & Townes
of Holland, Zealand, Brabant, Flanders, East Freizland, West
Freizland, Hambrough and the territories of the same or in
any of them riseing moved and to be moved, and to reforme,
decide, and pacify all manner of quest^s discords and variances,
between themselves, & between them or any of them and
other Merchants in the said Countries & Townes of Holland
&c. &c. (same as above) and all manner Trespasses, Hurts,
misprisons, Excesses, violences, and injuries to Merch^{ts} Strangers
in the said Foreign Countries or in any of them done by the
said Merch^{ts} of the said Fellowship or Corporation or by any
of them to repayre restore and amend and like restitutions, reparations and amends of other Merch^{ts} Strangers
or of their Dep^s to require ask, and receive.   And further,
we for us our Heirs & Successors doe by these presents
graunt to the said Govr Assist^s & Fellowship of Merch^{ts} Adv^{trs}
of England and their successors that it shall and may be
Lawfull to the Govr of the said Fellowship for the tyme being
and to every of them at all tyme and tymes hereafter and from
tyme to tyme for ever to call, assign appoint and assemble
courts and Congregations of all the said Fellowship of Mers.
Adv^{trs} of England as well as the place or places of old

tyme accust^d within the City of London and elsewhere within this our Realms as alsoe in the said Flanders, East and West Friezland, Hambrough and the territoreyes of the same or in any of them as after and whensoever as the said Govr Dep or Dep^s for the tyme being or to any of them it shall seeme and be thought expedient for the weale of the said Fellowship of Merchants Adventurers of England. And moreover We for us our heirs and Successors doe by these presents give power and Authority to the said Governor Assistants & Fellowship of Merchants Adventurers of England that the same Gov. or his Dep. or Dep^s and the said Four & Twentie Assistants or the more part of them for the tyme being and all manner of persons being of the said Fellowship of Mer^s Adv^{trs} of England which shall be admonished or warned at any tyme or tymes by their officer or officers to come and appeare at any assembly, Court, or Congregation from thenceforth to be appointed by the said Govr or his Dep. or Dep^s for the tyme being or any of them and which shall not come and appeare at the hour and place, to them or any of them by the said officer or Officers to be appointed or Assigned for his or their non-appearance and disobedience in that behalf or for any other offence done or to be done against the Commonweale of the said Fellowship or against any of the Priveleges to them heretofore or by these presents graunted to send and comitt to the Goale or Prison there to remayne without bayle or main prize and to be further punished by Fine or Fines after the quallity of their trespasses as the said Govr or his Dep. or Dep^s for the tyme being together with the said Fower & Twentie Assistants or Thirteen of them at the least shall be ordeyne and award. And further we for us our heirs and Successors will graunt ordeyne and establish by these presents that if any person or persons which now is or at any tyme hereafter shall be free of the said Fellowship of Mers. Adv^{trs} of England shall at any tyme or

tymes hereafter marry and take to wife any woman borne out
of this Realme of England and other our Domin^s or shall at
any tyme or tymes hereafter purchase, obteyn gett or have to
himself or to any person or persons to his use or upon any
confidence or trust any Lands tenements or heriditaments in
any of the said Ports or Places beyond the Seas out of our
Domin^s, that then and from thenceforth imediately after such
marriage or purchase so to be had or made the same person
and persons which soe shall marry or purchase as is aforesaid
shall be ipso facto disfranchized off and from the said Fellowship and shall not be at any tyme after reputed, received,
accepted, or used by the said Govr Assist^s and Fellowship of
Mers. Adv^trs of England or their Successors or by any other
person or persons as one of the said Fellowship or Free of the
same, but shall from thenceforth in all and every place or
places be utterley excluded of and fr. all Liberties, Traffiques,
trade of Merchandizes, preheminences, Jurisdictions and Voyces
belonging unto the said Fellowship of Merchants Adventurers
of England, or to any person being free of the same. And
alsoe that such person or persons now or lately being free of
the said Fellowship of Mers. Adventurers lately tradeing the
said Countries of Holland, Zealand, Brabant Flanders and
other Places nigh adjoyning or any of them for Merchandize
and useing and exercising the Feate & Trade of Merchants
Adv^trs which before the date of these presents have marryed
any woman borne out of our said Realme of England and
other our Domin^s and doe and shall by himself or his wife
inhabit out of our said Realme and Domin^s or that heretofore
have Purchased Obteyned or gotten to him or themselves or to
any other Person or Persons to his or their use or upon any Confidence or Trust any Lands, tenements, heriditaments, lying in
any parts or places beyond the seas out of our Domin^s shall
not in any wise from henceforth during so long tyme as he and

his wife shall inhabit out of this our Realme and Domin^s dureing so long tyme as he or they or any other Person or Persons to his or their use or upon any Confidence or trust shall be seazed of any lands, Tenements or heriditaments in the said Parts beyond the Seas out of our Domin^s Assemble amongst the said Fellowship or be present at any Consultation, Conference, Councell to be had by or amongst the said Govr or Dep. Assist^s and Fellowship of Mers. Adventurers of England or any of them anything before in these presents conteyned or any other matter or thing whatsoever to the contrary in any wise notwithstanding. And moreover wee greatly minding that discreet, honest and decent Gov^t heretofore used among the Merchants Adventurers, Lately tradeing into the said Countries of Holland, Zealand, Brabant, Flanders & other places nigh adjoyning for Merchandize should be kept con^d & had by the Govr Assist^s and Fellowship of Mers Ad^s of England, In as great estimation as in tymes past it hath beene of our more abundant Grace certeyn knowledge and mere motion for us our heirs & Successors, doe by these presents graunt to the Govr Assist^s Fellowship of Mers Adv^{trs} of England & to their Successors that the said Govr or his Dep. or Dep^s or the said Assistants and their Successors for the tyme being or Thirteen of them which shall be resiant as is aforesaid from tyme to tyme and at all tymes from henceforth shall and may enact, establish, allow and confirme and alsoe revoake, disannulle and repeale all and every Act and Acts Law & Ordinance heretofore had or made by the said Govr or Dep. & Assist^s of the said Fellowship of Merchants Adventurers lately tradeing in the said Countries of Holland, Zealand, Brabant, Flanders & other places nigh adjoyning for Merchandizes or heretofore to be made or used by or amongst the said Govr Assist^s & Fellowship of Merchants Adventurers of England And alsoe in the said Countries & Townes of

Holland be (as above) East Freizland, West Freizland, Hambrough, and in the territoryes of the same or in any of them and in such part of the same where the said Fellowship of Merch^{ts} Adv^{trs} of England shall repayre and be resient for the sale of their Merchandizes, shall and may from henceforth from tyme to tyme at all tymes hereafter for ever enact, make, Ordeyn and establish, Acts, Laws, Constitutions & Ordinances as well for the good Governmente, Rule & Order of the said Govr Assist^s & Fellowship of Merchants Adventurers of England and their successors and every Merchant & particular Member of the same Fellowship, Body Corporate, As Alsoe of all and every other subject and subjects of us our heirs & Successors, Intermedling, exercising & useing the Feate or Trade of the said Merchants Adventurers by any Meanes in the said Countries & Townes of Holland, Zealand, Brabant, Flanders, East & West Friezland, Hambrough and the Territoryes of the same or in any of them, so that the said Acts, Laws, Constitutions, Statutes & Ordinances be not hurtful to any the Rights of the Crowne, honour, dignity, Royall or prerogative or the diminuition of the Common Weale of this our Realme or contrary to any our Lawes & Statutes, And that the said Governor, his Dep. or Dep^s and the said Assistants and their Successors or the more part of them for the tyme being shall and may at this tyme and at all tymes hereafter for ever, so often as occasion shall serve put their said Acts and Orders & Rules & Ordinances so in forme aforesaid to be made in due execution as well within this our Realme as in the said Countries and Townes of Holland, Zealand, Brabant, Flanders, East & West Friezland, Hambrough and the Territoryes of the same and in every of them and shall and may alsoe at all tymes hereafter for ever so often as occasion shall serve within the said Foreign Countries & Townes and every of them freely and Lawfully put in due execution as well upon as against, and amongst all and every person & persons being or that hereafter shall be, a Member or Members of the same Fellowship or Body Corporate of Gov[r] Assist[s] & Fellowship of Mers. Adv[trs] of England, As alsoe against all and every Person & Persons, Intermedling with exercising or useing or that hereafter shall intermeddle with exercise or use the Feate or Trade of the said Mers. Adventurers by any wayes or meanes in the said Forreign Countries & Townes & in any of them all and singular, such Act & Acts Orders, Rules Lawes & Ordinances whatsoever, as have been heretofore had, made, or used by the said Gov[r] Dep. & Assist[s] of the said Fellowship of Mer[s] Adv[rs] Lately tradeing the said Countries of Holland, Brabant, Zealand, & Flanders, and other places nigh adjoyning for Merchandize by force of any priveleges, Powers, Liberties, Graunts, preheminences or Authorityes hereafter to be graunted or made to the said Gov[r] Assist[s] and Fellowship of Mer[s] Adv[s] of England or their Successors by any the Lord or Lords, Gov[r] or Gov[rs] of the said Forreign Countries & Townes or of any of them or of any part of them, be made, used, or established and shall and may allsoe compell such as be not of the same Fellowship of Merchants Adventurers of England and occupying exercising, or useing the Trade of Merchants Adventurers in any of the said Countries & Places beyond the seas to obey & performe all and every the said Acts, orders, Rules, Lawes & Ordinances by all or any the wayes or meanes aforesaid, made or to be made and every of them And that the said Governor &c. &c., shall and may take order with every the subject or subjects of us our heirs and subjects not being of the said Fellowship of Merch[ts] Adv[trs] of England and tradeing or haunting the said Countries, or Places, beyond the seas or any of them for Merchandize in the trade of a Merchant Adventurer and to compell every of them by Fines, Forfeitures, penalties, Emprisonments or otherwise to obey, hold and performe all such orders, Acts, and Ordinances that hereafter shall be ordeyned, made, allowed, or confirmed by the said Govr or his Dep. or Dep^s and the said Assistants and their successors or the more part of them for the Good Gov^t Rule, Order, & Condition of the said Subj. or Sub^s so as the State of the said Fellowship of Mer^s Adv^{trs} of England or any of them be not by them impeached or hindred but by all meanes and wayes maintained & con^d And that all such Forfeitures, Fines, Penalties and Amerciments so to be Leavied and taken shall be for evermore to the use and behoof of the said Govr Assist^s and Fellowship (of the Mer^s Adv^{trs}) of England and to their Successors for the tyme being.   AND furthermore Wee of our more abundant Grace for us our heirs and Successors doe will and streghtly charge & Command, as well all & every person or persons being or that hereafter shall be a Member or Members of the said Body Corporate of Govr Assist^s & Fellowship of Merchants Adventurers of England and all and every other Person or Persons Intermedling with, exerciseing or useing or that hereafter shall intermedle with, exercise or use the Feate or Trade of the said Merchants Adventurers by any wayes or meanes in the said Countries and Townes of Holland, Zealand, Brabant, Flanders East & West Friezland Hambrough, and Territoryes of the same or in any of them, that they and every one of them submit themselves and in all things be obedient to the said Govr Dep. or Dep^s and assist^s and their successors and every of them and to all and every the Acts, Orders, Rules, Lawes, & Ordinances had or made or hereafter to be had or made as is aforesaid without declineing from renounceing or disobeying the power or authority of them or of any of them and without any further appeale or Provocation whatsoever, As alsoe that all Mayors, Sheriffs, Bayliffs, Constables, and other officers, & Ministers of this our Realme and every of them for the tyme being Doe from tyme to tyme for ever support and assist and ayde the said Govr his Dep. and Dep^s and Assist^s for the tyme being and their Successors and their Ministers & Officers and every of them in the due Execution of the said Lawes Acts & Ordinances and in punishing the offender and transgressors of the same by the paines and penalties Limits & App^d or to be Limited and app^d in the Lawes, Acts, and Ordinances, And if the said Govr or his Dep. or Dep^s or his or their Successors for the tyme being with the consent of the said Assistants or the more part of them shall commit or send any of the said Fellowship of Merchants Adventurers of England or any other Subj. of us our heirs & Successors being not of the same fellowship to any Ward, Goale, or Prison, for breaking or doeing against any of the said Acts, Ordinances, or Orders made or to be made then our Will & Commandiment is, And for us our (heirs) & Successors Wee doe alsoe graunt unto the said Govr Assist^s and Fellowship of Merchants Adventurers of England and to their Successors that soe often tymes and from tyme to tyme the Warders Gaolers or Keeper, of the same Wards, Gaoles or Prisons, shall receive into his or their Prisons all and every such person or Persons so offending as shall be sent or committed to him or them and those shall safely keep the Person or Persons so committed at the proper costs and charges of the said person or persons so committed without Bayle or Maineprize untill such tyme as such offender or offenders shall be discharged of the said imprisonment by the said Govr or his Dep. or Dep^s and Assistants or the more part of them or their Successors. And that wee our heirs Successors will not in any wise discharge or release out of ward or Prison upon Surety Bayle, or Maineprize or otherwise any such offender or offenders without the consent of the said Govr or of his Dep. or Dep^s and Assist^s or of the more part of them for the tyme being or of their Successors untill such tyme and they and every of

them so imprisoned shall have bothe obeyed and fullfilled all
thinges according to the said Acts, Statutes, and Ordinances
made or to be made as is aforesaid.   And alsoe shall have paid
all and every such Fine & Fines penalties and forfeitures and
Amerciments which they shall be adjudged to pay by the said
Gov[r] &c. &c, for any such their trespasses abuse or offence
comitted or to be comitted as aforesaid against any of the Acts,
Statutes, Rules, and Ordinances made and to be made concerning the said trade and Feate of Merchandize.   The said
Fines & Fines, penalties, forfeitures & Amerciaments and every
of them to be demaunded levyed and received.   To the uses
of the said Gov[r] Assist[s] & Fellowship of Merchants Adventurers
of England and of their Successors for ever,   And alsoe that
it shall and may be lawful to the said Gov[r] or his Dep. or
Dep[s] and the said Fower & Twentie Assistants and their
Successors for the tyme being and Twenty of them whereof
the said Gov[r] or his Dep. to be one to amove, displace put out
and disfranchise out of the said Fellowship or Co. all and every
such Person or Persons which shall commit or perpetrate any
Greate trespas, abuse, offence and Contempt against any of the
said Acts, Lawes, Statutes, and ordinances made or to be made
as is aforesaid in that behalf.   Moreover Wee for us our heirs
& Successors Will by these presents graunt unto the said Gov[r]
Assist[s] and Fellowship of Merchants Adventurers of England,
and to their Successors that the said Gov[r] or his Dep. or Dep[s]
and Assist[s] for the tyme being or the more part of them shall
have full power and Lawfull Authority for ever to assign,
Constitute, make and ordeyne one officer or divers officers,—
as well within our City of London and in all other places
within this our Realme and other our Domin[s] as alsoe in the
said Countries and places beyond the seas or in any of them
to take, receive, leavy, and gather, all manner of Fines,
forfeitures, Penalties and Mulcts of every Person and persons

of the said Fellowship &c. or of any other person &c. not being
of the said Fellowship offending or breaking any Statutes &c.
made or to be made by the said Govr &c &c., And will and
graunt that the said officer shall have full power and authority
for default of payment or for disobedience in that behalf if
need be to arrest as well the Body and Bodeyes as the Goods
of such Offenders and Transgressors in all and every place
within this our Realme and Domin^s and in the said parts
beyond the seas or in any of them where the same can be
found and the same to reteyn and keep irreplevisable until they
Shall have satisfied for their offence or misdemeanour or otherwise agreed for the same with the Govr &c. &c.   And also Wee
for us our heirs and Successors doe give and graunt unto the
said Govr &c. &c. for our full power and Authority, that the
said Govr &c. &c. for ever shall and may choose and ordeyne
and Assigne within the said Countries and Townes of Holland,
Z. B. F. & E. & W. Freizland, H. & the Territoryes of the
same and in every of them Weighers, Porters, Measurers,
Ployers and Packers at their Liberties and pleasures to serve
onely for their Merchandizes, without any lett or impediment
of any of our officers or of any other person whatsoever.
Furthermore of our more ample and abundant Grace, certeyn
knowledge and mere motion, We have given, graunted, and
confirmed and by these presents for us our heirs and Successors
doe give and graunt and confirme unto the Said Govr &c. &c.
and to their successors and every of the said Fellowship for the
tyme being shall and may henceforth for ever have hold,
occupie, use and enjoy, exercise, preceave and take to and by
them and their successors and to and by every of them for ever
as well within our Realme of England and all our other Domin^s
as in the said Countries & Townes of H. Z. B. F. E. & W.
Freizland, & H. and in the Territories of the same and every
of them all and singular such like and the same graunts,

Liberties, Franchises, Immunities, preheminences, powers, Authorityes, Jurisdiction, Priveleges, Customes, usages, beenefits and all other thinges whatsoever comprised, specifyed, declared or graunted, in any Letters, Patents, heretofore made by our said Right noble Grandfather or any other our Noble progenitors or by any other Foreign Prince, Potentate &c. &c. of the said Countries of H. Z. B. F. and other places nigh adjoyning for Merchandize or any of them thereby have had, used or enjoyed by reason of any Custome, usage, or Prescription, any forfeiture, non-user, or misuser of the same or any part thereof had made or suffered or any other matter or thing whatsoever to the contrary in anywise notwithstanding. PROVIDED always that these our Letters, Patents, or anything in them conteyned shall not in any wise be prejudiciall or hurtfull to the Mayor, Constables, and Fellowship of Merchants of the Staple of England or to their successors or to any particular person of the same Fellowship, that now is or hereafter shall be but that they and every of them shall and may have and enjoy all and every such Graunts, Liberties, and Priveleges as heretofore have been graunted to them by us or any of our Progenitors, or as they or any of them heretofore hath lawfully used or had in as large and ample manner and Forme as they or any of them might before the date of these presents any cause, Article or restraint in these presents conteyned to the contrary notwithstanding. WHEREFORE we will and comand you and every of you to whome in this case it shall or may apperteyn, that you and every of you permit and suffer the said Govr Assist^s & Fellowship of Merchants Adventurers of England, and their Successors, and every Person or Persons now being or which hereafter shall be a member of the same Corporation fully and peaceably to use, perceive and enjoy the full and whole effect of this our Corporation and graunt without any manner your Lett impediment, deny all vexation or contradiction. And furthermore for us our heirs and Successors we will and streghtly charge and comand all and singular Officers, Ministers, true Liege men and subjects of us our heirs and successors, that unto the said Governor &c. &c. in the useing exerciseing, performing and fullfilling of all and singular the premisses, that they and every of them be favouring ayding, and assisting in all thinges, and at all tymes so as we may laud and comend them for due obeysuance, and for the contrary besides our indignations to answer with us at their extreme perills. PROVIDED always that if it shall seeme good to us at any tyme to revoake, upsett, make frustrate this our present graunt and Letters Patents or any Article, matter or cause herein conteyned that then it shall and may be lawfull for us at all tymes and from tyme to tyme dureing our Lyfe by our other Letters Patents under our Greate Seale of England to be directed to the said Govr or his Dep. or Assist^s for the tyme being, to revoake, repeale, and make void these our Letters Patents and every Graunt, Clause, and Article in the same conteyned or so much thereof as to us shall seeme meete and convenient to be repealed And that then these Our Letters Patents, or so much herein conteyned as we at any tyme or tymes dureing our Life shall by other our Letters under our Great Seale of England signify and declare to the said Govr or his Dep. and Assistants for the tyme being that our pleasure is to have to be repealed and made void shall from hence-forth be utterly void and of none effect, To all intents and purposes anything in these presents conteyned to the contrary hereof in any wise notwithstanding. And further our pleasure is, And We for us our heirs and Successors will and graunt by these presents that if Wee at any tyme hereafter shall repeale these our Letters Patents or any Graunt, Clause, or Article in the same conteyned that yet nevertheless, the said Govr Assist^s and Fellowship of Merchants

Adventurers of England by what name or names soever they were or be called, or knowne before the making hereof shall and may from henceforth have, use, hold, and enjoy all such Graunts, Liberties, Priveleges, Franchises, Jurisdictions, and usages, as they or any of them before the makeing of these presents ever had used or Lawfully enjoyed, or hereafter shall have use or enjoy by vertue of any other Graunt or Lycense heretofore to them had or made by any of our noble progenitors or by any other Foreign Prince or Potentate as hereafter to them by us by any Graunt to be made or by any Lawfull usage, Prescription, or Custome, anything in the said Repeale hereafter to be had and made or any other matter or thing or cause whatsoever to the contrary thereof in anywise notwithstanding.

And further our Will and pleasure is that the said Govr &c. &c. shall have these our Letters Patents under our Greate Seale of England without any Fine or Fee Greate or small to us our heirs and Successors, or to the use of us our heirs and Successors in our Hamper or elsewhere, to be given or paid therefor for that expres mention of the full and playne words of the Corporation of the Fellowship of Merchants Adventurers of England or of every or any particular name or names of the same Corporation or of the Merchants of the aforesaid Fellowship or of the Certeyntye of any other the premises or of any other guift or Graunt by us or any our Progenitors, to the said Governor Assistants & Fellowship of Merchants Adven^{trs} or to any person or persons now being or which hereafter shall be free of the same Fellowship or to any of them heretofore made and graunted is not in these presents fully and particularly had made and specified or any Laws, Statute, Custome or any other matter cause, ambiguity, thing doubt or question whatsoever, to the contrary hereof in any wise notwithstanding.

IN WITNESS whereof We have caused these our Letters to

be made Patents, Witnes our self at Westminster the eighteenth day of July in the Sixt yeare of our Reigne.

III.—SPECIMEN OF A STUART CHARTER (CHARLES II.).

HIS MAJESTY'S ROYAL CHARTER TO THE GOVERNOR AND COMPANY OF HUDSON'S BAY.

Charles the II., by the grace of God king of England, Scotland, France, and Ireland, defender of the faith, etc., to all to whom these presents shall come, greeting: Whereas our dear entirely beloved cousin, Prince Rupert, Count Palatine of the Rhine, Duke of Bavaria and Cumberland, etc., George, Duke of Albemarle, William, Earl of Craven, Henry, Lord Arlington, Anthony, Lord Ashley, Sir John Robinson, and Sir Robert Vyner, knights and baronets, Sir Peter Colleton, baronet, Sir Edward Hungerford, Knight of the Bath, Sir Paul Neele, Sir John Griffith, Sir Philip Carteret, and Sir James Hayes, knights, John Kirke, Francis Millington, William Prettyman, John Fenn, esquires, and John Portman, citizen and goldsmith of London, have, at their own great cost and charges, undertaken an expedition for Hudson's Bay, in the north-west parts of America, for the discovery of a new passage into the South Sea, and for the finding of some trade for furs, minerals, and other considerable commodities, and by such, their undertaking, have already made such discoveries as do encourage them to proceed farther in pursuance of their said design, by means whereof there may probably arise great advantage to us and our kingdoms.

And whereas, The said undertakers, for their farther encouragement in the said design, have humbly besought us to incorporate them, and grant unto them, and their successors, the whole trade and commerce of all those seas, straits, and bays, rivers, lakes, creeks, and sounds, in whatsoever latitude they shall be, that lie within the entrance of the straits commonly called Hudson's Straits, together with all the lands, countries, and territories, upon the coasts and confines of the seas, straits, bays, lakes, rivers, creeks, and sounds aforesaid, which are not now actually possessed by any of our subjects, or by the subjects of any other Christian prince or state.

Now know ye, That we, being desirous to promote all endeavors that may tend to the public good of our people, and to encourage the said undertaking, have, of our especial grace, certain knowledge, and mere motion, given, granted, ratified, and confirmed, and by these presents for us, our heirs, and successors, do give, grant, ratify, and confirm, unto our said cousin Prince Rupert, George, Duke of Albemarle, William, Earl of Craven, Henry, Lord Arlington, Anthony, Lord Ashley, Sir John Robinson, Sir Robert Vyner, Sir Peter Colleton, Sir Edward Hungerford, Sir Paul Neele, Sir John Griffith, Sir Philip Carteret, and Sir James Hayes, John Kirke, Francis Millington, William Prettyman, John Fenn, and John Portman, that they, and such others as shall be admitted into the said society as is hereafter expressed, shall be one body corporate and politic, in deed and in name, by the name of the governor and company of adventurers of England, trading into Hudson's Bay, and them by the name of the governor and company of adventurers of England, trading into Hudson's Bay, one body corporate and politic, in deed and in name, really and fully forever, for us, our heirs, and successors, we do make, ordain, constitute, establish, confirm, and declare, by these presents, and that by the same name of governor and company of adventurers of England, trading into Hudson's Bay, they shall have perpetual succession, and that they and their successors, by the name of governor and company of adventurers of England, trading into Hudson's Bay, be, and at all times hereafter shall be, personable and capable in law to have, purchase, receive, possess, enjoy, and retain, lands, rents, privileges, liberties, jurisdiction, franchises, and hereditaments, of what kind, nature, or quality soever they be, to them and their successors ; and also to give, grant, alien, assign, and dispose lands, tenements, and hereditaments, and to do, execute all and singular other things by the same name that to them shall or may appertain to do. And that they, and their successors, by the name of the governor and company of adventurers of England, trading into Hudson's Bay, may plead, and be impleaded, answer, and be answered, defend, and be defended, in whatsoever courts and places, before whatsoever judges and justices, and other persons and officers, in all or singular actions, pleas, suits, quarrels, and demands, whatsoever, of whatsoever kind, nature, or sort, in such manner and form as any other our liege people of this our realm of England, being persons able and capable in law, may, or can have, purchase, receive, possess, enjoy, retain, give, grant, demise, alien, assign, dispose, plead, defend, and to be defended, do, permit, and execute. And that the said governor and company of adventurers of England, trading into Hudson's Bay, and their successors, may have a common seal to serve for all the causes and businesses of them and their successors, and that it shall and may be lawful to the said governor and company, and their successors, the same seal, from time to time, at their will and pleasure, to break, change, and to make anew, or alter, as to them shall seem expedient.

And farthermore, We will, and by these presents for us, our heirs, and successors, we do ordain that there shall be from henceforth one of the same company to be elected and appointed in such form as hereafter in these presents is expressed, which shall be called the governor of the said company.

And that the said governor and company shall and may elect seven of their number in such form as hereafter in these presents is expressed, which shall be called the committee of the said company; which committee of seven, or any three of them, together with the governor or deputy governor of the said company for the time being, shall have the direction of the voyages of and for the said company, and the provision of the shipping and merchandises thereunto belonging, and also the sale of all merchandises, goods, and other things returned in all or any the voyages or ships of or for the said company, and the managing and handling of all other business affairs and things belonging to the said company. And we will ordain and grant by these presents for us, our heirs, and successors, unto the said governor and company, and their successors, that they the said governor and company and their successors shall from henceforth forever be ruled, ordered, and governed according to such manner and form as is hereafter in these presents expressed, and not otherwise ; and that they shall have, hold, retain, and enjoy the grants, liberties, privileges, jurisdictions, and immunities, only hereafter in these presents granted and expressed, and no other. And for the better execution of our will and grant in this behalf, we have assigned, nominated, constituted, and appointed by these presents for us, our heirs, and successors, and we do assign, nominate, constitute, and make our said cousin, Prince Rupert, to be the first and present governor of the said company, and to continue in the said office from the date of these presents until the 10th of November then next following, if he, the said Prince Rupert, shall so long live, and so until a new governor be chosen by the said company in form hereafter expressed. And also we have assigned, nominated, and appointed, and by these presents for us, our heirs and successors, we do assign, nominate, and constitute, the said Sir John Robinson, Sir Robert Vyner, Sir Peter Colleton, Sir James Hayes, John Kirke, Francis Millington, and John Portman to be the seven first and present committees of the said company, from the date of these presents until the said 10th of November then also next following, and so until new committees shall be chosen in form hereafter expressed.

And farther, We will and grant by these presents for us, our heirs and successors, unto the said governor and their successors, that it shall and may be lawful to and for the said governor and company for the time being, or the greater part of them present at any public assembly commonly called the court general, to be holden for the said company, the governor of the said company being always one, from time to time to elect, nominate, and appoint one of the said company to be deputy to the said governor; which deputy shall take a corporal oath before the governor and three more of the committee of the said company for the time being, well, truly, and faithfully to execute his said office of deputy to the governor of the said company, and after his oath so taken shall and may from time to time in the absence of the said governor exercise and execute the office of governor of the said company in such sort as the said governor ought to do.

And farther, We will and grant by these presents, for us, our heirs, and successors, unto the said governor and company of adventurers of England trading into Hudson's Bay, and their successors, that they, or the greater part of them, whereof the governor for the time being, or his deputy, to be one, from time to time and at all times hereafter, shall and may have authority and power, yearly and every year between the first and last day of November, to assemble and meet together in some convenient place, to be appointed from time to time by the governor, or in his absence by the deputy of the said governor, and the said company for the time being and the greater part of them which then shall happen to be present, whereof the governor of the said company, or his deputy, for the time being, to be one, to elect and nominate one of the said company which shall be governor of the said company for one whole year, then next following, which person being so elected and nominated to be governor of the said company, as is aforesaid, before he be admitted to the execution of said office shall take a corporal oath before the last governor, being his predecessor or his deputy, and any three or more of the committee of the said company for the time being, that he shall from time to time well and truly execute the office of governor of the said company in all things concerning the same ; and that immediately after the same oath so taken he shall and may execute and use the said office of governor of the said company for one whole year from thence next following.

And in like sort, We will and grant that as well every one of the above named to be of the said company or fellowship as all others hereafter to be admitted or free of the said company, shall take a corporal oath before the governor of the said company or his deputy for the time being, to such effect as by the said governor and company, or the greater part of them, in any public court to be held for the said company, shall be in reasonable and legal manner set down and devised, before they shall be allowed or admitted to trade or traffic as a freeman of the said company. *And farther*, We will and grant by these presents for us, our heirs and successors, unto the said governor and company, and their successors, that the said governor or deputy governor and the rest of the said company and their successors for the time being, or the greater part of them, whereof the governor or deputy governor, from time to time, to be one, shall and may from time to time and at all times hereafter have power and authority yearly and every year between the first and last day of November, to assemble and meet together in some convenient place from time to time to be appointed by the said governor, or in his absence by his deputy. And that they, being so assembled, it shall and may be lawful to and for the said governor and his deputy, and the company for the time being, or the greater part of them, which then shall happen to be present, whereof the governor of the said company, or his deputy for the time being, to be one, to elect and nominate seven of the said company, which shall be a committee of the said company as aforesaid, before they be admitted to the execution of their office, shall take a corporal oath before the governor or his deputy and any three or more of the said committee of the said company, being the last predecessors, that they and every of them shall well and faithfully perform their said office of committees in all things concerning the same, and that immediately after the said oath so taken, they shall and may execute and use their said office of committees of the said company for one whole year from thence next following.

And moreover, Our will and pleasure is, and by these presents for us, our heirs and successors, we do grant unto the said governor and company, and their successors, that when and as often as it shall happen, the governor or deputy governor of the said company for the time being, at any time within one year after that he shall be nominated, elected, and sworn to the office of the governor of the said company as is aforesaid, to die or to be removed from said office, which governor or deputy governor not demeaning himself well in his said office, we will to be removable at the pleasure of the rest of the said company, or the greater part of them, which shall be present at their public assemblies, commonly called their general courts holden for the said company ; that then it shall and so often may be lawful to and for the residue of the said company, for the time being, or the greater part of them within a convenient time after the death or removing of any such governor or deputy governor, to assemble themselves in such convenient place as they shall think fit, for the election of the governor or deputy governor of said company ; and that the said company, or the greater part of them, being then and there present, shall and may then and there, before their departure from the said place, elect and nominate one other of the said company to be governor or deputy governor for the said company in the place or stead of him that so died or was removed ; which person being so elected and nominated to the office of governor or deputy governor of the said company shall have and exercise the said office for and during the residue of the said year, taking first a corporal oath, as is afore-said, for the due execution thereof; and this to be done from time to time so often as the case shall so require.

And also, Our will and pleasure is, and by these presents for us, our heirs, and successors, we do grant unto the said governor and company, that when and as often as it shall happen, any person or persons of the committee of the said company for the time being, at any time within one year next after that they or any of them shall be nominated, elected, and sworn to the office of committee of the said company as is aforesaid, to die or to be removed from the said office, which committee not demeaning themselves well in their said office, we will to be removable at the pleasure of the said governor and company, or the greater part of them, whereof the governor of the said company for the time being, or his deputy, to be one ; that then and so often it shall and may be lawful to and for the said governor and the rest of the company for the time being, or the greater part of them, whereof the governor for the time being, or his deputy, to be one, within convenient time after the death or removing of any of the said committees, to assemble themselves in such convenient place as is or shall be usual and accustomed for the election of the governor of the said company, or where else the governor of the said company for the time being or his deputy shall appoint. And that the said governor and company, or the greater part of them, whereof the governor for the time being, or his deputy, to be one, being then and there present, shall and may then and there, before their departure from the said place, elect and nominate one or more of the said company in the place or stead of him or them that so died, or was or were so removed. Which person or persons so nominated and elected to the office of committee of the said company, shall have and exercise the said office for and during the residue of the said year, taking first a corporal oath, as is aforesaid, for the due execution thereof, and this to be done from time to time so often as the case shall require.

And to the end the said governor and company of adventurers of England trading into Hudson's Bay may be encouraged to undertake and effectually to prosecute the said design of our more especial grace, certain knowledge, and mere motion, we have given, granted, and confirmed, and by these presents for us, our heirs and successors, do give, grant, and confirm unto the said governor and company and their successors, the sole trade and commerce of all those seas, straits, bays, rivers, lakes, creeks, and sounds, in whatsoever latitude they shall be, that lie within the entrance of the straits commonly called Hudson's Straits, together with all the lands and territories upon the countries, coasts, and confines of the seas, bays, lakes, rivers, creeks, and sounds aforesaid, that are not already actually possessed by the subjects of any other Christian prince or state, with the fishing of all sorts of fish, whales, sturgeons, and all other royal fishes, in the seas, bays, inlets, and rivers within the premises, and the fish therein taken, together with the royalty of the sea upon the coasts within the limits aforesaid, and all mines royal as well discovered as not discovered, of gold, silver, gems, and precious stones, to be found or discovered within the territories, limits, and places aforesaid, and that the land be from henceforth reckoned and reputed as one of our plantations or colonies in America called Rupert's Land.

And further, We do by these presents for us, our heirs and successors, make, create, and constitute the said governor and company for the time being, and their successors, the true and absolute lords and proprietors of the same territories, limits, and places aforesaid ; and of all other the premises, saving always the faith, allegiance, and sovereign dominion to us, our heirs and successors, for the same to have, hold, possess, and enjoy the said territories, limits, and places, and all and singular other the premises hereby granted as aforesaid, with their and every of their rights, members, jurisdictions, prerogatives, royalties, and appurtenances whatsoever, to them the said governor and company and their successors forever, to be holden of us, our heirs, and successors, as of our manor of East Greenwich, in the county of Kent, in free and common socage, and not *in capite* or by knight's service ; yielding and paying yearly to us, our heirs and successors, for the same, two elks and two black beavers, whensoever and as often as we, our heirs and successors, shall happen to enter into the said countries, territories, and regions hereby granted.

And farther, Our will and pleasure is, and by these presents, for us, our heirs and successors, we do grant unto the said governor and company, and to their successors, that it shall and may be lawful to and for the said governor and company

and their successors from time to time, to assemble themselves
for or about any the matters, causes, affairs, or businesses of
the said trade, in any place or places for the same convenient,
within our dominions or elsewhere, and to hold court for the
said company and the affairs thereof; and that also it shall
and may be lawful to and for them, or the greater part of them,
being so assembled, and that shall then and there be present
in any such place or places, whereof the governor or his deputy
for the time being to be one, to make, ordain, and constitute
such and so many reasonable laws, constitutions, orders, and
ordinances as to them, or the greater part of them, being then
and there present, shall seem necessary and convenient for the
good government of the said company and of all governors of
colonies, forts, and plantations, factors, masters, mariners, and
other officers employed or to be employed in any the territories
and lands aforesaid, and in any of their voyages; and for the
better advancement and continuance of said trade or traffic
and plantations, and the same laws, constitutions, orders, and
ordinances so made, to be put in use and execute accordingly,
and at their pleasure to revoke and alter the same or any of
them as the occasion shall require. And that the said governor
and company, so often as they shall make, ordain, or establish
any such laws, constitutions, orders, and ordinances, in such
form as aforesaid, shall and may lawfully impose, ordain, limit,
and provide such penalties and punishments upon all offenders
contrary to such laws, constitutions, orders, and ordinances, or
any of them, as to the said governor and company for the time
being, or the greater part of them, then and there being present,
the said governor or his deputy being always one, shall seem
necessary or convenient for the observation of the same laws,
constitutions, orders, and ordinances; and the same fines and
amerciaments shall and may by their officers and servants, from
time to time to be appointed for that purpose, levy, take, and

have, to the use of the said governor and company and their successors, without the officers and ministers of us, our heirs and successors, and without any account thereof to us, our heirs and successors, to be made. All and singular which laws, constitutions, orders, and ordinances so as aforesaid to be made, we will to be duly observed and kept under the pains and penalties therein to be contained; so always as the said laws, constitutions, orders and ordinances, fines and amercia- ments, be reasonable, and not contrary or repugnant, but as near as may be agreeable to the laws, statutes, or customs of this our realm.

And farthermore, of our ample and abundant grace, certain knowledge and mere motion, we have granted, and by these presents for us, our heirs and successors, do grant unto the said governor and company and their successors, that they and their successors, and their factors, servants, and agents, for them and on their behalf, and not otherwise, shall forever here- after have, use, and enjoy not only the whole, entire, and only liberty of trade and traffic, and the whole, entire, and only liberty, use, and privilege of trading and traffic to and from the territories, limits, and places aforesaid; but also the whole and entire trade and traffic to and from all havens, bays, creeks, rivers, lakes, and seas, into which they shall find entrance or passage by water or land out of the territories, limits, and places aforesaid; and to and with all the natives and people, inhabitants or which shall inhabit within the territories, limits, and places aforesaid; and to and with all other nations in- habiting any the coasts adjacent to the said territories, limits, and places aforesaid, which are not already possessed as afore- said, or whereof the sole liberty or privilege of trade and traffic is not granted to any other of our subjects.

And of our farther royal favor, and of our more especial grace, certain knowledge, and mere motion have granted, and by these presents for us, our heirs and successors, do grant to the said governor and company and to their successors, that neither the said territories, limits, and places hereby granted as aforesaid, nor any part thereof, nor the islands, havens, ports, cities, towns, and places thereof, or therein contained, shall be visited, frequented, or haunted by any of the subjects of us, our heirs or successors, contrary to the true meaning of these presents, and by virtue of our prerogatives royal, which we will not have in that behalf argued or brought into question; we straightly charge, command, and prohibit for us, our heirs and successors, all the subjects of us, our heirs and successors, of what degree or quality soever they be, that none of them directly do visit, haunt, frequent, or trade, traffic, or adventure, by way of merchandise, into or from any the said territories, limits, or places hereby granted, or any or either of them other than the said governor and company, and such particular persons as now be or hereafter shall be of that company, their agents, factors, and assigns, unless it be by the license and agreement of the said governor and company in writing first had and obtained under their common seal, to be granted upon pain that every such person or persons that shall trade and traffic into or from any of the countries, territories, or limits aforesaid, other than the said governor and company and their successors, shall incur our indignation, and the forfeiture and the loss of the said goods, merchandises, and other things whatsoever, which so shall be brought into this realm of England or any the dominions of the same, contrary to our said prohibition or the purport or true meaning of these presents, or which the said governor and company shall find, take, and seize, in other places out of our dominions, where the said company, their agents, factors, or assigns shall trade, traffic, or inhabit by virtue of these our letters patent, as also the ship and ships, with the furniture thereof, wherein such goods, merchandises, and other things shall be brought or found, the one half of all the said forfeiture to be to us, our heirs and successors, and the other half thereof by these presents clearly and wholly for us, our heirs and successors, give and grant unto the said governor and company and their successors. And farther, all and every the said offenders, for their said contempt, to suffer such punishment as to us, our heirs and successors, shall seem meet or convenient, and not to be in any wise delivered until they and every of them shall become bound unto the said governor for the time being in the sum of one thousand pounds at the least, at no time then after to trade and traffic into any of the said places, seas, bays, straits, ports, havens, or territories aforesaid, contrary to our express commandment in that behalf set down and published.

And farther, of our more especial grace, we have condescended and granted, and by these presents for us, our heirs and successors, do grant unto the said governor and company, and their successors, that we, our heirs and successors, will not grant liberty, license, or power to any person or persons whatsoever, contrary to the tenor of these our letters patent, to trade, traffic, or inhabit unto or upon any of the territories, limits, or places afore specified, contrary to the meaning of these presents, without the consent of the said governor and company or the most part of them.

And, of our more abundant grace and favor to the said governor and company, we do hereby declare our will and pleasure to be, that if it shall so happen that any of the persons free or to be free of the said company of adventurers of England trading into Hudson's Bay, who shall, before the going forth of any ship or ships appointed for a voyage or otherwise, promise or agree, by writing under his or their hands, to adventure any sum or sums of money towards the furnishing any provision or maintenance of any voyage or voyages, set forth or to be set forth, or intended or meant to be set forth, by the said governor and company, or the more part of them, present at any public assembly commonly called the general court, shall not within the space of twenty days next after warning given to him or them by the said governor and company, or their known officer or minister, bring in and deliver to the treasurer or treasurers appointed for the company, such sums of money as shall have been expressed and set down in writing, by the said person or persons subscribed with the name of said adventurer or adventurers, that then and at all times after it shall and may be lawful to and for the said governor and company, or the more part of them present, whereof the said governor or his deputy to be one, at any of their general courts or general assemblies, to remove and disfranchise him or them, and every such person or persons, at their wills and pleasures ; and he or they so removed and disfranchised, not to be permitted to trade into the countries, territories, or limits aforesaid, or any part thereof; nor to have any adventure or stock going or remaining with or among the said company, without special license of the said governor and company, or the more part of them present at any general court, first had and obtained in that behalf, anything before in these presents to the contrary thereof in any wise notwithstanding.

And our will and pleasure is, and hereby we do also ordain, that it shall and may be lawful to and for the said governor and company, or the greater part of them, whereof the governor for the time being, or his deputy, to be one, to admit into and be of the said company, all such servants or factors of or for the said company, and all such others as to them or the most part of them present at any court held for the said company, the governor or his deputy being one, shall be thought fit and agreeable with the orders and ordinances made and to be made for the government of the said company.

And farther, Our will and pleasure is, and by these presents for us, our heirs and successors, we do grant unto the said governor and company, and to their successors, that it shall and may be lawful in all elections and by-laws to be made by the general court of the adventurers of the said company, that every person shall have a number of votes according to his stock, that is to say, for every hundred pounds by him subscribed or brought into the present stock, one vote, and that any of those that have subscribed less than one hundred pounds may join their respective sums to make one hundred pounds, and to have one vote jointly for the same, and not otherwise.

And further, of our especial grace, certain knowledge, and mere motion, we do for us, our heirs and successors, grant to and with the said governor and company of adventurers of England trading into Hudson's Bay, that all lands, territories, plantations, forts, fortifications, factories, or colonies, where the said companies, factories, or trade are or shall be, within any the ports or places afore limited, shall be immediately and from henceforth under the power and command of the said governor and company, their successors and assigns ; saving the faith and allegiance due and to be performed to us, our heirs and successors, as aforesaid ; and that the said governor and company shall have liberty, full power, and authority to appoint and establish governors and all other officers to govern them ; and that the governor and his council of the several and respective places where the said company shall have plantations, forts, factories, colonies, or places of trade within any the countries, lands, or territories hereby granted, may have power to judge all persons belonging to the said governor and company, or that shall live under them in all causes,

whether civil or criminal, according to the laws of this kingdom, and to execute justice accordingly.

And, in case any crime or misdemeanor shall be committed
in any of the said company's plantations, forts, factories, or
places of trade within the limits aforesaid, where judicature
cannot be executed for want of a governor and council there,
then in such case it shall and may be lawful for the chief factor
of that place and his council to transmit the party, together
with the offence, to such other plantations, factory, or fort,
where there shall be a governor and council, where justice may
be executed, or into the kingdom of England, as shall be
thought most convenient, there to inflict such punishment as
the nature of the offence will deserve.

And moreover, Our will and pleasure is, and by these presents for us, our heirs and successors, we do give and grant
unto the said governor and company and their successors free
liberty and license in case they conceive it necessary to send
either ships of war, men, or ammunition, into any their plantations, forts, factories, or places of trade aforesaid, for the
security and defence of the same, and to choose commanders
and officers over them, and to give them power and authority
by commissions under their common seal, or otherwise, to
continue or make peace or war with any prince or people
whatsoever, that are not Christians, in any places where the
said company shall have any plantations, forts, or factories, or
adjacent thereunto, as shall be most for the advantage and
benefit of said governor and company, and of their trade ; and
also to right and recompense themselves upon the goods,
estate, or people of those parts, by whom the said governor
and company shall sustain any injury, loss, or damage, or upon
any other people whatsoever, that shall any way, contrary to
the intent of these presents, interrupt, wrong, or injure them in
their said trade, within the said places, territories, or limits

granted by this charter. And that it shall and may be lawful to and for the said governor and company and their successors, from time to time and at all times henceforth, to erect and build such castles, fortifications, forts, garrisons, colonies or plantations, towns or villages, in any parts or places within the limits and bounds granted before in these presents, unto the said governor and company, and their successors, from time to time ; and at all times from henceforth to erect and build such castles, fortifications, forts, garrisons, colonies or plantations, towns or villages, in any parts or places within the limits and bounds granted before in these presents unto the said governor and company, as they in their discretion shall think fit and requisite ; and for the supply of such as shall be needful and convenient, to keep and be in the same, to send out of this kingdom, to the said castles, forts, fortifications, garrisons, colonies, plantations, towns, or villages, all kinds of clothing, provision of victuals, ammunition, and implements necessary for such purpose, paying the duties and custom for the same, as also to transport and carry over such number of men being willing thereunto or not prohibited, as they shall think fit, and also to govern them in such legal and reasonable manner as the said governor and company shall think best, and to inflict punishment for misdemeanors, or impose such fines upon them for breach of their orders, as in these presents are formerly expressed.

And farther, Our will and pleasure is, and by these presents, for us, our heirs and successors, we do grant unto the said governor and company and their successors, full power and lawful authority to seize upon the persons of all such English or any other subjects which shall sail into Hudson's Bay, or inhabit in any of the countries, islands, or territories hereby granted to the said governor and company, without their leave and license in that behalf first had and obtained, or that shall

contemn or disobey their orders, and send them to England;
and that all and every person or persons, being our subjects,
any ways employed by the said governor and company, within
any the parts, places, or limits aforesaid, shall be liable unto
and suffer such punishments for any offences by them committed in the parts aforesaid as the president and council for
the said governor and company there shall think fit and the
merit of the offence shall require as aforesaid; and in case any
person or persons being convicted and sentenced by the president and council of the said governor and company, in the
countries, lands, or limits aforesaid, their factors or agents
there, for any offence by them done, shall appeal from the
same; and then and in such case, it shall and may be lawful
to and for the said president and council, factors or agents, to
seize upon him or them, and to carry him or them home
prisoners into England, to the said governor and company,
there to receive such condign punishment as his cause shall
require, and the law of this nation allow of; and for the better
discovery of abuses and injuries to be done unto the said
governor and company, or their successors, by any servant, by
them to be employed in the said voyages and plantations, it
shall and may be lawful to and for the said governor and company, and their respective presidents, chief agent, or governor
in the parts aforesaid, to examine upon oath all factors, masters,
pursers, supercargoes, commanders of castles, forts, fortifications, plantations, or colonies, or other persons, touching or
concerning any matter or thing, in which by law or usage an
oath may be administered, so as the said oath and the matter
therein contained be not repugnant but agreeable to the laws
of this realm.

And, We do hereby straightly charge and command all and
singular, our admirals, vice-admirals, justices, mayors, sheriffs,
constables, bailiffs, and all and singular other our officers,

ministers, liege men, and subjects whatsoever to be aiding, favoring, helping, and assisting to the said governor and company, and to their successors, and to their deputies, officers, factors, servants, assignees, and ministers, and every of them, in executing and enjoying the premises, as well on land as at sea from time to time, when any of you shall thereunto be required ; any statute, act, ordinance, proviso, proclamation, or restraint heretofore made, set forth, ordained, or provided, or any other matter, cause, or thing whatsoever to the contrary in any wise notwithstanding. In witness whereof, we have caused these our letters to be made patents ; witness ourself at Westminster, the second day of May, in the two and twentieth year of our reign.

By Writ of Privy Seal.   (Signed)   PIGOTT.

IV.—SPECIMEN OF A REVOKED CHARTER.

PROCLAMATION OF JAMES I. DISSOLVING THE ANCIENT COMPANY OF MERCHANT ADVENTURERS OF ENGLAND.

By the King.

A proclamation prohibiting the Merchant Adventurers Charter from henceforth to be put in practise or execution, either within the Kingdome, or beyond the Seas.

As there is no great Action, which tendeth to the Advancement of a publique good, but it requireth certaine degrees of timely proceeding, and neverthelesse meeteth with divers impediments ; some by Accident and some by practise : so is there nothing that doeth more adorne the true Majestie and Greatenesse of Sovereigne Princes, then to be constant in their wel-grounded Resolutions, and by their policie and lawfull power, to scatter and beat downe all difficulties, and undue oppositions, until they have conducted their Actions to a good and happy end : Wee therefore having propounded unto Our-selves, as a principall worke of our times to ordeine and pro-vide, that the great commoditie of Broad Cloth, being one of the principall dowries of Our Kingdome may receive the due Manufactures of Dying and Dressing within the Realme, did to that end publish Our Royall Proclamation, dated the three and twentieth July prohibiting and ordeyning, That no Broad Cloth, of what sort soever, made here within this Our Kingdome of England, should be exported Undried and Undrest, after the second day of November next, ensuing the date of Our said Proclamation : which time was given, as well for the Mer-chant Adventurers to vent their whites, which might be upon their handes, as for the preparing of divers thinges, necessary to the settling of the new Trade of Died and Dressed Clothes.

And wee did further by our said Proclamation provide *in the word of a King* to all Our loving subjects, that should under-take to export the said Brod-Clothes in their true Manufactures that neither the Charter of the Merchant Adventurers nor any other Licences or Dispensations by *non obstantes* contrary to Our Lawes, heretofore granted by us, or any of our pre-decessors, should be any manner of prejudice, impeachment ; disturbance, or interruption to such as should after time afore-said vent the said Clothes Died and Dressed, according to Our said Royall Ordinance And Constitution ; but should be from the said second day of *November* declared to be annihilated, and made void to all intents and purposes. At which time of the publishing of Our said Proclamation, We did expect that the said Charter of the Merchant Adventurers should, before the said second day of *November*, have beene in due form of Law surrendered ; But after, finding the said Company of Merchant Adventurers make difficulty concerning the Surrender of their Patents, Wee have beene enforced through their Wilfulnesse and inconformitie, as well to order a Legall Course to be taken for the over-throwe of their said Patent : As also to licence divers of Our loveing subjects, that have very worthily and with great alacrity, undertaken to set up and manage the said Trade of Dyed and Dressed Clothes, to export also whites in the meanwhile until such time as the said Patent of the Merchant Adventurers shall be by judgment evicted, and some respite of time afterwards, lest there might have ensued some stand of the vent of Cloth before the New Trade were settled : But for as much as the course of judiciall proceeding, though in a case never so clear and plaine, must have due formes and times observed according to the rules of Law, and for that time in this case is exceeding precious and that it is not possible for the new intended Company, to goe on with that confidence and incouragement ; that in so great a businesse were fit, as long as the Charter of the Merchant Adventurers is put in order and practise.

Therefore to remove and discharge all discouragements and impediments ; Wee doe by these presents prohibite, forbid, constitute and ordeine, That from henceforth the Charter of the said Merchants Adventurers, and all powers, Lycences, Authorityes, privileges, formes of Government contained in the same, or otherwise all usages holdings of Courts, meetings, Assemblies, and all other proceedings, by colour or vertue thereof, together with all the dependances, be not from henceforth put in any maner of practise or execution, either in the parts beyond the Seas or here within Our kingdome. And to that end, Wee doe not only notifie and publish this Our Royall prohibition and Ordinance, as well to all Foreiners, as to all Our loving subjects, to whome it may appertaine : But doe furthermore straitly and expresly charge and comaund, as wel the Governour, Deputie or Deputies, and Assistants of the said Company of Merchants Adventurers, as the whole bodie of them, and also every of them in particular, And all their Factors, Servants, and Ministers, as wel beyond the seas, as on this side, within Our Kingdome and Dominions. That from this time forwards, they doe in no wise presume directly or indirectly, to doe, performe, or execute any Trade, Traffique or Merchandizing into or from any the Countryes or places where the said Merchant Adventurers are or have beene privileged, or any point or thing whatsoever, by vertue or Colour of their said Charter, or by vertue of any former treatie or treaties, betwixt our Noble Progenitors or Predecessors and any Prince or Potentate, Citie or Politique Government or former usages, upon paine of our high indignation, imprisonment, and other punishment, which by Our Lawes or Prerogative Royall, may bee inflicted upon them : Letting them know that Wee shall proceede against every such Offender, as a Contemner of our Royall Commandement, and a disturber of so excellent a worke, wherein we have so farre declared ourselves for the Universall Weale, and comfort of Our people.

Provided neverthelesse, that where Our Treasurer of England hath directed his Letters to the Officers of Our Custome-house, and Posts giving libertie of importation onely until the last of this present month of *December:* That these presents shall not any way countermaund the said limitation of time so prefixed, and no longer ; But that the said Merchant Adventurers may during that time importe accordingly, anything before in these presents to the Contrary notwithstanding.

Given at our Court at Newmarket the second day of December, in the twelfth yeare of Our Raigne of England, France, and Ireland, and of Scotland the Eight and fourtieth. (A.D. 1614.)

God save the King.

V.—SPECIMEN OF A RESTORED CHARTER.

PROCLAMATION OF JAMES I. RESTORING THE ANCIENT COMPANY OF MERCHANT ADVENTURERS.

By the King.

A proclamation for restoring the Ancient Merchantes Adventurers to their former Trade and Priviledges.

Whereas heretofore Wee declared Our desires to have brought to passe as a principall Worke of Our times, the Manufactures of Dying and Dressing of Broad-Cloths within this Realme, and to that end did publish Our severall proclamations, the one 23rd. July 12 of Our Raigne, the other 2nd. December following, for the encouragement of such of our subjects then undertooke to set up and manage the said Trade; But finding that time discovreth many inhabilities, which cannot at first be seene, and being willing to have it knowne to all Our loving subjects, that Wee intend not to insist and stay longer upon specious and faire shewes, which produce not the fruit Our Actions ever aime at, which is the general good of this Our State and Kingdome : Wherefore perceiving that the former grounds proposed to Us, by the Undertakers of that worke, consisted more in hopes than in effectes ; and finding the Worke is felte to bee too great to bee brought to passe in any short time, by reason of the many difficulties accompanying the same, and that as the State of Trade now stands there will bee greater losse in the Cloth-making of the Kingdome, then gaine in the Dying and Dressing thereof, which Wee may not suffer, the Comoditie of Broad-cloath being one of the principall Dowries of this Our State and which hath brought great wealthe and honour to the same ; And having the experience of many ages to ground Our selves upon, that the Ancient Company of Merchant Adventurers have ever managed their

Trade, as with profite to the Comon-Wealthe, so with much praise to their Company, in taking off and venting the Cloathes of this Kingdome, whereby they deserve both grace and encouragement from us. Therefore no longer to Withdraw Our Countenance from them, but to quicken and give a new life unto them. Wee doe hereby signifie and declare that Wee have already restored and given backe unto them All and every their Charters, anywise touching theire Incorporation, forme of Government and Trade, or any Powers, Licences, Authorities, or Priviledges concerning the same ; And them have and doe hereby settle and redintigrate in their former estate and degree to all purposes ; Willing it to be knowne that none of the Charters of the said Co., were ever by Us annihilated, or by Law avoyded, but onely suspended and sequestered, till Our further pleasure (be) knowne. And therefore Wee doe by these presents declare constitute and ordeine, That the said Co., of Merchants Adventurers shall and may from henceforth practise, and put in execution all and every their Powers, Lycences, Authorities, Privileges and forme of Government contained in all or any their said Charters : And all usages, holding of Courts, Meetinges, Assemblies, and all other proceedinges by vertue of them, or any of them, together with all the dependances, either in the parts beyond the Seas, or here within the Kingdome.

And further Wee doe hereby intimate and declare, letting it to be knowen to all Foraine Princes and States in whose Dominions, the said Merchants Adventurers now have or heretofore shall have any recourse in the exercise of their Trade : That (notwithstanding any former signification of Our pleasure otherwise) Wee have againe fully, and really enabled them to maintaine, hold, possess, and enjoy all and every their former Imunities, Rights, Powers, and Privileges in any foraine parts beyond the Seas, with free libertie and power as heretofore to deale, contract, and agree with any Prince, State or City in Germany or the Low Countries, for and touching any further, or other Priviledges to be had and obtained in those parts touching their Trade : Hereby giving and graunting and allowing unto the said Merchants Adventurers from time to time, free liberty and choice to make and appoint such and so many places of their residence in foraine parts, as to them shall seeme convenient ; And those at their pleasure to change and remove, as shall and may stand best with their Comoditie and profite, And that the said Merchants Adventurers may henceforth goe on and exercise their said Trade, with better confidence and encouragement, which is best effected by removing and discharging all impediments, Wee doe by these presents straightly prohibit, forbid and constitute, and ordaine, That from henceforth no Interloper, nor other person or persons, not free of the said Co., upon paine of Our high Indignation, and such other paines and penalties, as by the Charters of the said Company or any of them are or shall be provided for transgressors in that kind, which that it may have the better effect, Wee doe hereby straightly charge and Comand all Mayors, Sheriffes, Bailiffes, Constables ; especially all Customers and Searchers and other Officers of Our Customes, as well in the Port of London, as in all other Ports of this Kingdome. That they be aiding and assisting to the said Co., and the Officers thereof in the execution of their said Charters, and that they nor any of them in their several places passe out any goods or Merchandizes into any the parts of Germanie, or the Low Countries, nor unto any other parts beyond the seas where the said Co., now have, or hereafter shall have any priviledges graunted unto them contrary to the true meaning of their said Charters upon paine of Our displeasure, and the loss of his or their Offices that shall offend therein.

Given at Our Court at Ashton the 12 of August in the 16th. yeere of Our Reigne of England France and Ireland and of Scotland the 51st. (1617.)

God save the King.

VI.—SPECIMEN OF A PETITION.

(CHARLES II., 1660.)

PETITION.

To the King's most Excellent Majesty,

The Humble Pet. of the Govr and Deputy Assistants and Fellowship of Merchants Adventurers of England

Showeth. That your Majesty's Royall predecessors did first introduce the manufacture of clothing into this Realme and afterwards still persisted, as to crush the same that they made a full request of that untill their foreign fabriques. That having obtained the same they by Good Lawes were still carefull, both to regulate the true making thereof at home, and also to provide for the vent of such surplusage as could not be consumed within the Kingdome, unto Foreign Parts. And to this end, did not only in diverse Treatyes with the House of Burgundy, and severall States of Germany, make the one speciall point thereof, but also so promote the same did by their charters under the Great Seale of England incorporate the Merchants of England who reported their manufactures, that by Good Gov^t both at home and abroad the increase and esteeme thereof might be acquired and mayntained.

That these Charters were confirmed and enlarged as the times required, from King Henry 4th, by all the Kings and Queens of this Realme, except Edw. 5th unto the

Reigne of your Majesties Most Royall Father of our Blessed Memory.

That this last Charter 15 of King James of Glorious Memory, Your Majesties Most Royall Grandfather was so Compleate, as it required noe more, but to be duely observed and putt in execution and to this end your Majesties Royall Father did sett forth two severall Proclamations in the years 1634 & 1636.

But during the late unhappy trouble of this Nation, this Gov\ hath relaxed, and divers encroachments have been made thereupon, both abroad and at home.

And therefore for the restablishment thereof with the Glorious Restauration of your Majesty to the Royall Throne of your Ancestors.

The Pet^rs· most humbly beseech your Majesty to Graunt them your Royall Charter, under your Greate Seale of Confirmation of the said lost Letters Patents of your Royall Grandfather King Jas : as also a like Proclamation for the ratifying thereof, as they obtained from your said Royall Father.

And for these matters wherein their priveleges in foreigne parts have been also changed and violated through the Advantage hath been taken by the late dissensions at home, that the Pet^rs· may have your Gracious permission to seeke the Remedy thereof from these Honble Com^rs your Majesty shall appoint to renew your Alliances with the Ambass^drs of the Respective Princes and States of the Dominions that are within the Limits of your Pet^rs· Chrtre according to the severall Capitulacons and Agreements in the annexed Catalogue.

And the Pet^rs as in duty bound shall dayly pray &c.

(Signed)　　Richard Lord & Governor.
(Signed)　　Charles Llyod Deputy.

APPENDIX III.

CHARTER OF INCORPORATION OF THE BRITISH SOUTH AFRICA COMPANY.

VICTORIA by the Grace of God, of the United Kingdom of Great Britain and Ireland, Queen, Defender of the Faith.

To all to whom these presents shall come, Greeting:

WHEREAS a Humble Petition has been presented to Us in Our Council by THE MOST NOBLE JAMES DUKE OF ABERCORN Companion of the Most Honourable Order of the Bath; THE MOST NOBLE ALEXANDER WILLIAM GEORGE DUKE OF FIFE Knight of the Most Ancient and Most Noble Order of the Thistle, Privy Councillor; THE RIGHT HONOURABLE EDRIC FREDERIC LORD GIFFORD, V.C.; CECIL JOHN RHODES, of Kimberley, in the Cape Colony, Member of the Executive Council and of the House of Assembly of the Colony of the Cape of Good Hope; ALFRED BEIT, of 29, Holborn Viaduct, London, Merchant; ALBERT HENRY GEORGE GREY, of Howick, Northumberland, ESQUIRE; and GEORGE CAWSTON, of 18, Lennox Gardens, London, ESQUIRE, Barrister-at-Law.

20

AND WHEREAS the said Petition states amongst other things :—

That the Petitioners and others are associated for the purpose of forming a Company or Association, to be incorporated, if to Us should seem fit, for the objects in the said Petition set forth, under the corporate name of The British South Africa Company.

That the existence of a powerful British Company, controlled by those of Our subjects in whom we have confidence, and having its principal field of operations in that region of South Africa lying to the north of Bechuanaland and to the west of Portuguese East Africa, would be advantageous to the commercial and other interests of Our subjects in the United Kingdom and in Our Colonies.

That the Petitioners desire to carry into effect divers concessions and agreements which have been made by certain of the chiefs and tribes inhabiting the said region, and such other concessions agreements grants and treaties as the Petitioners may hereafter obtain within the said region or elsewhere in Africa, with the view of promoting trade commerce civilization and good government (including the regulation of liquor traffic with the natives) in the territories which are or may be comprised or referred to in such concessions agreements grants and treaties as aforesaid.

That the Petitioners believe that if the said concessions agreements grants and treaties can be carried into effect, the condition of the natives inhabiting the said territories will be materially improved and their civilization advanced, and an organization established which will tend to the suppression of the slave trade in the said territories, and to the opening up of the said territories to the immigration of Europeans, and to the lawful trade and commerce of Our subjects and of other nations.

That the success of the enterprise in which the Petitioners are
engaged would be greatly advanced if it should seem fit to
Us to grant them Our Royal Charter of incorporation as
a British Company under the said name or title, or such
other name or title, and with such powers, as to Us may
seem fit for the purpose of more effectually carrying into
effect the objects aforesaid.

That large sums of money have been subscribed for the purposes
of the intended Company by the Petitioners and others,
who are prepared also to subscribe or to procure such
further sums as may hereafter be found requisite for the
development of the said enterprise, in the event of Our
being pleased to grant to them Our Royal Charter of incorporation as aforesaid.

NOW, THEREFORE, We having taken the said Petition
into Our Royal consideration in Our Council, and being
satisfied that the intentions of the Petitioners are praiseworthy
and deserve encouragement, and that the enterprise in the
Petition described may be productive of the benefits set forth
therein, by Our Prerogative Royal and of Our especial grace,
certain knowledge and mere motion, have constituted erected
and incorporated, and by this Our Charter for Us and Our
Heirs and Royal successors do constitute erect and incorporate
into one body politic and corporate by the name of The
British South Africa Company the said James Duke of Abercorn, Alexander William George Duke of Fife, Edric Frederic
Lord Gifford, Cecil John Rhodes, Alfred Beit, Albert Henry
George Grey and George Cawston, and such other persons and
such bodies as from time to time become and are members of
the body politic and corporate by these presents constituted,
erected and incorporated with perpetual succession and a
common seal, with power to break alter or renew the same at

discretion, and with the further authorities powers and privileges conferred, and subject to the conditions imposed by this Our Charter: And We do hereby accordingly will, ordain, give, grant, constitute, appoint and declare as follows (that is to say) :—

1. The principal field of the operations of The British South Africa Company (in this Our Charter referred to as 'the Company') shall be the region of South Africa lying immediately to the north of British Bechuanaland, and to the north and west of the South African Republic, and to the west of the Portuguese Dominions.

2. The Company is hereby authorized and empowered to hold, use and retain for the purposes of the Company and on the terms of this Our Charter, the full benefit of the concessions and agreements made as aforesaid, so far as they are valid, or any of them, and all interests, authorities and powers comprised or referred to in the said concessions and agreements. Provided always that nothing herein contained shall prejudice or affect any other valid and subsisting concessions or agreements which may have been made by any of the chiefs or tribes aforesaid. And in particular nothing herein contained shall prejudice or affect certain concessions granted in and subsequent to the year 1880, relating to the territory usually known as the District of the Tati, nor shall anything herein contained be construed as giving any jurisdiction, administrative or otherwise, within the said District of the Tati, the limits of which district are as follows, viz. : from the place where the Shasi River rises to its junction with the Tati and Ramaquaban Rivers, thence along the Ramaquaban River to where it rises, and thence along the watershed of those rivers.

3. The Company is hereby further authorized and empowered, subject to the approval of one of Our Principal

Secretaries of State (herein referred to as ' Our Secretary of State '), from time to time, to acquire by any concession agreement grant or treaty, all or any rights interests authorities jurisdictions and powers of any kind or nature whatever, including powers necessary for the purposes of government, and the preservation of public order in or for the protection of territories, lands, or property, comprised or referred to in the concessions and agreements made as aforesaid or affecting other territories, lands, or property in Africa, or the inhabitants thereof, and to hold, use and exercise such territories, lands, property, rights, interests, authorities, jurisdictions and powers respectively for the purposes of the Company and on the terms of this Our Charter.

4. Provided that no powers of government or administration shall be exercised under or in relation to any such last-mentioned concession agreement grant or treaty, until a copy of such concession agreement grant or treaty in such form and with such maps or particulars as Our Secretary of State approves verified as he requires, has been transmitted to him, and he has signified his approval thereof either absolutely or subject to any conditions or reservations, And provided also that no rights, interests, authorities, jurisdictions, or powers of any description shall be acquired by the Company within the said District of the Tati as hereinbefore described without the previous consent in writing of the owners for the time being of the Concessions above referred to relating to the said District, and the approval of Our Secretary of State.

5. The Company shall be bound by and shall fulfil all and singular the stipulations on its part contained in any such concession agreement grant or treaty as aforesaid, subject to any subsequent agreement affecting those stipulations approved by Our Secretary of State.

6. The Company shall always be and remain British in

character and domicile, and shall have its principal office in Great Britain, and the Company's principal representative in South Africa, and the Directors shall always be natural born British subjects or persons who have been naturalized as British subjects by or under an Act of Parliament of Our United Kingdom ; but this Article shall not disqualify any person nominated a Director by this Our Charter, or any person whose election as a Director shall have been approved by Our Secretary of State, from acting in that capacity.

7. In case at any time any difference arises between any chief or tribe inhabiting any of the territories aforesaid and the Company, that difference shall, if Our Secretary of State so require, be submitted by the Company to him for his decision, and the Company shall act in accordance with such decision.

8. If at any time Our Secretary of State thinks fit to dissent from or object to any of the dealings of the Company with any foreign power and to make known to the Company any suggestion founded on that dissent or objection, the Company shall act in accordance with such suggestion.

9. If at any time Our Secretary of State thinks fit to object to the exercise by the Company of any authority, power or right within any part of the territories aforesaid, on the ground of there being an adverse claim to or in respect of that part, the Company shall defer to that objection until such time as any such claim has been withdrawn or finally dealt with or settled by Our Secretary of State.

10. The Company shall to the best of its ability preserve peace and order in such ways and manners as it shall consider necessary, and may with that object make ordinances (to be approved by Our Secretary of State) and may establish and maintain a force of police.

11. The Company shall to the best of its ability discourage and, so far as may be practicable, abolish by degrees, any

system of slave trade or domestic servitude in the territories aforesaid.

12. The Company shall regulate the traffic in spirits and other intoxicating liquors within the territories aforesaid, so as, as far as practicable, to prevent the sale of any spirits or other intoxicating liquor to any natives.

13. The Company as such, or its officers as such, shall not in any way interfere with the religion of any class or tribe of the peoples of the territories aforesaid or of any of the inhabitants thereof, except so far as may be necessary in the interest of humanity and all forms of religious worship or religious ordinances may be exercised within the said territories and no hindrance shall be offered thereto except as aforesaid.

14. In the administration of justice to the said peoples or inhabitants, careful regard shall always be had to the customs and laws of the class or tribe or nation to which the parties respectively belong, especially with respect to the holding, possession, transfer and disposition of lands and goods and testate or intestate succession thereto, and marriage divorce and legitimacy and other rights of property and personal rights, but subject to any British laws which may be in force in any of the territories aforesaid, and applicable to the peoples or inhabitants thereof.

15. If at any time Our Secretary of State thinks fit to dissent from or object to any part of the proceedings or system of the Company relative to the peoples of the territories aforesaid or to any of the inhabitants thereof, in respect of slavery or religion or the administration of justice, or any other matter, he shall make known to the Company his dissent or objection, and the Company shall act in accordance with his directions duly signified.

16. In the event of the Company acquiring any harbour or harbours, the Company shall freely afford all facilities for or to

Our ships therein without payment except reasonable charges for work done or services rendered or materials or things supplied.

17. The Company shall furnish annually to Our Secretary of State, as soon as conveniently may be after the close of the financial year, accounts of its expenditure for administrative purposes, and of all sums received by it by way of public revenue, as distinguished from its commercial profits, during the financial year, together with a report as to its public proceedings and the condition of the territories within the sphere of its operations. The Company shall also on or before the commencement of each financial year furnish to Our Secretary of State an estimate of its expenditure for administrative purposes, and of its public revenue (as above defined) for the ensuing year. The Company shall in addition from time to time furnish to Our Secretary of State any reports, accounts, or information with which he may require to be furnished.

18. The several officers of the Company shall, subject to the rules of official subordination and to any regulations that may be agreed upon, communicate freely with Our High Commissioner in South Africa and any others Our officers, who may be stationed within any of the territories aforesaid, and shall pay due regard to any requirements suggestions or requests which the said High Commissioner or other officers shall make to them or any of them and the Company shall be bound to enforce the observance of this Article.

19. The Company may hoist and use on its buildings and elsewhere in the territories aforesaid, and on its vessels, such distinctive flag indicating the British character of the Company as Our Secretary of State and the Lords Commissioners of the Admiralty shall from time to time approve.

20. Nothing in this our Charter shall be deemed to authorize the Company to set up or grant any monopoly of trade ; pro-

vided that the establishment of or the grant of concessions for banks, railways, tramways, docks, telegraphs, waterworks, or other similar undertakings or the establishment of any system of patent or copyright approved by Our Secretary of State, shall not be deemed monopolies for this purpose. The Company shall not, either directly or indirectly, hinder any Company or persons who now are or concern or venture within the said District of the Tati hereinbefore described, but shall by permitting and facilitating transit by every lawful means to and from the District of the Tati across its own territories or where it has jurisdiction in that behalf and by all other reasonable and lawful means encourage assist and protect all British subjects who now are or hereafter may be lawfully and peaceably engaged in the prosecution of a lawful enterprise within the said District of the Tati.

21. For the preservation of elephants and other game, the Company may make such other regulations and (notwithstanding anything hereinbefore contained) may impose such license duties on the killing or taking of elephants or other game as they may think fit : Provided that nothing in such regulations shall extend to diminish or interfere with any hunting rights which may have been or may hereafter be reserved to any native chiefs or tribes by treaty, save so far as any such regulations may relate to the establishment and enforcement of a close season.

22. The Company shall be subject to and shall perform and undertake all the obligations contained in or undertaken by Ourselves under any treaty agreement or arrangement between Ourselves and any other State or Power whether already made or hereafter to be made. In all matters relating to the observance of this Article, or to the exercise within the Company's territories for the time being, of any jurisdiction exercisable by Us under the Foreign Jurisdiction Acts, the

Company shall conform to and observe and carry out all such directions as may from time to time be given in that behalf by Our Secretary of State, and the Company shall appoint all necessary officers to perform such duties, and shall provide such Courts and other requisites as may from time to time be necessary for the administration of justice.

23. The original share capital of the Company shall be £1,000,000 divided into 1,000,000 shares of £1 each.

24. The Company is hereby further specially authorized and empowered for the purposes of this Our Charter from time to time—

> (i.) To issue shares of different classes or descriptions, to increase the share capital of the Company, and to borrow moneys by debentures or other obligations.

> (ii.) To acquire and hold, and to charter or otherwise deal with, steam vessels and other vessels.

> (iii.) To establish or authorize banking companies and other companies, and undertakings or associations of every description, for purposes consistent with the provisions of this Our Charter.

> (iv.) To make and maintain roads railways telegraphs harbours and any other works which may tend to the development or improvement of the territories of the Company.

> (v.) To carry on mining and other industries, and to make concessions of mining forestal or other rights.

> (vi.) To improve develop clear plant irrigate and cultivate any lands included within the territories of the Company.

> (vii.) To settle any such territories and lands as afore-said, and to aid and promote immigration.

(VIII.) To grant lands for terms of years or in perpetuity, and either absolutely, or by way of mortgage or otherwise.

(IX.) To make loans or contributions of money or money's worth, for promoting any of the objects of the Company.

(X.) To acquire and hold personal property.

(XI.) To acquire and hold (without license in mortmain or other authority than this Our Charter), lands in the United Kingdom, not exceeding five acres in all, at any one time for the purposes of the offices and business of the Company and (subject to any local law) lands in any of Our Colonies or Possessions and elsewhere, convenient for carrying on the management of the affairs of the Company, and to dispose from time to time of any such lands when not required for that purpose.

(XII.) To carry on any lawful commerce, trade, pursuit, business, operations, or dealing whatsoever in connection with the objects of the Company.

(XIII.) To establish and maintain agencies in Our Colonies and Possessions, and elsewhere.

(XIV.) To sue and be sued by the Company's name of incorporation, as well in Our Courts in Our United Kingdom, or in Our Courts in Our Colonies or Possessions, or in Our Courts in Foreign countries or elsewhere.

(XV.) To do all lawful things incidental or conducive to the exercise or enjoyment of the rights, interests, authorities and powers of the Company in this Our Charter expressed or referred to, or any of them.

25. Within one year after the date of this Our Charter, or such extended period as may be certified by Our Secretary of State, there shall be executed by the Members of the Company for the time being a Deed of Settlement, provided so far as necessary for—

> (I.) The further definition of the objects and purposes of the Company.
>
> (II.) The classes or descriptions of shares into which the Capital of the Company is divided, and the calls to be made in respect thereof, and the terms and conditions of Membership of the Company.
>
> (III.) The division and distribution of profits.
>
> (IV.) General Meetings of the Company ; the appointment by Our Secretary of State (if so required by him) of an Official Director, and the number qualification appointment remuneration rotation removal and powers of Directors of the Company, and of other officers of the Company.
>
> (V.) The registration of Members of the Company, and the transfer of shares in the capital of the Company.
>
> (VI.) The preparation of annual accounts to be submitted to the Members at a General Meeting.
>
> (VII.) The audit of those accounts by independent auditors.
>
> (VIII.) The making of bye-laws.
>
> (IX.) The making and using of official seals of the Company.
>
> (X.) The constitution and regulation of Committees or Local Boards of Management.
>
> (XI.) The making and execution of supplementary deeds of settlement.

(XII.) The winding up (in case of need) of the Company's affairs.

(XIII.) The government and regulation of the Company and of its affairs.

(XIV.) Any other matters usual or proper to be provided for in respect of a chartered Company.

26. The Deed of Settlement shall, before the execution thereof, be submitted to and approved by the Lords of Our Councils, and a certificate of their approval thereof, signed by the Clerk of Our Council, shall be endorsed on this Our Charter, and be conclusive evidence of such approval, and on the Deed of Settlement, and such Deed of Settlement shall take effect from the date of such approval, and shall be binding upon the Company, its Members, Officers and Servants, and for all other purposes whatsoever.

27. The provisions of the Deed of Settlement or of any supplementary Deed for the time being in force, may be from time to time repealed, varied or added to by a supplementary Deed, made and executed in such manner as the Deed of Settlement prescribes. Provided that the provisions of any such Deed relative to the official Director shall not be repealed, varied or added to without the express approval of Our Secretary of State.

28. The Members ot the Company shall be individually liable for the debts contracts engagements and liabilities of the Company to the extent only of the amount, if any, for the time being unpaid, on the shares held by them respectively.

29. Until such Deed of Settlement as aforesaid takes effect the said James Duke of Abercorn shall be the President; the said Alexander William George Duke of Fife shall be Vice-President; and the said Edric Frederick Lord Gifford, Cecil John Rhodes, Alfred Beit, Albert Henry George Grey, and George Cawston, shall be the Directors of the Company: and

may on behalf of the Company do all things necessary or proper to be done under this Our Charter by or on behalf of the Company : Provided always that, notwithstanding anything contained in the Deed of Settlement of the Company, the said James Duke of Abercorn, Alexander William George Duke of Fife, and Albert Henry George Grey, shall not be subject to retire from office in accordance with its provisions but shall be and remain Directors of the Company until death, incapacity to act, or resignation, as the case may be.

30. And we do further will, ordain and declare that this Our Charter shall be acknowledged by Our governors and Our naval and military officers and Our consuls, and Our other officers in our colonies and possessions, and on the high seas, and elsewhere, and they shall severally give full force and effect to this Our Charter, and shall recognise and be in all things aiding to the Company and its officers.

31. And We do further will, ordain and declare that this Our Charter shall be taken construed and adjudged in the most favourable and beneficial sense for, and to the best advantage of the Company as well in Our courts in Our United Kingdom, and in Our courts in Our colonies or possessions, and in Our Courts in foreign countries or elsewhere, notwithstanding that there may appear to be in this Our Charter any non-recital, mis-recital, uncertainty or imperfection.

32. And We do further will, ordain and declare that this Our Charter shall subsist and continue valid, notwithstanding any lawful change in the name of the Company or in the Deed of Settlement thereof, such change being made with the previous approval of Our Secretary of State signified under his hand.

33. And We do further will, ordain and declare that it shall be lawful for us Our heirs and successors and We do hereby expressly reserve to Ourselves Our heirs and successors the

right and power by writing under the Great Seal of the United Kingdom at the end of 25 years from the date of this Our Charter, and at the end of every succeeding period of ten years, to add to alter or repeal any of the provisions of this Our Charter or to enact other provisions in substitution for or in addition to any of its existing provisions. Provided that the right and power thus reserved shall be exercised only in relation to so much of this Our Charter as relates to administrative and public matters. And We do further expressly reserve to Ourselves, Our heirs and successors the right to take over any buildings or works belonging to the Company, and used exclusively or mainly for administrative or public purposes on payment to the Company of such reasonable compensation as may be agreed, or as failing agreement may be settled by the Commissioners of Our Treasury. And We do further appoint direct and declare that any such writing under the said Great Seal shall have full effect, and be binding upon the Company, its members, officers and servants, and all other persons, and shall be of the same force, effect, and validity as if its provisions had been part of and contained in these presents.

34. Provided always and We do further declare that nothing in this Our Charter shall be deemed or taken in anywise to limit or restrict the exercise of any of Our rights or powers with reference to the protection of any territories or with reference to the government thereof should We see fit to include the same within Our dominions.

35. And We do lastly will, ordain and declare, without prejudice to any power to repeal this Our Charter by law belonging to Us Our heirs and successors, or to any of Our courts ministers or officers independently of this present declaration and reservation, that in case at any time it is made to appear to Us in our Council that the Company has substantially failed

to observe and conform to the provisions of this Our Charter, or that the Company is not exercising its powers under the concessions agreements grants and treaties aforesaid, so as to advance the interests which the Petitioners have represented to Us to be likely to be advanced by the grant of this Our Charter, it shall be lawful for Us Our heirs and successors, and We do hereby expressly reserve and take to Ourselves our heirs and successors the right and power by writing under the Great Seal of Our United Kingdom to revoke this Our Charter, and to revoke and annul the privileges powers and rights hereby granted to the Company.

In Witness whereof We have caused these Our Letters to be made Patent.

Witness Ourself at Westminster, the 29th day of October, in the fifty-third year of Our reign.

By warrant under the Queen's Sign Manual.

MUIR MACKENZIE.

The
Great Seal
of the
United
Kingdom.

INDEX.

A.

AFRICAN COMPANIES. See Guinea Companies

Albany River, occupied by the Hudson Bay Company, 165

Alfred, King, his account of Ohthere's and of Wulfstan's voyages of discovery, 32, 60

Amboyna first visited by the English, 91 ; its unpleasant memories, 91, 102

Andros, Sir E., Governor of New England, fails to seize the Connecticut and Rhode Island charters, 213

Anne, Queen, her tripartite indenture, 118

Anglo-Canadian half-breeds, their constituent elements, 183 ; their physical and mental qualities compared with those of the Franco-Canadian trappers and traders, 183

Antwerp, the Staplers' first mart, 18 ; a station of the St. Thomas à Becket Fraternity, 22 ; saved from the Inquisition by the Merchant Adventurers, 25

Archangel visited by Chancellor, 33

Archduke Philip, his commercial treaty with Henry VII., 23

Astoria, Columbia river, its origin and history, 190

B.

Baffin attempts the North-West Passage, 155

Bantam, a station of the East India Company, 107

Barbary Company, its Elizabethan charter, 236 ; privileged by the Sultan of Marocco, 236

Barbary corsairs, their origin, 68 ; obstruct the trade of the Mediterranean lands, 68

Barras, on the command of the sea, 135

Batton attempts the North-West Passage, 155

Benkulen, its relations with the East India Company, 107

Bergen, English traders outraged at, by the Hanseatics, 8

Bermuda or Somers Isles Company incorporated by James I., 241

Bezoar-stones, meaning and derivation of, 98

Billingsgate, tolls levied at, by Ethelred, 5 note

Bishopsgate to be kept in repair by the Hanseatics, 6, 7

'Blues,' the North-West Company's people, why so named, 187

'Boston men,' meaning of the expression, 180

Boghar, Persia, visited by Jenkinson, 36

Boscawen, 'Admiral, occupies St. Thomé, 128

Bowes, Sir J., at the Court of Tsar Feodor, 41

Bonaparte, his designs on India thwarted, 135

Bourbon River. See Nelson

Brotherhood of St. Thomas à Becket, origin of, 15 ; history of, 20 et seq.

Bruges, a mart of the Staplers, 19 ; the staple for English exports under Edward III., 21

215, 216; to Georgia, 222; to the four Guinea (Africa) Companies, 228-235; to the Marocco Company, 236; to the Canary Company, 236, 237; to the Guiana Company, 238; to the Bermuda Company, 241; to the China (Cathay) Company, 242, 243

Chartered companies, their disputes with the Interlopers, 23

'Charter Oak,' Connecticut, why so named, 214

Child, Sir J., on the Eastland Company, 66; on the trade of the East India Company, 107

China Company. See Cathay Company

Choktaws, address of their chief to Oglethorpe, 226

Churchill River occupied by the Hudson Bay Company, who here erect a great stronghold, 164, 165. See also Port Prince of Wales

Cicero, on the command of the sea, 129

Clive wrests the Carnatic from the French, 132; captures Chandernagore, 133; avenges the 'Black Hole' atrocity, 133; his jaghir, 137; quits India leaving the East India Company masters of Bengal, 138

Cockayne's Patent, its history, 28, 29

Companies, joint stock and regulated, 9-13

Combe, Mr., his account of the Lapérouse expedition to Hudson Bay, 175, 176

Connecticut first settled by the Dutch, 211; its English charter, 211; rescued from Governor Andros by Captain W. Wadsworth, 213,¦214

Coureurs des bois, meaning of the expression, 181

Cossim Ali Khan, his wars and transactions with the East India Company, 137

Cromwell, his attitude towards the East India Company, 103

D.

Davis attempts the North-West Passage, 155

D'Avenant, Dr., defends the East India exclusive trade, 115

Delaware, its charter, 203

Delaware, Lord, Governor of South Virginia, 203

Delft, a station of the Merchant Adventurers, 31

Denmark, her possessions in India, 130

Ditmarsch, joins the Hanseatic League, 4

Dobbs, Mr., his controversy with the Hudson Bay Company, 172-174

Dort, a central station of the Merchant Adventurers, 30

Dupleix, his schemes of conquest, 128

Dutch, their possessions in India, 130, 134; driven from the Ganges by Clive and Forde, 133, 134

E.

Easterlings, meaning of the word, 6

East India Company, its origin and history, 86 *et seq.*; its first charter, 87-89; its first ventures, 90; its first factory at Surat, 90; first naval battles with the Turks and Portuguese, 91-93; extend their operations to Japan, 92; costly exports to and imports from India, 93; erect Fort St. George at Madras, 94; first collision with the Great Moghul, 94; alliance with Shah Abbas, 94; drive the Portuguese from Ormuz, 94, 95; their political status recognised by James I., 95; their profitable trade at this time, 95, 96; their privileges encroached upon by Charles I., 100; settlement of their differences with the Dutch East India Company (1654), 101, 102; their privileges revoked and restored by Cromwell, 103, 104; their powers enlarged by Charles II., 105, 106; constituted a sovereign State, 106; acquire Bombay, 106; their possessions in Malaysia, 107; objections to their exclusive trade under Charles II., 108, 109; extend their operations to China and the Pacific Ocean, 109, 110; their fifth charter from Charles II., 111; their first war with the Great Moghul, 111-113; erect Fort William at Calcutta, 113; accused of corrupt practices under William and Mary, 114; violent agitation against them in public and in Parliament, 115-117; an opposition company incorporated, 116, 117; rivalries and reconciliation, the tripartite indenture, 117-119; their funded stock consoli-

Tomochechi, chief of the Uchee tribe, his address to Oglethorpe, 225

Trading charters, their relation to local charters, 2 ; their influence on the development of foreign trade, 3

Trinity Island, its fishing-grounds, 49 ; granted to the Corporation of Hull, 49

Turkey Company, its origin and history, 67 *et seq. ;* its first charter, 68, 69 ; promotes English interests in the Levant, 70, 71 ; introduces Eastern fruits and other commodities, 71 ; stimulates shipping and navigation, 71 ; compounds with the Barbary corsairs, 72 ; fights naval battles with the Spaniards, 72 ; its second charter with enlarged privileges, 72, 73 ; its first trading expedition to India, 73 ; its profitable trade under James I., 76 ; its powers increased in 1643 by Act of Parliament, 77, 78 ; receives fresh concessions from Sultan Mahomet IV., 79 ; its complaints against the East India Company, 80-82 ; its decline and extinction, 84, 85

V.

Virginia, original meaning of the word, 198 ; North and South, 198. See also South Virginia

Virginian Company, its origin, first charter and history, 197 *et seq. ;* its Caroline charter of 1625, 204

Voyageurs, Franco-Canadian, meaning of the expression, 181

W.

Wesley, John, his visit to Georgia, 226, 227

Weston, Thomas, his charter, 208

Wheeler, J., on the St. Thomas à Becket Fraternity, 22 ; his account of the Merchant Adventurers, 27, 28

Whitefield, George, his visit to Georgia, 226, 227

White Sea, the route known to King Alfred, 32

Willoughby, Sir H., his disastrous expedition, 33

Windford, Norway, English traders murdered at, by the Hanseatics, 7, 8

Williams, Rev. R., obtains the Rhode Island charter from Parliament, 212

Wool, English ports of export for, in the fourteenth century, 19

Wootton, Sir H., his negotiations, with Holland about the Greenland and North Sea fisheries, 46, 47

Wulfstan, his voyage to the East Sea, 60

X.

X. Y. Company, its origin, quarrels, and fusion with the North-West Company, 186

Y.

Yeardley, G., Governor of South Virginia, 203

Z.

Zamindar, derivation and meaning of, 149

THE END.